Write Choices
Elements of Nonfiction Storytelling

Sue Hertz
University of New Hampshire

Los Angeles | London | New Delhi
Singapore | Washington DC | Boston

Los Angeles | London | New Delhi
Singapore | Washington DC | Boston

FOR INFORMATION:

CQ Press

An Imprint of SAGE Publications, Inc.

2455 Teller Road

Thousand Oaks, California 91320

E-mail: order@sagepub.com

SAGE Publications Ltd.

1 Oliver's Yard

55 City Road

London EC1Y 1SP

United Kingdom

SAGE Publications India Pvt. Ltd.

B 1/I 1 Mohan Cooperative Industrial Area

Mathura Road, New Delhi 110 044

India

SAGE Publications Asia-Pacific Pte. Ltd.

3 Church Street

#10-04 Samsung Hub

Singapore 049483

Printed in the United States of America

A catalog record of this book is available from the Library of Congress.

ISBN 978-1-4522-3085-6

This book is printed on acid-free paper.

Acquisitions Editor: Matthew Byrnie

Editorial Assistant: Janae Masnovi

Production Editor: Bennie Clark Allen

Copy Editor: Deanna Noga

Typesetter: C&M Digitals (P) Ltd.

Proofreader: Laura Webb

Indexer: Sheila Bodell

Cover Designer: Glenn Vogel

Marketing Manager: Liz Thornton

15 16 17 18 19 10 9 8 7 6 5 4 3 2 1

Brief Contents

Contents

Preface

EVER SINCE THE TERM CREATIVE NONFICTION was coined in the early 1990s, nonfiction storytelling has enjoyed unprecedented attention and innovation. Open any magazine, literary journal, or online publication and you will find a rich array of compelling tales of fact that employ literary techniques. Personal essays, memoir, travelogue, opinion, and journalistic explorations of timely and timeless events line the table of contents. Just look at a recent New Yorker: Readers choose between memoir (writers remember their times with J.D. Salinger), personal essay (John McPhee ponders the death of his father while fishing for pickerel), opinion (Hendrik Hertzberg reacts to a presidential speech), and narrative journalism (Jon Lee Anderson chronicles one Haitian woman's effort to save her community). Log on to your computer or iPad, and not only must you choose among the panoply of text stories, but also related videos, audio slideshows, and interactive graphics. Narratives of fact have never been so varied.

Given the seemingly infinite variety of ways to tell true stories, emerging writers feel often overwhelmed. They find themselves so tangled in labels and forms — Is the piece a profile or character essay? Is a first person tale rich in research considered memoir or literary journalism? Is a newspaper feature narrative? Is a radio essay? — that they lose sight of what is really important: telling a good story, taking a reader on a journey that educates as well as entertains, that strikes viscerally as well as intellectually.

"Write Choices" blasts through these boundaries, exploring the decisions all writers confront when crafting any kind of factual narrative — from a reflective essay to a Rolling Stone profile to an 80,000-word memoir to a video script. Rather than isolating each of these forms, "Write Choices" celebrates the decisions faced by all nonfiction storytellers. The book takes emerging writers step by step from idea to revision, analyzing the questions they will face along the way. What makes a compelling idea? What do you want to learn? What will your reader learn? What is the central mystery? What information do you need? What sources must you seek? Who are your main characters? What is the structure?

What is the narrative arc? Who is the narrator? What scenes best illustrate the message? Is dialogue appropriate? Which details are significant? Which are superfluous?

"Write Choices" asks emerging writers to ignore the labels and instead focus on telling the best story possible, to find the form that fits the content. In short, "Write Choices" serves as a commonsense approach by celebrating the universal elements shared by all true stories told with a narrative arc. The mission for us all, from the memoirist to the magazine writer, is to weave accurate and creative narratives, with a journalist's drive for content, a poet's eye for imagery, and a fiction writer's sense of drama. And in this digital age, to recognize the ways technology can enhance — not replace — our words. Because as New Yorker editor David Remnick said at a forum called "Long Form Storytelling in a Short Attention Span World," language remains our greatest invention.

WHO IS THIS BOOK FOR?

"Write Choices" targets writers of all levels, from undergraduates testing the narrative nonfiction waters to graduate students stretching their writing muscles to seasoned practitioners seeking inspiration from the masters. Based on interviews with over 60 print and digital storytellers as well as my own decades of teaching and publishing factual narratives, "Write Choices" provides insights from a wide variety of voices. Emerging writers will learn how these veterans determine critical issues, such as how Ryan Van Meter identifies a memoir's focus or how Cynthia Gorney selects the narrator's point of view for a story about child brides or the moments Phillip Toledano seeks to illustrate in his photo essays. By following the pros on their literary quests, the book's readers will acquire tools necessary to help them choose the best path for their own narratives, whether they chase a Montaigne-like idea (Is lying less sociable than silence?), an image (What did the glass castle her father talked of building symbolize about Jeannette Walls' chaotic childhood?), or an external conflict (Why would a high school sophomore stab his classmates?).

"Write Choices" will assist students in any course — be it labeled journalism or creative nonfiction — that celebrates factual tales employing narrative techniques. Or to borrow a phrase from Creative Nonfiction magazine: "True stories, well told."

It will also assist them to think digitally. While most writers may not prove as adept with a camera as they are with a pen, recognizing how sound and images can enrich the reading experience is vital in this digital age. Online publications such as Atavist may employ a team of tech stars to integrate timelines and interactive maps and videos with text, but the writer, the story's engine, can best dictate what will enhance and not detract. Besides, as online journals and e-books expand our opportunities to publish, new and seasoned writers alike will benefit from learning how multimedia artists approach their storytelling. And perhaps how they, the steadfast writers, might too employ their computer and smart phones as creative tools.

HOW TO USE THE BOOK

"Write Choices" follows chronologically the choices writers make as they craft their narratives. Each chapter is devoted to a major decision. Chapter One explores what makes a worthy subject. Chapter Two asks what form is best for the subject. Succeeding chapters cover selecting content, focus, structure, and components. The journey ends at drafting and revision. Along the way readers will encounter how multimedia artists confront the same challenges, a reminder that regardless of medium, regardless of form, we all worry about organization, tension, and rich characters.

Each chapter breaks down the choice into digestible pieces, embellished with the insights and experiences of the veteran writers as well as excerpts from their work. Scattered throughout each chapter are writing exercises based on a particular challenge. For example, following a discussion of point of view, writers are offered prompts that test their skills at telling a story through multiple narrators. By asking student writers to act on what they have just learned rather than wait until the chapter's end will, hopefully, keep them engaged and bolster their confidence. As they try and wobble, then try again and succeed, they collect the skills necessary to launch them into the next round of choices. Writers learn by writing.

Each chapter also includes two features. The first, "Challenging Choices," highlights one particular writer's experience wrestling with that chapter's central choice. Speaking in his or her own voice (Studs Terkel oral history style), the writer will tell how he or she navigated through the challenges of choosing a focus, or structuring a narrative, or revising a mishmash of a rough draft. This feature allows the reader to hear the writers walk through a dilemma in their own words rather than through the narrator's filter. By the end of the book, the emerging writer will have a working knowledge of choices made by a wide range of narrative artists.

The second feature, "Web Choices," details the decisions involved in creating a digital story or essay or a multimedia complement to a prose narrative. As with "Challenging Choices," a craftsman — which in this case could be a videographer, or a photographer, or a scriptwriter — explains how he or she tackled that chapter's choice while creating a multimedia project. How do you build character in a video? How do you narrow the focus of an audio slideshow? While "Write Choices" is aimed at an audience who loves words, and telling stories with words, it also hopes to expand the writer's understanding of narrative nonfiction in the digital age. Through "Web Choices," the text's readers will gain insights into the similarities — and yes, differences — encountered while building a narrative based on images or sound, or both.

A FEW WORDS ON TERMINOLOGY AND SOURCES

While different scholars have different definitions of what constitutes an essay or a story, "Write Choices" emphasizes that the lines have blurred. Certain writings are clearly essays — the narrator explores an idea, untangles an intellectual puzzle — and others stories that lead the reader scene by scene to an epiphany. Yet many true tales could fall into both camps. Consequently, often in "Write Choices," the two terms are used interchangeably. More often, the more-inclusive term *narrative* is used. Narrative, after all, covers stories told with a beginning, middle, and end, stories that employ literary techniques such as scene and dialogue. A nonfiction narrative is not a litany of facts or a news report but a carefully carved tale that takes the reader on an intellectual and emotional journey through its inventive style and colorful content.

To avoid gender favoritism, hypothetical writers mentioned throughout the book alternate between male and female. Sometimes the writer is a he and sometimes a she.

Internal refers to narratives or parts of narratives based on the writer's own experience and reflections. *External* means content gleaned from other people's experiences and reflections and sources such as books, media, databases, and court records.

Most of the direct quotes included in "Write Choices" were acquired during my conversations with the storytellers. These interviews were conducted by phone, e-mail, and in person. The sources of all other quotes are stated directly in the text. A list of chapter-by-chapter references can be found in this book's final pages.

FINAL THOUGHTS

As in many narratives, the message of this book is best expressed in a scene:

The season was late winter, the setting my office. The graduate student across from me scrunched up her face in concentration, her fingers pressing against her temples. We sat knee to knee in my office, the afternoon sun illuminating her like a spotlight. Yet neither the sun's warmth nor anything I said soothed her anxiety. "Where," she said, pausing between each word, "am ... I ... in ... this ... story?"

A writer with a distinctive narrative voice, an ear for dialogue, and a passion for the personal essay, this student was most comfortable writing about her own experiences. Yet the project we discussed, the project causing her so much agita, had nothing to do with her past adventures. Rather, the idea she pursued — why baseball doesn't attract African-American players — was about other people, a whole slew of other people. The goal of our conference was to whittle down this huge topic into something manageable. Yet she was paralyzed. If she was not front and center in the story, she couldn't envision how the narrative would unfold, let alone grasp how to begin.

What we worked on that afternoon was what "Write Choices" is all about — recognizing that crafting the project she proposed, one based on research, employed the same tactics she used to pen the kind of essays she had always written. The content may be different but the process was identical. Whether she was exploring baseball diversity or her memories of summer school, she faced the same choices from beginning to end.

At the end of our conference she looked a little less strained, relieved, it seemed, to have vented. More important, she had a plan. And that plan looked surprisingly familiar. "I can do this," she said.

And she did.

Acknowledgments

First and foremost, I am indebted to Jane Harrigan, who encouraged me to write this book and helped build its foundation. With her trademark good cheer and blue edits, she guided this project from a possibility into a reality. Thanks, too, to Charisse Kiino of CQ Press, for her enthusiasm and confidence, and to Matt Byrnie of SAGE Publications for stepping in and shepherding "Write Choices" through to completion. He is an editor of great common sense, patience, and, most important, humor.

A round of applause, too, for the friends and students who read pieces of this manuscript, including Evelyn Iritani and Lisa Meerts-Brandsma, and two rounds for Janet Schofield, who read the whole blasted thing. Janet's sharp eye for detail and deep understanding of both fiction and nonfiction narratives provided the questions and insights needed to frame the revision. No amount of scarves or sushi lunches could properly thank her.

Last of all, my deepest gratitude to all the nonfiction storytellers I interrupted from their storytelling to talk to me about their craft. Many, many thanks to Cynthia Gorney, the three Kates (Kate Bolick, Katie Campbell, Katy Butler), Rolf Potts, Todd Balf, John Sutter, Amy Ellis Nutt, Chris Jones, Sarah Schweitzer, Tom French, Phillip Toledano, Ann Silvio, Neil Swidey, Dinty W. Moore, Chelsea Conaboy, Joe Mackall, Jacqueline Salmon, Jennie Latson, Galen Clarke, Bonnie Rough, Ryan Van Meter, Faith Adiele, Joan Wickersham, Bruce Ballenger, John Bresland, Stephen Maing, Andrew DeVigal, Eric LeMay, Amy O'Leary, Sheila Anne Feeney, Thomas Larson, Joshuah Bearman, Ben Montgomery, and all the others who were so very generous with their time and thoughts about how they spin facts into art.

About the Author

Sue Hertz is an associate professor of English and nonfiction writing at the University of New Hampshire where she teaches in both its graduate and undergraduate writing programs. Author of "Caught in the Crossfire: A Year on Abortion's Front Line," she has published essays and stories in numerous national and regional publications, including Redbook, House Beautiful, Walking, New England Monthly Magazine, Boston Magazine, The Boston Globe Magazine, and Parenting. Before she began the double life of teacher-writer, she was a feature writer for the Hartford Courant, the Seattle Post-Intelligencer, and The Herald in Everett, WA.

For Bill, Luke, and Jordy Steelman

1

What's the Big Idea?

Overview

Finding an idea that is as compelling to the reader as it is to the writer looms often as daunting a task as scaling Kilimanjaro — barefoot.

Yet sources of inspiration are all around if we know where to look and what questions to ask. In this first chapter, we examine the paths that could lead to narrative topics, including brainstorming, the writer's passions, conversations, observations, reading, reflection, and web cruising. Once we have a subject, we ask ourselves the hard questions — Where lies the conflict? What's surprising? Is this idea timely or timeless? — to ferret out the fresh angle.

THE INVITATION WENT SOMETHING LIKE THIS: Please attend a potluck dinner to which you will bring a taste treat for the guests and a book idea for the hostess.

A Book Raising party, I called it. And because the only folks invited were writers and because writers, or at least all the writers I know, will put up with pretty much anything for food, I predicted that I'd host a full house. Which was a good thing because I desperately needed help. In my early 30s, I had moved from newspaper feature writing to magazine article writing and longed to leap into the world of tens of thousands of words, to dive deeply into a topic, expand my skills, and surface an author. For the past year I'd explored a variety of ideas that for one reason or another — too depressing, too simple, too boring — tanked. I hoped that the combined creative genius of my writer friends would produce a project far more electric than the ones I'd thought up on my own.

And so they arrived to this brainstorming session with zucchini casseroles and spinach salads and chocolate-raspberry cupcakes. At the door they signed a waiver conceding to the hostess all rights to all ideas. One friend, a feature writer for the Boston Herald, needed story suggestions for a Monday meeting with her editor and refused to sign. I didn't blame her. She and her hummus were still allowed in. We ate, we drank, we laughed, and then we got down to business. By the end of the evening I had what I thought were two intriguing book ideas to pitch to my literary agent.

While he loved the concept of the book raising party, he dismissed one of the two ideas, and was only mildly interested in the second. Still, he contacted an editor, who, within minutes of hearing the pitch, said it wasn't for her, thanks and hung up. Still on the line, I sighed, frustrated, muttering that I wanted to write about social issues, but that it felt like I would never land the right idea. "Sure you will," my agent said. "What you need is a vehicle."

"Like what?" I asked.

He paused, thinking. "Like a year in the life of an abortion clinic."

"Yuck," I said.

"No, it is great," he said. "Think about it."

I did, and 2 years later Prentice Hall published "Caught in the Crossfire; A Year on Abortion's Front Line," my narrative nonfiction account of how the politics and the protests on the outside affected the staff and patients on the inside of Preterm Health Services in Brookline, Massachusetts. What my agent had known, and I was in too much of a hurry to appreciate, was that subjects are everywhere, but *ideas* require a hook, or as he called it, a vehicle. My writer friends and I could talk until we were breathless about potential topics — shoe trends, addictive video games, sibling rivalry — but without a specific approach to those topics, we were merely treading water, flapping around but not moving forward. Yes I wanted to write about social issues, and sure enough, abortion is a social issue, but what about abortion did I want to learn? What angle could I pursue that would surprise? What could I discover that was new?

As writers, we are always searching for stories to tell, whether those stories are about our own lives and experiences, or the experiences and lives of others. Whether we hope to write a short essay, a 5,000-word magazine narrative, a thick book or text for a digital slide show. Yet so often we find ourselves staring into the abyss, a big empty vat, when we try to summon ideas to pursue. Our literary quests would be so much easier if we trained ourselves to think in terms of questions rather than subjects.

Subjects, indeed, float all around. A subject to explore on the page could be a hobby (fly fishing, scrapbooking) or a fear (small places, slithering snakes).

A subject could be a memory (a father's rage) or an event (a trip to Istanbul). Subjects emerge from daily media stories (small town racism, wheelchair basketball) or observations (territorial winter surfers, over-friendly dog walkers). Conversations breed potential subjects — a casual chat about willful toddlers or a ferocious brainstorming session that yields a slideshow of embarrassing middle school memories. Sometimes subjects surface when we least expect them — soaking in a steaming tub, driving on a rural back road, half-asleep on the hammock — any occasion, really, when our racing brains relax. As we let our thoughts ramble, the inner critic shuts down and from our subconscious bubble concerns (plastic bag pollution), pleasures (Red Sox tickets), recollections (sailing on a stormy Lake Michigan).

An idea for a narrative, however, is not based on a subject, but rather on a question about the subject. What do you want to learn about the impact of your father's rage? How do territorial surfers affect the sport? What's new in your town about the effort to ban plastic bags? Is a seat at Fenway Park worth the cost and hassle?

A reporter by trade and by nature, I'm an annoying fountain of queries, as my friends and family will attest. I ask about their day and their health. I ask about their feelings toward a proposed historic district. I ask why the elementary school abolished morning recess. I ask whether the wind turbine keeps them awake at night. And as a result of three decades of telling true stories, I ask myself what I want to learn from topics assigned to me and topics I drum up on my own. Ask any writer and he will tell you the same thing: Every story begins with a question.

So let's begin this journey into nonfiction storytelling by first fishing for subjects and then directing our energies into applying a hook, into discovering the mystery we want to solve about the subject. Picture yourself in a car, settling into your comfy leather seat, ready to go. First you decide on your destination. Then you figure out a route. In the craft of telling true stories, the question you pursue is your GPS. But the best part is that you don't need to tinker with an electronic tracking device to launch your idea. The only ingredient required is curiosity.

WHERE LURK SUBJECTS?

Flannery O'Connor once said, "Anybody who has survived his childhood has enough information about life to last him the rest of his days." In other words, anyone over 12 has plenty of subject matter for literary pursuits. Branch out beyond one's own life and potential topics sprout as thick as tallgrass on a prairie.

The first step toward identifying whether a subject has enough inherent drama to spawn a narrative is to stomp to shreds that noisy internal editor, the voice that shoots down every idea, every suggestion. Not all topics will be winners but you won't know what could prove fruitful if you nix rather than nurture.

And what would be easier to nurture than something that fires you up? First stop for the subject sensor: your passions.

Find subjects in passions

"I say, follow your bliss and don't be afraid, and doors will open where you didn't know they were going to be."

~ Joseph Campbell in an interview with
Bill Moyers for the documentary "The Power of Myth"

When the mythologist Joseph Campbell coined the phrase "Follow your bliss" to help guide his students and readers toward a richer life, he could also have been speaking to writers in search of ideas. If you're bored by a topic, no doubt your reader's attention will drift off to favorite YouTube videos by Paragraph Two — so it only makes sense that writers seek ideas within subjects about which they are passionate.

Todd Balf is an avid outdoorsman. He loves to bike and run and kayak and hike. He loves sports, all sports, and is fascinated by how humans push themselves physically and emotionally in pursuit of a dream. Little wonder, then, that he has made a career out of writing and editing for adventure magazines, such as Outside, Esquire, and Men's Journal. His first book, "The Last River," was about a tragic kayak trip taken by some of the top U.S. paddlers down the Tsangpo River Gorge in Tibet, his second, "The Darkest Jungle" about the failed 1854 expedition to find a route across the isthmus of Panama, and his third, "Major," a biography of one of the earliest stars in competitive bicycling, an African-American named Marshall Major Taylor. "I get my ideas mostly from what I'm passionate about," says Balf. "Because I'm not particularly expert in anything, I use my inexpertise and curiosity to feed ideas." While he cheerfully admits that his passion is adventure and travel, he adds that his definition of adventure is broad. "It could mean growing a really good tomato or it could be trudging across a jungle in Panama," he says. "The mindset is always the same; you have something that you aren't sure you can do, you're committed to wanting to do it, and then you write about that experience and journey to getting to it or not getting to it."

When asked how they come up with ideas, writers will often say one word: "theme." Just as athletes migrate to specific sports and chefs to certain cuisines, writers have favorite topics they pursue again and again. Tracy Kidder, for one, spent his early energies writing books about process — the process of building a computer, of building a house, of educating fifth graders. Susan Orlean has devoted decades to writing about people and their obsessions, be they a New York City fishmonger or a Spanish bullfighter. Born of a Nigerian father and Finnish mother, Faith Adiele centers much of her writing on identity.

As much as I'd like to call myself a generalist, with a portfolio containing tales ranging from problem feet to ghost hunts, the subjects that ignite my curiosity inevitably involve people confronting adversity. Parents of homicide victims learning to cope. Parents of young children learning to juggle child-raising with caring for their aging parents. Scientists struggling to conduct their research amid political turmoil that threatens their life's work.

What are your passions? Are you an avid road biker? Traveler? Family genealogist? Quilter? Egyptologist? Are you fascinated by architecture? African-American history? Do you find yourself flipping to magazine stories about women struggling to balance ambition and family? To stories of survival? To entrepreneurs creating life-altering devices and services? What subjects pique your curiosity? Harbor mystery and fascination, perhaps even frustration? Often we write best about topics that perplex us the most.

Find subjects in conversations

During my years as a regular contributor to Boston Magazine, an editor once asked me to write a BIG story on day care. The father of a toddler, he found himself in frequent conversations with other parents about problem nannies and overcrowded day care centers, and he figured that if that many of his peers were obsessing about child care, then so were plenty of Boston Magazine's subscribers. He didn't have a specific angle; finding one was my job. Ordinarily, I would have been happy with the freedom, but in this case, I clutched. Single at the time, I lived alone, my daily contact with children limited to waving to my landlord's

---

TRY THIS

1. What do you love? Fashion? Rock climbing? Vintage cars? Reggae? Think of an experience involving that passion. Perhaps you recall a huge fight you had with a parent about a clothing choice, or a terrifying moment as you dangled from a ledge, your mountaineering harness coming loose. Now what about that moment, that experience do you want to understand? The passion is the subject. What you want to learn is the angle, the idea. Start writing, beginning with the critical moment. Where does it lead?

2. Flip through CNN.com. What topics enrage you? Annoy you? Entertain you? What do you want to learn about the issue? Research stats, facts, and other people's experiences about that topic. Where does the research lead? What central question surfaces? If the topic is gun control, what do you want to learn about firearm rights? How a local group is waging war against the National Rifle Association? How your grandfather's devotion to hunting changed your mind about gun owner's rights?

two young daughters who lived on the first floor of our apartment building. What I knew about daycare was what everyone knew — that finding someone to care for your child with love and humor and healthy snacks and lots of outdoor time was tough. But a story about the trials of finding quality day care wouldn't make it past the pitch. Too trite. Too obvious. Frustrated, I vented to my carpool mate Barb en route to our teaching jobs at the University of New Hampshire. "What about a story from the day care provider's side?" she suggested. Her mother-in-law owned and directed a day care center just north of Boston, and while she prided herself on the attention and education she offered at her center, the visits and inquisitions and demands she received from the state were daunting at best. Ever since Tookie the Clown had been arrested and found guilty of child abuse in another Massachusetts center, the state had been relentlessly aggressive in monitoring the men and women who cared for other people's children. Some might say too aggressive. What, then, were the challenges of providing quality care in an era of hyper state vigilance and helicopter parents?

"Brilliant!" I said. The surprise factor was great; who thought of the day care provider's perspective? The editor agreed. After weeks of shadowing both sides — the day care providers and the social workers assigned to assess childcare centers' safety and quality, as well as talking to parents and dependent care experts, I had the answer to my central question: While all parties agreed that child safety was paramount, the state would better serve providers, and thus children, if it served as an advocate rather than adversary. Between the low pay, long days, constant criticism by parents, and social workers demanding pounds of paperwork, more fans, and fewer electric cords, the providers were run ragged. "Who Cares for the Child?" offered all sides but leaned sympathetically toward the women and men who care for children as a livelihood. Had my carpool mate Barb never mentioned her mother-in-law, I would have missed this angle.

One of my grad students, too, profited well from a conversation. During a casual chat with a friend, she heard the story of a dramatic winter rescue on Mt. Washington, New Hampshire's notorious tallest peak that until recently, held the world record for strongest recorded winds. A group of volunteers, skilled climbers from the North Country, faced the brutal gales and below-zero temperatures to recover a stranded hiker. Amy, an athletic blonde who loves being outdoors in all kinds of weather, perked up, her story antennae erect. What was the name of the volunteer group? she asked. Mountain Rescue Service. How long have they operated? Since 1972. Why would anyone risk his life in the legendary wind, cold, and snow of the White Mountains to rescue unprepared hikers? No answer. Amy decided to find out and spent the next year learning how the Mountain Rescue Service climbers operated, and the next year following them out on rescues. The answer to that original question proved the pulse of her MFA thesis, a portion of which became an article for the Appalachian Mountain Club's magazine.

Dialogue prompts reflection, and reflection can lead to a piece of memoir, or a personal essay. Bonnie Rough and her new husband spent many an hour debating the wisdom of having their own children, weighing the risk of passing on a rare condition for which Rough was a carrier. The discussions inspired an essay that was published in the New York Times Modern Love column and later a memoir titled "Carrier."

While working at the front info desk of Powell's Books in Portland, Oregon, Kevin Sampsell exchanged words with a customer that led him to mull his own life choices, which led him to write the essay "I'm Jumping Off the Bridge." The customer, a "frazzled-looking young guy" named Chris, stood before Sampsell and announced that he was going to hurl himself off the Burnside Bridge. Sampsell kept him talking and called for help, and 30 minutes later an ambulance arrived. Chris was safe, at least for the moment, but for months afterward, Sampsell ruminated about his failed relationships, his responsibility to his son, his depression. He, too, contemplated suicide. But instead he wrote about the experience and his epiphany: he needed to live to love his son. The end to his essay circles back to that initial conversation with Chris:

> *The next morning I woke up and shaved and took a shower and drank my coffee. I went to work and took my position behind the info desk. The store opened two hours late because it was New Year's Day. Customers came filing in, looking for books, looking for stories. Looking for the bathroom. I sat there, feeling fresh-faced and feeling like a survivor. I was ready to help anyone who needed it.*

Conversations with friends, colleagues, aunts, uncles, classmates, and even siblings could guide one to rich territory. With a nudge, most people will share their opinions, their news, their dreams, their worries. If a neighbor complains about the effects of a juice cleanse, chances are others have suffered ill experiences, and a story is born. Or perhaps the chatter will lead the writer to try her own cleanse and write about it.

To catch provocative conversations, one need go only as far as one's laptop or smartphone; Cyberspace is awash in complaints, postures, and bold statements. Anonymity protects and lifts the filter. Online publications post reader comments, and while some of those commenting hope only to stir debate, perhaps there's a kernel of an essay idea lodged in a tirade about Michelle Obama's love of kale chips. Facebook and Twitter provide plenty of fodder to peruse as friends and followers converse digitally. About what are people complaining? Rejoicing? What kinds of comments surface when you search for random topics, such as "movies," "shoe trends," or perhaps something timely such as "legalize marijuana"? Many media writers troll aggregator sites such as Reddit for ideas. A news brief might grab them — say "Man killed wife, parrot because they talked too much" — and they start mulling story options, such as how do pets impact relationships? What are the most bizarre reasons for crime in this region? Or one of the site's "SubReddits" (categories such as jokes, music, creep, fitness) might spark an idea for a personal essay. A title such as "Instagram Sunglasses — yay or nay?" could launch a reflective piece about the role of social media in our daily routines. Where are the boundaries?

Find subjects in observations

Writers notice things. Perhaps it is because we are fascinated by human nature, by what people do and why they do it. Perhaps it is because we have developed a keen sense of the absurd, or just the unusual. Or perhaps it is because we are just nosey. Regardless of the reason, writers observe, and often out of those observations sprout story ideas. While watching women's soccer on television several years ago, the author and journalist Gay Talese became fascinated with a young Chinese woman who missed a shot and lost the game against the United States. How does she endure? he wondered. He flew to China to interview her and write her story. Earlier in his career, Talese, a New Yorker, became fascinated with the building of the Verrazano Bridge, imagining what it was like to work on something so high, so dangerous. "The Bridge" chronicled the building from the workers' perspective.

TRY THIS

1. Gather three friends and ask them to each write down five things people do that annoy them. You, too, make a list. Then start talking. For each topic that flares red, write down a question that you might pursue in an essay. How do you deal with coworkers who text during dinner? How do you feel about casual sex? Should you stay friends with someone who can't keep secrets?

2. Think of a conversation you once had that left you with more questions than answers. Write down the questions and ponder how they could be approached on the page. Of these questions, isolate the ones that pose the most promise for a thorough exploration that will lead to understanding. For instance, not long ago, an aging relative told me that my father's side of the family was Jewish, that most of his relatives, including his parents, had left Germany in the 1930s to escape the concentration camps, not because they thought business was better in the United States, which was the story I had always heard. Since all the players, including my dad, were dead, I had a litany of questions. Why the cover up? How many relatives died in gas chambers? But the prompt I would choose for an essay, the question that would lead to a layered exploration would be: "How has this knowledge impacted my sense of self and family?"

Likewise, Jon Krakauer was intrigued enough by the sight at an Arizona mini-mart of women dressed in 19th century garb that he began asking questions. Who are these women, he asked the locals, wearing high-collared, long-sleeved, ankle-length dresses on a sweltering summer day? To his surprise, he learned that the nation's largest community of Mormon fundamentalists, a group who believed entry into heaven required polygamy, lived in Colorado City, Arizona, not Utah. Several thousand polygamists lived in the town under the control of a former tax accountant, the husband of over 75 women. "Under the Banner of Heaven," an examination of religious fundamentalism, resulted.

Observations don't have to involve thousands of polygamists to provide idea ammunition; often something we notice in our daily routines will crank the engine. Reflecting on random moments with his children — his toddler daughter insisting she walk alone, his son explaining why he dumped sand on the patio, his oldest daughter, now a Tibetan Buddhist nun, explaining at six that she and the man she spoke with were "not the same person" — Will Baker wrote the essay "My Children Explain the Big Issues." The frustration and humiliation of being unable to access her gynecologist's examination table from her wheelchair prompted Nancy Mairs to write "Sex and the Gimpy Girl," an essay exploring the ways our culture views women with disabilities specifically and women as a sex in general.

A sign I spotted every time I drove or biked through Ipswich, a neighboring town near my home on the North Shore of Massachusetts, launched my freelance relationship with The Boston Globe Magazine. "Voice Lessons: All Kinds," the sign read. Considering that during party sing-a-longs I was relegated to the kitchen and that years later my own son would say to me, "Mommy, when you sing you make babies cry," the thought that voice lessons would be of any value was, well, laughable. But as I sat that Friday afternoon at the desk of a Boston Globe Magazine editor prattling off Big idea after Big idea, watching her head shake like a bobble toy at all my story pitches, I blurted, "What if I take singing lessons?"

She stopped rifling through her papers. "Take singing lessons and write about it?" she asked.

I nodded, eyeing her warily.

"Yes!!!" she said exuberantly. "People love those kinds of stories."

The opening line of the essay that followed: *I sing like a mule.*

Find subjects in reading

While observation kickstarted my Boston freelance career, reading launched my Seattle writing life. Fresh out of college and new to the Pacific Northwest, I needed ideas to pitch to newspaper editors with the hope that first they'd hire me as a freelancer, and then, wowed by my skill, or at least my willingness to write for cheap, they'd hire me as staff. At least that was the plan. But first I needed ideas. So I buried myself in the Seattle Public Library's periodical rack and there, in the classifieds of the Seattle Weekly, was the ad. "Hire a Wife," it said. "Will clean, buy groceries, pick up theatre tickets, anything a wife would do except have sex." I called the phone number, interviewed the woman behind the ad, and won the lottery. Not only was her work noteworthy, but also so was she: The author of the ad was the daughter of actor Anthony Quinn, (Think "Zorba the Greek"). Tired of California, Christina Quinn had packed everything she owned into a VW bug and drove north. Without a job, she needed income, and watering other people's plants and feeding their cats was one way. The idea became an assignment, which led to more assignments, which led, eventually, to a staff feature-writing job — with health benefits!

Read everything, in print and online. Read what you don't usually read, what the people you want to write about read. Gems of ideas lurk in all kinds of text in all kinds of places. In the classifieds. In news briefs. In medical journals. In Car and Driver. In court files. During a one-day conference called "Law School for Journalists," an assistant attorney general for the state of New Hampshire told his audience that while most journalists were interested in only three or four high profile cases of murder for hire and cop killing, the state's court filing cabinets were teeming with fascinating cases. Jennie Latson, who covered courts and cops for a variety of newspapers, including the Houston Chronicle, nodded her head enthusiastically at the suggestion; some of her best stories, she said, came from rifling through files buried in court cabinets, directing her to assaults and robberies and lawsuits that had escaped media attention. Not as sensational as the high profile cases, they were nevertheless quirky and complicated and dramatic enough to make good reads.

Jonathan Harr's book "The Lost Painting" sprang from a short article in The New York Times about the unveiling in Dublin of a Caravaggio painting that had been missing for centuries. Likewise, Adrian Nicole LeBlanc discovered the idea for "Random Family," her acclaimed saga of crime, love, drugs, and poverty in the South Bronx, in a Newsday brief about the trial of a fabulously successful heroin dealer. Susan Orlean reads specialized publications — dog magazines, hunting magazines — to find people with specific interests. My editor at the Hartford Courant snagged most of his ideas from reading newspapers and magazines from other cities. One morning as he read a story in the Dallas Morning News featuring a man complaining that no one took him seriously because he was too good-looking, lighting struck. "How about a story on what it is like being a drop-dead handsome man?" my editor said, turning to me. Please no, I responded. But he prevailed, and I spent the next few days asking female coworkers to recommend men they deemed not just attractive, but gorgeous. Jon Hamm or Jamie Foxx dazzling. I called the candidates, playing it straight, using the same neutral tone I used when talking to high school principals, as I asked them to explain the hardships (and benefits) of sporting looks that others envied. After a pause, then a guffaw, most of the guys agreed. They talked about the burden of friends using them as bait at bars, of women propositioning them at parties, of colleagues assuming that they are bubbleheads. I'd like to think that my stories on more pressing issues, say elder abuse in wealthy suburbs, earned more attention, but I fear that "Drop Dead Handsome" was my best read story during my tenure at the Courant.

Find subjects Web cruising

Essayist Eula Biss found inspiration navigating the web. Fascinated by telephone poles, she gleaned from the hundreds of websites she perused that telephone poles had been used for lynching, which fed into her interest in racism. The essay "Time and Distance Overcome," a meditation on race and connection and telephone poles, resulted, and is the opening essay in her prize-winning collection "Notes from No Man's Land."

No telling what an afternoon of online reading or listening or viewing will birth. Start with digital publications, from literary journals (Brevity, River Teeth), to media sites (Salon.com, NPR.org), to individual writer's sites (Rottin' in Denmark), or aggregators such as Longreads.com that publish what their editors deem the best narratives of the past and present. Let the variety of subjects, of approaches wash over you. What thoughts emerge? Does the essay on comfort food inspire memories of past meals, past relationships? How about the piece on the alcoholic lawyer whose addiction imperiled his clients? Thoughts on other professionals plagued by demons? Does the essay about the fraternity guy's gay experience spawn questions about sexuality and gender?

Dig deep. On media sites, particularly those with a hyperlocal focus (Patch.com, Uptown Messenger, Buffalo Rising), click on the links to individual stories. What are the pressing issues in Buffalo? New Orleans? Carlisle, Pennsylvania? Any similar controversies bubbling near you? Town-gown conflicts? Land use wars? Charter school vs. public school scuffles? David vs. Goliath encounters?

When searching for ideas on trends — what people are buying, doing, researching, studying, cooking, crafting — my undergraduate students are quick to hit the social network sites — Twitter, Facebook, Linked-In, Friendster.com. If they want to learn the latest in online gaming, they go to Hi5. If they want to learn more about environmental activism, they log into Care2. When they tire of those, they move onto blogs, seeking insight into the opinions found on Xanga.com, Blogspot, and WordPress. There's no guarantee that a diamond of an idea will evolve, but, hey, it is worth a try.

Cruise the blogosphere. Skip over the legions of vacation posts and baby photos, and ferret out blogs about people's fascinations. Google's Blogsearch can take you on a wide variety of trips through politics, sports, fashions, and odd hobbies. Blogs on media sites can provide a writer's insight into a subject about which he has been researching and writing, or it can serve as an ongoing conversation. The New York Times has dozens of blogs, ranging from a professional writer posting

stories and dialogue about the college process to Beltway analysis to car maintenance to monitoring the health care industry to parenting to climate change.
Searching through blogs is sort of like shopping at Marshall's; you know there are
great stories lurking but it may take a few visits to snag one. Be patient.

Find subjects in reflection

No one ever really knows why someone would take his or her own life, and when
that person is your father, your beloved father who bought you and your sisters
boxes of grapefruits the week before he shot himself but didn't leave a note, the
confusion and hurt is deep and lasts forever. And if you are a writer like Joan
Wickersham, you use your words to seek some answers, or at least some understanding. You start out in the genre that is most comfortable — fiction — but after
years of writing a novel around suicide and recognizing that the imagined parts
were weak while the parts based on your experience were rich and compelling, you
try telling the tale as nonfiction. And it worked; "The Suicide Index" is a memoir
so textured and elegant that it was nominated for the National Book Award.

Or you could be Jan Waldron, who was 15 and overwhelmed when she gave
up her infant daughter for adoption, only to reconnect with her girl 11 years
later, the beginning of a turbulent and extraordinary relationship. Through her
years studying literature and writing as both an undergraduate and graduate student, Waldron had written around this most complicated and central bond but
eventually realized that she needed to tell the whole story, completely, honestly
and thoroughly. "Giving Away Simone" earned Waldron a guest appearance on
"Good Morning America," hardback and soft cover editions, and years of grateful letters from readers wrestling with their own adoption issues.

Often, writers new to telling stories in the first person fret that their lives are
boring, that they don't have the dramatic history of a family suicide or teen pregnancy to share on the page. Yet they have experienced loss and success, family
complications (whose family isn't complicated?), rejection, acceptance, love, fear
— all the emotions and life events that harbor great literary potential.

When you think about it, all writing boils down to the same handful of
themes. Consider the events that have shaped you, challenges you have overcome, people you admire. Consider changes you have weathered, observed. Consider situations that have disturbed you. What key moments surface when you
close your eyes and reflect on your past? Your present?

As the essayist Ryan Van Meter says, "Life gives you one, maybe two essays, in
which you just have to write down what happened. Most of what you get from
life experience is anecdotes." And those anecdotes, those scenes of car crashes and
adolescent angst, require the author to explore further what they mean, to reflect,
make connections, perhaps between that anecdote and other anecdotes. "That's
the work," says Van Meter, "the figuring out."

TRY THIS

1. Make a list of five international recent events, five national events, five regional events, and five super-local events. Underneath each, make another list of how that event has influenced you or people you know. What questions simmer? How has immigration reform impacted the migrant workers in general and one migrant worker specifically at the local apple orchard? What do your friends and relatives from other countries think of the proposed changes in U.S. immigration laws? What is their experience in their adopted country? Or if you are new to this country, what is your experience?

2. Pick a Twitter message — say, Creative Nonfiction's tweet about how everyone gets rejection letters, even Kurt Vonnegut and Madonna — and write five questions about your own experience with the subject. In the case of rejection, #1: What was the hardest "No" you ever received? #2: What did you learn from the rejection? #3: How do others you know deal with rejection? #4: Who in your circle deals with rejection the worst? #5: What have you learned from his behavior? Which of these questions intrigues you the most? What scenes illustrate the situation?

WEB CHOICES

Videographer Ann Silvio Seeks the Story in the Subject

Her dream was to be a longform writer for The New Yorker, but the only job Ann Silvio could find when she arrived in New York in her mid-20s was as a fact checker for Esquire. She freelanced a bit, too, but when a better-paying job as a research editor at The Boston Globe Magazine presented itself, she jumped. Little did she know then that her new job would lead to a whole new vocation: multimedia storytelling. When the Globe decided to move wholeheartedly into new media and sought staffers interested in audio and video stories, Silvio raised her hand. Why not? she thought. Within 3 years, she became one of the newspaper's most adept and sought-out multimedia talents and documentary producers, so talented in fact that she was soon scooped up by "60 Minutes" and became the senior producer who launched the online "60 Minutes Overtime."

Like any good reporter, she recognizes that a video requires a tension thread and a narrative arc. But as a multimedia storyteller, she also knows that not all stories lend themselves to audio and video. Her mission on every assignment is to ferret out the angle that best lends itself to her medium. And that's not always easy.

For instance, in June of 2010, as the Boston Celtics battled the Los Angeles Lakers for the NBA title, Silvio was asked to accompany a print reporter to shoot a video of the World Feed

(Continued)

(Continued)

Truck parked just outside the TD Banknorth Garden's doors. The focus of the text story was the international marketing of the NBA games, and Silvio's video would illustrate the hub-bub in this truck in which technicians would broadcast feeds of the Boston Celtics vs. Los Angeles Lakers Game #3 all around the world. But what Silvio saw in the World Feed Truck — a bunch of American producers sitting in front of computers and soundboards, pressing buttons as they sent the game to media outlets around the planet — wouldn't work for her medium. The week after her video ran, she reflected on her reporting and editing choices and how she found the story:

Nothing visual, I thought. Where is the action? Where is the audio?

The reporter got a good quote out of the vice president of the world unit, but he was not interesting to watch. I miked him up and shot him but didn't use any of it.

The game started, and I didn't have enough to tell the story. So I took my equipment, walked over to the Garden and started poking around. I began seeing these guys, none of whom spoke English, in separate rooms broadcasting the game. These guys were so animated, both physically and in the sound of their voices. There was this comic element, this cacophony of sounds, of these guys yelling in Italian and Japanese and Spanish. I asked, "Is this okay?" and started shooting. I thought, This is my video! This is my lede!

But then I had tech problems. I had this great footage of these guys but I couldn't hear over the roar of the crowd. I spent part of the night hunting down cables to plug into their audio feeds. I went into each room to get isolated sound from them, which took an hour and a half.

When I came back to the Globe, my editor asked how it went. I find that the first thing out of my mouth in conversation with editors after returning from the field is usually my best material. "Pretty good," I said. "I captured all these announcers speaking their languages doing play by play for their home audiences."

The first thing I did was watch all my interviews, which create the spine of the story. Interviews are the A roll. B roll is all footage that isn't interview. If you don't have a B roll to support the interviews, you don't have enough. You need interesting visuals and sounds. You're always trying to get variety since people get bored watching someone talking.

You quickly scrub your B roll to get a sense of what is there. You grab some clips, build a time line, a rough cut, and show it to the editors. We call that chunking up a story. You establish mini chapters by creating a time line of chunks. In the NBA story, I started with the French guys, then the Japanese guys, then the Spanish guys. I came up with the order of chunks, moving from one section to another. I put the voice over on a separate track. It took me 6 hours to edit and write a script for the NBA story. For me, that's fast.

WHAT'S THE QUESTION?

My sixth-grade teacher Mrs. Crawford summed up the heart of narrative when she said, simply, "Every story has a problem." And it is that problem, or question, that propels the reader from page to page; we read to find out how or if the problem was resolved, how the question is answered. As writers, we need to figure out long before we lower our fingers to the keyboard just what problem we hope to solve in our research or reflection. Otherwise, we sit in that car in those comfy leather seats, ready to go but with no destination. The central question the writer pursues directs the thinking and content collecting.

For Terry Tempest Williams, the question she pursued in her memoir "Refuge" was how do we find peace in change? In the spring that her mother was ill with ovarian cancer, the Great Salt Lake began to rise, threatening to flood the Bear River Migratory Bird Refuge, a spiritual haven for Williams. By weaving scenes from these two events, Williams takes the reader — and herself — on a journey to a greater understanding about control and release, about acceptance.

For John Branch, the question was how could a group of 16 elite skiers and snowboarders, many of whom knew the mountain intimately, get caught in an avalanche in western Washington? The answer, collected from months of interviews and research, is "Snow Fall: The Avalanche at Tunnel Creek," a multichapter narrative supported by interactive graphics, videos, and slideshows that explains how even the most experienced, most technologically savvy skiers can fall victim to nature.

For Chris Jones, the question was how do the remains of a soldier get from the sands of Iraq to a cemetery in Scottsburg, Indiana? After learning on CNN.com about the death of Sgt. Joseph Montgomery, Jones spent half a year tracing the route of the military man's final journey. His piece, "The Things that Carried Him," told the story in reverse — opening with his burial and concluding with the IED that killed Montgomery. By the time we meet Joey in the last pages, we understand the loss his family in particular and all military families in general endure.

Writing is an exploration, either of one's own experiences or someone else's. The question that launches the exploration can be factual (Chris Jones' pursuit of a soldier's final journey) or esoteric (Terry Tempest Williams' seeking insights into what it means to be human amid devastating change). The central question will lead to other questions, a plot and multiple subplots. Those subquests will lead the writer on various paths, but all flow back to the main thread, building context and support. Think of the main question as the spine and the subquestions as the vertebrae.

For some writers, the central query is inherent in the idea. Isabel Wilkerson interviewed over 1,000 people for her book "The Warmth of Other Suns" as she sought the answer to why thousands of African-Americans migrated from the South over a 56-year period. How does one enjoy the mundane after the loss of a child? asked Donald Murray in many essays he wrote after the death of his 20-year-old daughter. Why did I leave New York, asks Joan Didion in her essay "Good-Bye to All That?"

For others the idea is still fuzzy, and the challenge is how to zero in on that one angle. Often the answer lies in determining the core conflict.

Where lies the conflict?

Abby, a former grad student of mine, was a polished wordsmith who could wax eloquently on the page about politics, geography, and history. What she had yet to master was telling a story. An indefatigable researcher, she would plumb the Internet, interview, and observe for every subject she chose, and then she would write great blocks of background and scenes and dialogue. The only problem was, the stories meandered in all directions. While she had fascinating subjects and gobs of information, she didn't have a central question that she pursued. Without a central question, the stories offered no central message. Without a central message there was no narrative arc, and without an arc, there was no story.

One afternoon she appeared at my office door hoping to chat about her latest project. I was ready. Proposed subject: a woman who owned a small cosmetics company in New York City. "What about her?" I asked. "What's the question you'll chase in your research?"

Abby scrunched up her face. "I *hate* when you ask that," she said. She didn't have a question, she admitted, only the desire to write about this woman who faced competition from cosmetic Goliaths such as Macy's and Sephora. "Isn't that the question?" I asked.

She looked at her knees, her hands clasped tightly together. I pressed on. "Aren't you curious about how an independent small-time cosmetics boutique can survive?"

Well, she nodded slightly, yeah. And off she went, devoting most of her Thanksgiving break to interviewing and observing the woman entrepreneur in her Greenwich Village storefront, as well as researching background on the mascara and blush industry. What she learned was a testament to the will and creativity of the woman, as well as a keen business savvy, who figured out how to provide services that cosmetic chain stores cannot. In a few weeks, Abby submitted a draft that could have been titled "The Little Make-Up Company that Could."

At the heart of the journey of all nonfiction narratives, from reflective essays to personality profiles to true crime books, is some kind of conflict. The conflict provides the tale's tension, the thread that keeps the reader reading. Even a John McPhee essay on an object, say a river, explores inherent challenges, say how a proposed dam would impact the river and its ecology, not to mention those who use the river for livelihood and pleasure. Without that conflict, that thread, the story would be just blobs of information without a string connecting them.

Like you, your readers are busy. They are inundated with school and work and family demands. They are bombarded by different media screaming Watch me! Read me! Listen to me! It's your job, your writerly duty, to provide a strong enough angle into a subject that your readers will choose to devote their attention to your tale. You just can't say, "This subject interests me" and think that your reader will automatically agree. Instead, think of your reader. Why would a reader be interested in this subject? What will the reader learn? Terry Tempest Williams' "Refuge" was a personal tale that resonated universal themes about grief and denial and acceptance. Chris Jones pursued a timely tale that, too, illuminated how humans deal with death and tragedy. Both answered the most important question writers can ask themselves:

So what? Why would anyone want to read this?

Is the subject timely or timeless?

After "So what?" the next critical query is "Why now?" Clearly, if you write for a daily publication, either in print or online, the time element is critical. You are competing against other stories that are newsworthy that day, that week, and you need to update the reader, tell him what's new about the subject, what he doesn't know. If the time-sensitive issue is, say, a drought, stories might focus on who is affected (farmers, gardeners, children seeking swimming holes), and essays might ponder the author's reaction or reflections on water deprivation. If you write for publications that appear less regularly, say monthly, you have a bit more leeway but your reader — and editor — will still ask why. What about the drought will be relevant in two months?

Timeless subjects, too, require an angle, a question that will elicit fresh insights into subjects we have read about again and again. Tom French has built a career writing narratives about age-old issues — teenage relationships, murder, imprisonment — giving them life by viewing them through a specific lens. The murder of a mother and her two daughters vacationing in Florida had been covered ad nauseum by the daily press. But in French's hands, the facts became an

---

TRY THIS

Make a timeline of your life's major events. Zoom in on one that illustrates a choice you made and the consequence you experienced. Write the story (anecdote) of the choice and what happened afterward. Sit back and analyze. What have you learned from this experience? What do you want your reader to learn? How can you revise this to evolve from a central question that lures the reader from beginning to end?

exploration into good and evil, into trust and depravity. Instead of reporting just what happened, in the Pulitzer-winning "Angels and Demons," French shows the events through character, through the husband and father left behind, the detectives hell-bent on finding the killer who took the Rogers women out on his boat, bound them, assaulted them, tied a rope attached to an anchor around their necks, and then tossed them into Tampa Bay. Once the key suspect is arrested, we understand the drama through the eyes of the prosecutors. Through French's indefatigable research, the crime becomes a psychological drama, rich in emotion and complexity.

French tackled the concept of imprisonment by immersing himself in the daily routine of the Tampa's Lowry Park Zoo. Again, his intensive research provides a layered narrative that explores the universal themes of exile and loss, betrayal, extinction, and freedom, and the human's role in all of it. The angle is this specific zoo populated with its specific people and animals.

On a more personal level, one of my grad students announced one afternoon in his second year that his MFA thesis would center on another timeless topic: adoption. I waited, assuming that an elaboration would follow. But instead, silence. So I asked the obvious: What about adoption? What's new? What's a compelling angle?

He paused, rubbed a hand through his hair, and said that, well, he was adopted. He had found his birth mother, written to her, sent her a photo, but had never heard back. He tried again. Still, no answer. He knew that she had a family, two young daughters and a husband, and was a volunteer at her church and kids' schools. Intellectually, he recognized that she might have kept secret the son she bore as a college student, that she couldn't contact him for fear of what his existence could do to her family equilibrium. Emotionally, he was devastated. How could she not want to meet him?

I couldn't mend the wound, but I could help him think about what he wanted to write that might provide some healing insight. So we talked about what disturbed him most, and out of the list, which question might resonate most with an audience. His conclusion: How did open adoption laws and the resulting efforts to find birth children and parents impact the players? With that question in mind, he had an objective to guide his research and ultimately the writing of the thesis.

Curiosity fuels the narrative quest

In a talk Joan Didion gave at the University of California, a talk that later became her much-lauded essay "Why I Write," the revered writer spoke of writing to answer the images and questions in her head.

> *"I write entirely to find out what I'm thinking, what I'm looking at, what I see and what it means. What I want and what I fear. Why did the oil refineries*

TRY THIS

1. Timeless ideas are based on universal themes, such as grief, resilience, and perseverance. What friends, family members, or acquaintances have experienced one of life's major challenges? What is their story, and how can you tell it?

2. Timely ideas answer the questions so what? Why now? When stuck, think of a trend and how that trend impacts you, impacts others, or both. For instance, as more parents and professionals use Facebook to communicate with friends and colleagues, how have the original users — the under-25 set — reacted? How do your peers use social media? What is your relationship to current social media trends? What do you love and hate about them? What do others?

---

around Carquinez Straits seem sinister to me in the summer of 1956? Why have the night lights in the bevatron burned in my mind for twenty years? What is going on in these pictures in my mind?"

When considering the central question, tap into your own curiosity about the subject. After my initial conversation with my agent about a book on a year in the life of an abortion clinic, I pondered what I wanted to know. What was it like to work as a nurse in an abortion clinic, to park your car blocks away so that the protesters shouting outside your employer's door every morning wouldn't recognize the license plate and follow you home? What was it like to work as a doctor and receive daily threats to your life and your family's safety? What was it like to be a woman wrestling with the toughest decision of your life while navigating through a morass of bloody fetus posters and protestors screaming "Murderer!"? What was it like to await a Supreme Court decision to know whether or not you should show up for work, or for a scheduled appointment? When forced to provide one central question, I settled on this: How do the politics and protests on the outside affect the people on the inside of an abortion clinic?

And think of the essay, of how it originated with questions pondered by Michel de Montaigne as he sat in his French chateau overlooking the Bordeaux countryside. A lawyer by trade, he thought he'd let his mind rest when he retired, but instead he found his thoughts racing, questions bubbling like fizz in a fine champagne, and an urgent need to answer those questions in writing. What is a father's responsibility for his children? How does romantic love destroy a man's freedom? What did he think about vanity? About presumption? About glory? And so he wrote, and wrote, and wrote. Not solving anything, except his need to explore his thoughts on paper about this wide range of subjects.

Think, too, about the question behind every nonfiction narrative. In his book, "Among Schoolchildren," Tracy Kidder seeks to learn what it takes to motivate and educate 10-year-old students from a wide range of economic backgrounds. In "Soul of a New Machine" Kidder asks, "How is a computer created?" Susan Orlean wants to understand why her subjects find their chosen profession, or hobby, enthralling. The trick, Todd Balf knows, is to ferret out a fresh angle within a subject about which he cares deeply. In the case of his first book, "The Last River," he was among many writers vying to tell the story of the tragic venture. But one of the reasons that the paddlers chose Balf as their storyteller was that he wasn't interested in just rattling off the step-by-step account of what happened as they tried to be the first to ride "the Everest of rivers." Instead, he planned to explore the personal and professional impact on the kayakers of the loss of their friend and their failed excursion.

As my friend Sheila Anne Feeney says, if you have an organic interest in people and their experiences, you will always find that angle, that question. For Feeney, who has written for newspapers and magazines on both coasts, the central question always involves, as she says, "the people on the ground." When assigned to write a behind-the-scene feature about an NBA playoff game at Seattle Center, Feeney wrote about the tongue inspector, the woman who stood at the gate and asked attendees to open their mouths so that she could check for gum. A few years and a 3,000-mile move later, as she listened to her editors for a New York magazine discuss a proposed policy to prevent gay men and women from serving as foster parents, Feeney wondered what the kids in the foster care system thought. What she learned was that the kids *preferred* gay foster parents. In the kids' view, gay adults were less likely to want a foster child for money, and more likely to seek children to nurture, love, and shelter. As one boy in a do-rag and oversized pants told Feeney, gay parents spend money on them, pay attention to them, provide them with beds and clothes. "Yo man," he said, "they even buy you soy milk."

Now there's a story.

CHALLENGING CHOICES

The Washington Post's Jacqueline Salmon

Confronts The Bad Idea

Jacqueline L. Salmon has coauthored three books, including one about the U.S. military presence in Afghanistan that spent a month on The New York Times bestseller list, and written for numerous magazines, including GQ and Glamour. But it was during her 23 years as a reporter for the Washington Post that she learned best how to navigate around one of the inherent minefields of the writing life: the editor-generated bad idea. Any writer who has worked closely with an editor knows the trepidation when the boss opens with, "What about a story on ...." Holidays are particularly dicey, since Valentine's Day and Thanksgiving and Easter come every year, year after year. Original approaches are at a premium. At Christmas-time a while back, Salmon's editor suggested an idea that Salmon sensed wouldn't go any-where. Instead of agreeing then writing what she wanted, which would have irritated the editor, or agreeing and writing something she deemed lame, which would have irritated her, she enlisted a maneuver she learned waiting tables in high school.

When I was a teenager, I was a waitress at Howard Johnson's, where I was told never say no to a customer. When asked for an item that was not available, say a blueberry muffin, I would offer something else, like a corn muffin. Or a Danish. That's the atti-tude I take with editors. Never turn them down flat. Always present them with an alternative. So in December a few years ago, an editor came to me with an idea. He was not a parent but thought that because parents were working so much these days that they must be cutting back on Christmas. "I'd like you to do a story on how they cut back," he said to me.

"I think it is the opposite," I said. "I think parents are killing themselves to bring kids a bigger and better Christmas with as much homegrown stuff and activities as possible."

This was based on my gut feeling and what my friends were saying. I had the sense that my life and my friends' lives were pretty typical, but when I went out and did the reporting I made sure that I didn't focus on white, middle-class families. I went to immigrant centers that are racially diverse, ethnically diverse, and income diverse. Often reporters talk only to friends and people like them. I interviewed parents at day care centers and in grocery store parking lots. I introduced myself and asked, "How busy are you at Christmas?" My topic would grab them. If they were in a rush, I would ask for their name and number and called them later.

I was surprised by the length that parents would go to give their children a perfect childhood. I tried never to judge them, though, and instead let the readers judge.

The result was "Holiday Rush: A Tradition Some Can't Do Without," which opens like this:

There's no such thing as overdoing Christmas as far as Linda Osborne is concerned. She is mailing out more than 100 Christmas cards, buying 75 gifts for family and friends, baking dozens of cookies, throwing the holiday party for her 5-year-old daughter's class at school and organizing a holiday tour of her Silver Spring neighborhood.

Her pre-Christmas schedule is so jam-packed, Osborne said, that she had to string her outdoor lights at midnight a few days ago because it was the only free moment she had.

No matter. Osborne, 40, a full-time legal secretary, accepts this exhausting pace as one of the season's rituals. "I feel like I'm trying to do more and more," she said. "I don't know why. I'm crazy, I guess."

Chapter

2

What's the Form?

Overview

While this book celebrates the commonalities shared between different kinds of nonfiction storytelling, it is important to identify — and embrace — the range of forms available to writers of factual narratives. To that end, this chapter explores a variety of those forms, which include:

Internal Narratives

External Narratives

Internal and External Narratives

Length: Short Essay? Kindle Single? Full-Fledged Book?

Multimedia Options

LONG BEFORE TRUMAN CAPOTE PICKED UP The New York Times and read about the brutal murder of the Clutter family in Holcomb, Kansas, he had decided that he wanted to use his considerable fiction writing talents to spin a factual tale with tension, character, dialogue, and setting. A crime would be the perfect subject, he thought. So when he spotted the Times story on that November day in 1959, about the Saturday night slaughter of the Kansas farmer and his family in their home, he hit gold. He had a mystery, a small town shattered, and a police chase. All the key ingredients to create what would become the best-selling classic "In Cold Blood."

In Capote's case, the form came before the subject. Likewise, when Chris Jones is assigned a story for Esquire he understands the magazine has a style and length that he must accommodate. A men's magazine, Esquire expects a well-researched article told in either omniscient or first person point of view that runs from 3,000 to 9,000 words, depending on if it is a short personality profile or a back-of-the-book immersion feature. The voice can be cantankerous, or witty, or ruminative, or remorseful — anything as long as it is distinct. The piece can include sections of reflection, but unless it is a first-person feature — that is a story about Jones' experience and only his, say a reminiscence of renovating his old Victorian home near Lake Ontario — much of the content will be gleaned from interviewing, reporting, and observation. An Esquire writer serves as a guide, an interpreter, molding the content to support his point, sometimes leading the reader gently to a conclusion and sometimes forcefully.

As a narrative writer for the Tampa Bay Times, Ben Montgomery has the enviable job of devoting most of his workweek to pursuing his curiosities, which he defines as loneliness, the consequence of human choices, and the human collision that often results. He's pursued stories about everything from the lovable outlaw who stole Crystal Gale's van to a lynching of an innocent African-American man to unresolved deaths at a Florida boy's school. While he has the luxury to spin a tale scene by scene and to develop his sources into three-dimensional characters, he also knows that his readers (and editors) expect a format that is based on fact, less on perception, and explains early on why the story is newsworthy.

When essayist Dinty W. Moore created his online journal Brevity, he knew that he would only accept short — 750 words or less — essays that, as one guest blogger says, "use language and form in unexpected ways." No he said/she said fact, fact, fact newswriting. No lengthy memoir. Just, as Moore says, narratives that celebrate "concision, precision, density of language, the importance of intimate detail." As an essayist, Moore delves into subjects from his own perspective, twisting and turning them, examining them, and arriving at some kind of resolution, which is often no resolution. As an editor and reader, he delights in ruminations about a scene in McDonald's or the meaning of hair or a bad date. A successful essay is one that plays with image and meaning and language. An essay doesn't have to prove its newsworthiness. As Michel de Montaigne, considered one of the fathers of the modern essay, stated in the 16th century that *essai* in French means "to try." And that is what an essay does — tries to understand a question, a situation, an experience.

Certain writers specialize in certain forms — Ben Montgomery avoids first person narratives while Dinty W. Moore embraces them — but the beauty for most writers is the infinite possibilities of ways to spin a tale of fact. If the subject is a guy training for the "Triple Crown" of distance swimming — the English Channel, the Catalina, California channel, and around the island of Manhattan — Moore might write an essay exploring what it means to set goals. Montgomery might write a feature about one event and supplement the text with a video or audio slide show of the swim, the swimmer's arms slicing through the rolling waves. A longform narrative writer such as Chris Jones might invest the next 3 years in following the training and the events for a book.

While many writers don't know the form the narrative should take until they are neck-deep in research or have started to write — as Joan Wickersham says, a lot of blundering goes on before one hits the right chord — other writers find choosing a form in the early stage helpful. It serves as a guide. Like an architect designing a ranch rather than a Victorian mansion based on basic factors such as site size and budget, the writer weighs possible forms based on the subject and the writer's relationship with the subject. Todd Balf explores the impact of club soccer on parents in a first-person narrated essay because he is the parent of club soccer players. When chronicling an ill-fated kayak expedition in Tibet, he frames the story as a journey told through the eyes of those participating. He wasn't there. It isn't his story. Likewise, Joshuah Bearman wasn't in Iraq, a dry country, when a bar operated out of the U.S. fortress known as the Green Zone. Like Balf, he recreated the story from the point of view of those involved. But Bearman also considered multimedia forms that would complement his narrative "Baghdad Country Club" that ran in Atavist, a digital longform publication. Cartoons, timelines, maps, and videos are featured with the narrative that illustrates how this legendary bar thrived in a war zone.

Fortunately for the writer, it's a lot easier to switch forms than it is for an architect to reshape a house once the frame has been nailed into place. No decision for a writer is irreversible; somewhere down the line the subject she thought would mold neatly into a modest story proves complex enough to fill a book. Or that the subject she envisioned as a book lacked heft and was better off told as a Brevity short. Or the travel story she wanted to tell about hut-to-hut climbing in the White Mountains is richer as a personal essay on overcoming adversity.

When we talk about spinning narratives from fact we have distinct choices about form: Is the narrative internal (an exploration of the writer's experience)? Is the narrative external (an exploration of someone else's experience)? In cinematic terms, is the camera pointed in toward the writer or out toward another person or place? Or is the narrative both internal and external? Is the narrative based on the author's experience and supplemented with outside research? Or is the external subject complemented by the author's perspective and background?

Let's start by exploring the internal.

INTERNAL NARRATIVES

When I was a feature writer for the Hartford Courant, my apartment in a 3-story Tudor building on a busy street in a Connecticut suburb known for its fur coats and diamond tennis bracelets was robbed twice in a week. I felt so violated, so raw and vulnerable that I didn't know whether to chase down the guys I suspected (my neighbors) or hibernate behind padlocked doors. My losses — some jewelry and stereo equipment — earned only a yawn from the local police and a shrug from my landlady, who claimed that the octogenarian building manager and his blind poodle Susie kept the tenants safe. The only way I knew to gain control was to write, or as Joan Didion says, to learn what I thought. At first I planned to write a feature story about coping with crime. I'd talk to experts and other people who had suffered rape and burglary and gather statistics. But that seemed ordinary, and I was too close to the experience to even pretend impartial analysis. And so instead I wrote an essay about struggling with personal violation and shattered security.

Personal narrative. Self-reflection. Examining a life event. Examining one's reaction to someone else's life event. In internal writing, the camera is pointed at the author, and the author's mission is to dissect, to turn an experience, a thought, a reflection, a reaction inside and out from all possible angles. In a personal essay, Virginia Woolf studies a moth on her window and plumbs what it means to live, to die. Brenda Miller prepares for a date and ruminates about relationships and intimacy. In a memoir, a narrative that focuses on one aspect of the author's life, Jeanette Walls chronicles her turbulent childhood as she attempts to understand how her parents ended up eating out of dumpsters while she became a media celebrity. David Sheff traces the obsessive worry and wrenching self-doubt he felt as he sought to rescue his once joyous son from crystal meth addiction.

In the two primary internal forms, the personal essay and the memoir, the writer takes us on a personal journey that reveals a universal truth about the human experience.

Personal essay

The personal essay is one of the most versatile and malleable forms of nonfiction writing. From Montaigne pondering the different ways to raise children to David Sedaris remembering his drama days to an NPR "This I Believe" podcast about the power of spontaneity, the personal essay takes many shapes. Julia Powell's blogs about cooking her way through 524 Julia Child's recipes could be considered essays. Rebecca Solnit's rumination on the arrogance of men on TomDispatch.com is a personal essay. The common ingredient is the author's examination of an experience, or a thought, and what it means. After that, everything — the structure, the voice, the role of scene vs. reflection, the literary devices — is up for grabs.

The engine running what one of my grad students calls "The Montaigne Essay," is reflection, the author's ruminations connecting a life experience or observation to a larger theme, a universal truth. Instead of following scenes, you follow the writer's mind at work. As Phillip Lopate says, in a personal essay the writer chases a thought, dissecting it from all angles. In his essay "Against Joie de Vivre," Lopate tries to untangle why he resents people flaunting their efforts to live well. In "Book Marks" Rebecca McClanahan uses the comments people write in book margins as a vehicle to explore life choices and relationships:

> *And from what she has left behind on the pages of Levertov's poems, it appears that our hearts have worn down in the same places. This is the part that worries me. Though my heart has mended, for the time being at least, hers seems to be in the very act of breaking. A present-tense pain pulses through each marked-up poem, and the further I read the clearer it becomes what she is considering. I want to reach through the pages and lead her out.*

Her fascination with "marginalia" is the arc of this essay as she explores her habit's history, of claiming someone else's words as her own, and reflects on the connections between the comments, the books, and her own past emotional upheavals. "Book marks" serve as a metaphor for lives lived, and she uses the image to understand troubled times of her own. Her primary tool is reflection, more telling than showing:

> *For instance, you can leave, gather up what remains of yourself and set off on a journey much like the journey of faith Levertov writes of. Or, if that proves too difficult, you can send your self off on its own, wave goodbye, step back into childhood's shoes and refuse to go one step further. You can cut off your hair, take the pills the doctors prescribe and beg for more, then lose yourself daily in a gauzy sleep, surrounded by the books that have become your only food. His deferment dream did not materialize, so you have followed him to a military base where you know no one. Vietnam is still a possibility. Your heart is divided: you dread the orders yet pray for them. If they come, you will be able to retreat honorably to your parents' home. In the meantime, you have the pills and the books and the bed grown huge by his nightly absence — he is sleeping elsewhere now, with someone else, and he no longer even tries to hide it.*

Yet another breed of the personal essay depends as much, if not more, on showing. Life experiences are lived and examined scene by scene. Sometimes the author inserts himself to explain one scene before jumping into another, and sometimes the writers let the scenes speak for themselves. In "Writing & Publishing a Memoir: What in the Hell Have I Done?" Andre Dubus III ponders how his memoir of violence and abandonment will impact his mother and siblings, the very people he wrote about. We move from scenes of family conversations to scenes of audiences reacting to his reading, supported by passages of reflection and explanation. In describing one scene at a reading, Dubus pauses to examine the difference between characters in a novel and characters in a memoir and the effect on the author:

> *Years ago I read an interview with the writer Janet Burroway, in which she says that when readers go to the novel, what we're really saying to it is this: "Give me me." Most of us know this to be true. If the writer goes deeply enough into her characters and their stories, then they'll go deeply enough into us too, their own natures resonating with ours, like an easterly breeze moving wind chimes on a porch we'd never even known about. But with creative nonfiction/memoir, the breeze seems to be even more direct, the wind chimes closer to the front door of the house in which we live.*
>
> *"Hey, don't tell me but I know who the Murphy brothers really are. The Pecker Street gang."*
>
> *The man who said that wore a dark sweater and Dickie work pants, broken capillaries blooming across his upper cheeks. He was my age, and looked pleased with himself, and I liked him right away.*

Dubus moves seamlessly between exposition — pondering the meaning of writing about real people and the impact your story will have on them — and action, the scenes that illustrate this conflict.

In his essay "My Children Explain the Big Issues," Will Baker ruminates about what he has learned from his children in scenes, depicting lessons his two daughters and sons have taught him through action and no reflection. In the first scene he is walking with his 23-month-old daughter, who is dressed only in a diaper, a floral print bonnet, and cowboy boots, up a long hill. This is the longest walk his daughter has ever taken, and when Baker sees sweat sprout on her nose, he offers to carry her. She declines. She falls on loose gravel. She pauses. "But quickly she scrambles up and slaps at the dirty places on her knees, then looks at me sidelong with a broad grin. See?"

No reflection necessary. The action says it all.

Blogging

Anyone with an Internet connection can blog. Friends blog about their trip to Ghana, their home renovation, their new puppy. Aspiring chefs blog about their recipes. Aspiring novelists blog about their work-in-progress. Journalists blog about their beat — the White House, local schools, transportation. Book lovers blog about books. And moms — moms from Oregon to Maine, Mississippi to

TRY THIS

1. What makes you feel vulnerable? State the source in one word (e.g., the unknown, parking garages, loneliness). List three anecdotes that illustrate moments when you felt anxious. List three reasons why you might have reacted this way. List two examples of other people reacting similarly and two examples of people reacting dissimilarly. Sleuth a little on the Internet for videos or expert opinions, anything pertaining to the source of anxiety. Write an essay exploring this reaction. What do you learn about yourself specifically and human behavior in general?

2. Spend 20 minutes roaming social media sites — Twitter, Facebook, Instagram, Pinterest. What themes do you notice? Thoughtless rantings? Bawdy jokes? Compromising photos? Self-congratulations? List the themes and ask questions of each. Why does online self-indulgence make you yearn for Walden Pond? Should Instagram be more selective about the photos it runs? Should social media sites delete some of the rants? Try writing an essay that answers one of these questions.

Minnesota — blog about parenting products, parenting tips, parenting traps, parenting resources. They blog for camaraderie, and they blog to share what they've learned.

It has been argued that these blogs are not literature, or at least not in the same league as personal narratives that have been revised and edited and published in established journals and magazines. While fresh and spontaneous, a self-published blog is often more passion than polished prose, the argument goes, a chain of incomplete thoughts and awkward sentences. Editing is not a service provided by a blogging platform such as WordPress or Blogger.

While this may be true for your neighbor's blog about tackling crabgrass or a former roommate's postings about favorite musicians, it is not true for the myriad sites that publish personal reflections as finely tuned as any New Yorker essay. Log on to blog posts for sites such as The Dish, Huffington Post, Vox, Slate, or The Rumpus and you'll find focused, tightly composed, and thoughtful narrative commentary. For instance, Brian McGuigan's "I Wasn't the White Boy Everyone Thought I Was" from The Rumpus, reads like a polished memoir:

I stared at the line of boxes under the Race and Ethnicity section of my college application unsure of which to check. Based on my features alone, I was just another white boy: pale skin, brown hair, and freckles. They were all traits I shared with my mother, who sat beside me at our rickety kitchen table.

I hadn't planned to apply for college. Few of my friends from the neighborhood — the ones who hadn't already dropped out — were going. I wanted to find a job, had even talked about joining the Navy like my grandfather, but my mother shot that down. She'd enrolled in college after graduating high school, went back before she had me at 32, then night school once I was old enough to be home alone. But she never finished ....

My eyes ticked down the options; none seemed applicable to me. My mother must've suspected I'd struggle. Before I could turn to her for help, she tapped a pencil beside Hispanic/Latino and said, "This one."

McGuigan employs scene, character, dialogue, and plot in his essay about claiming his ethnic identity. The sentences are crisp, the emotion ripe, and the pace fluid. Likewise, on Andrew Sullivan's blog, The Dish, posts are articulate assessments of issues from the Common Core standardized tests to pollen pollution to atheism. The reader feels that he is on a lively and engaging intellectual journey. Sullivan, a writer and editor who has worked for some of the biggest names in nonfiction, including The New Republic and The New York Times Magazine, is not among the writers dissing blogs as rambling online narcissism. Instead, he argues that blogging has become a literary art form. In a column for The Atlantic called "Why I Blog," Sullivan stated that while blogging's "truths are provisional, and its ethos collective and messy," the interaction blogs enable between writer and reader "is unprecedented, visceral, and sometimes brutal." Blogging is to writing, he says, "as sports are to athletics: more free-form, more accident-prone, less formal, more alive. It is, in many ways, writing out loud."

Memoir

Unlike an autobiography, which marches a reader through key events from birth to present, a memoir hones in on a slice of the writer's life. Frank McCourt's infamous "Angela's Ashes" recounts the tragic and comic path of his family's immigration from Ireland to New York. Darin Strauss' "Half a Life" contemplates the lasting effects of a car accident years before. He was 18, a month shy of graduating, when a bike rider, a girl from his high school, inexplicably rode her bike across two lanes of traffic and rammed into the car Strauss was driving. She died hours later. Despite being deemed innocent by the police, the courts, and the community, Strauss couldn't shake the guilt — until he wrote about it 18 years after that horrific spring day. Kelly Corrigan was in the middle of intensive chemotherapy for breast cancer when she, the mother of an infant and a toddler, learned that her father, her idol, her best friend, had testicular cancer. How else to process the emotional chaos but to write about it? Her memoir, "The Middle Place," focuses on the year she and her father battled cancer, a reflection on what it means to be both a daughter and a mother, and a daughter and a wife, facing mortality.

And unlike the fact-checkable autobiography, a memoir is based on scene-by-scene construction punctuated by reflections. Rather than just telling the story of a person's life, a memoir offers the reader universal themes. A rambling of I-did-this-I-did-that, regardless of how graceful the prose, means little to the reader if there is no meaning. Without a direction, a narrative arc of a beginning, middle, and end, the scene is a journal entry; it holds no meaning for an outside audience. Scenes without arc, without theme, are journal entries.

How much those themes are illuminated in scene vs. the summation is up to the writer. Mary Karr's "The Liar's Club" is told primarily from the child's point of view, depending on action and dialogue rather than reflection. From the opening scene of the local East Texas sheriff carrying away the child Mary and her sister Lecia from their home in the middle of the night, Karr shares the story of her chaotic childhood as a camera chronicling key moments with just enough reflection for the action to make sense:

> *On the night the sheriff came to our house and Mother was adjudged more or less permanently Nervous, I didn't yet understand the word. I had only a vague tight panic in the pit of my stomach, the one you get when your parents are nowhere in sight and probably don't even know who has a hold of you or where you'll wind up spending the night.*
>
> *I could hear the low hum of neighbor women talking as we got near the front door. They had gathered on the far side of the ditch that ran before our house, where they stood in their nightclothes like some off-duty SWAT team waiting for orders. The sheriff let go of my hand once we were outside. From inside the tall shadow of his hat, with my sister still wrapped around him in bogus slumber, he told me to wait on the top step while he talked to the ladies. Then he went up to the women, setting in motion a series of robe-tightenings and sweater buttonings.*

The narrator tells us that her mother was deemed Nervous, but that at the moment, the child Mary didn't know what that meant, only the panic she felt with all these strangers in her house. And then she takes us outside and shows us the sheriff, the neighborhood women in their bathrobes, and her sister pretending to be asleep in the sheriff's arms. A tight ballet of show and tell.

In contrast, Darin Strauss' narrative uses scene to launch lengthy passages of exposition in which he analyzes what he was feeling in the hours, days, months, and years following the accident in which his car struck a classmate on a bicycle:

> *My father arrived. Someone must have called him, though this was before cell phones. It was the sight of my dad that day, the clean sadness on his face, that turned this real, finally. All this had happened to me; I had done this; I was his*

son. Dad was somehow like a new circuit in the fuse box. He arrived, emotion could flow. In his hug I went out all at once into tears, as I never had before and haven't since. I don't remember how long we'd all been there, whether I'd gone to look at Celine's excessively pale face again. (A psychologist later told me such memory skips have been installed for our own protection. Trauma makes a spark that in a white glow washes out details, guilt, shame — a flare that throws the recent past into shadow and deep obscurity.)

His father arriving is the action. But then the narrator steps in to interpret the meaning of his father's presence, the implication to the younger Darin. In the balance of show and tell, Strauss leans more on the tell.

What is the difference between memoir and personal essay? Sometimes nothing. Both can be scene-based and offer a reader a rich experience. But unlike a personal essay, which can entail a writer musing about the power of gun ownership, or marriage, or the plight of a moth, a memoir is based on memory. The name itself, after all, stems from the Latin *memoria*, meaning memory or reminiscence.

And while memory may be enough to form the narrative arc, few humans can recall all the minute details — the brand of cake mix a grandmother used, the population of a favorite Wyoming town — that are essential to the story. When reminiscence fails, research enters and the internal tale looks to the external for support.

EXTERNAL NARRATIVES

"But I don't want to write about myself," pleaded one of my students in an undergraduate essay writing course. A biology major, Katie loved research and had grown weary of writing about growing up with grandfather's honey business and her mother's depression. While many of her classmates were thrilled to ponder the meaning of their life experiences, to tap their memories as their only source, Katie's interests pointed outward. Yet she fretted that she hadn't studied journalism, that she didn't want to be a reporter, but that she did want to write about subjects other than, well, Katie.

Easy enough. The beauty of narrative nonfiction is that any subject has potential, and one's own experiences are merely one area to plumb. Turn the camera and one's curiosity outward and a whole universe awaits investigation. Admittedly, I am far more interested in learning about the lives of others than I am in examining my past. Through observing and hearing of the challenges, successes, expertise, and interests of homicide detectives, mussel farmers, day care providers, life coaches, child crossword puzzle champions, and any one of the hundreds of people I have written about, I learn just a little more about the planet, about the human connection, about why people do what they do. Writing about

TRY THIS

Since all narratives depend on conflict, and all lives are filled with conflicts big and small, a memoirist has years of material to mine. For starters, here are some prompts to help turn those past problems into audience-worthy stories:

1. Changes are a huge source of conflict, either in the anticipation, the process, or the aftermath. Think of changes you've encountered — income changes, relationship changes, health changes, changes in beliefs. Pick one. List scenes that represent the three stages. Scenes that show the problem that forced the change and how you felt at the prospect. Scenes that show you in the midst of the alteration and scenes that illustrate what happened afterward. What did you learn from the experience? What would others learn from your experience? Try writing a 500-word essay about this change, showing the switch and also explaining what you learned then and now as you reflect back.

2. Adolescence is ripe with problems. Mull places you frequented in your middle school years. The cafeteria? The city basketball courts? Your grandmother's apartment? The floating dock at summer camp? Choose one that evokes memories. What happened at this place? What made you anxious? Happy? Explore the why. Write three scenes that illustrate either the delight or the anxiety. Who were the other players? How did they behave? Arrange and rearrange the scenes. Note the patterns. What did you learn about kindness and relationships? Try weaving your insights into the scenes. Voila. An essay draft.

3. On one piece of paper write a defining life event. A parent's death? A college rejection? A civic award? A mentor's suggestion to change jobs? On a second piece of paper write how that event changed you, what you learned from the experience. On a third piece of paper write what someone who doesn't know you would learn from reading about this event and your insights. Identify scenes that will illustrate this message. Write the essay.

"other" is like an anthropological dig; by studying someone else's lifestyle and decisions, we expand our knowledge of culture. Or, as the writer Ted Conover, who has built a career writing about hoboes and prison guards and Nigerian truck drivers, says in an interview in the "New New Journalism," "There are many ways of looking at the world."

For many writers, the fear of research, of combing through databases and books and magazines and journals, of talking to people to gather content, is paralyzing. Like Katie, they fear that if they haven't studied newswriting and reporting, if they haven't written for their school newspaper or interviewed for the local cable channel, that they can't possibly write about something other than themselves, use sources other than their memories and reflections.

It's funny, especially to those of us who started our careers writing for the media, that the prospect of — yikes! — interviewing a human could pose such an obstacle. Journalism has such a harsh sound to some, so intimidating. But all that we're talking about is focusing on a subject other than oneself and gathering the content needed to tell that story. Sometimes the level of content needed is minimal. When John Jeremiah Sullivan was assigned by GQ to cover the Creation Festival, a multiday Christian rock event on a farm planted in a valley in rural Pennsylvania, his goal was to learn why tens of thousands of Evangelical fans would travel for days to listen to these bands. Instead, the guys he intended to profile caused him to reflect on his own (brief) past as an Evangelical teen and the research became part reporting, part observation, part just sitting around playing guitar and chatting with these guys, and part reflection. Readers of "Upon this Rock" learn as much about the author as they do about the festival.

When Katherine Boo writes about poverty in a Mumbai slum in her book "Behind the Beautiful Forevers," the camera is on the slum and its residents. When Ben Montgomery builds a narrative about the lynching of an innocent black man, his eyes are on the man, his accusers, the culture that bred the venom. In these narratives, the writer's physical presence isn't necessary.

Gary Smith, a writer for Sports Illustrated, has a gift for spinning tales of others in distinctive ways. In "Shadows of a Nation," he takes the reader on a journey into the complex world of a Native American reservation and its pull on the young men by focusing on a talented basketball player, who is wooed by the outside world, but keeps returning to the reservation and succumbing to alcoholism and sex that leads to early fatherhood. He opens in second person, shifts to third and omniscient and ends in second person. In "The Man Who Couldn't Read," he tells the whole story through the main character's point of view, the story of a man who made it through high school and college, and built a successful real estate career, without knowing how to read. This piece is mind-boggling in detail, and one can only imagine the hours of interviewing devoted to extracting the specifics from someone else's memory to recreate these scenes.

None of them understood what night sweat could do to a man. If he needed one badly enough, was there any charade a man couldn't play? John remembered a spring day back in fourth grade, back when the realization that he would be forever different from everyone else had begun to come over him. He had run out of class at 3:00 p.m., aching for some arena in which to prove he wasn't really the boy who sat at his desk, stupid and silent as a stone, and then had felt his legs moving toward the school's ball field, even though he was too young to play. Standing behind the batting cage with his glove on his hand, he watched the game with hungry eyes, noticing that neither team wore uniforms and there was no outfield fence, and how the big kid on the other school's team belted the ball over the right fielder's head his first two times up.

A memoirist could just reach back in his memory to extract this kind of sensory detail, but Smith had to ask his subject to resurrect the fourth grade moment. He had to ask his subject what he felt like as a kid sitting at a school desk, unable to read the text in front of him. He had to ask how he dealt with the shame. What did he do? How did he react? Could he recall a specific moment when his affliction became clear? Storytellers of external tales must dig deep to gather the specifics — the night sweats, standing behind the batting cage — that make a narrative strike an emotional chord.

INTERNAL AND EXTERNAL NARRATIVES

In the old days, a stark division lay between reporters and writers. Reporters scribbled on little notebooks, their pen flying across the page, capturing quotes and facts from crime witnesses, politicians, rape survivors, garbage collectors, city clerks, and gas station attendants. Back in the newsroom, they carved those notes into fact-filled stories, writing from a distant, objective point of view. Rarely did the reporter ever physically appear in a story, divulge her life experiences, her perspective, her interactions.

In contrast, writers ruminated. Like Montaigne, they sharpened their pencils, stared out the window, and carved beautiful metaphors out of their insights about friendship and nature and crushing loss. They wrote elegant essays from their point of view, infusing the prose with their voice, their wisdom, their feelings, making connections between their experiences and greater themes. Think

TRY THIS

1. Read the headlines of a daily media site such as Slate.com or your local newspaper. Pick three stories. What is the local impact or connection? How might these issues affect people in your community? Make a list of possible story ideas to pursue. For instance, for a headline about the inadequate response to sexual assaults on many of the nation's college campuses, one story idea could be a local college's response to increased federal pressure to update the sexual assault protocol. Another story could be profiling a survivor of sexual assault whose case was ignored. Or a story of a young woman or man who changed his or her school's attitude toward sexual assault.

2. Interview someone you don't know well about an event that changed his or her life. Ask enough questions to gather specific detail to recreate the key moments. Where was she? What did the room look like? What did she feel? What did she say? What else was happening in the scene? What were other people doing? Write the scene. What other details are needed to make it complete?

of the classic "Once More to the Lake," as E. B. White ponders his mortality during a visit with his son to the lake he had enjoyed with his own father.

It's not that writers who gathered content from sources other than their own memories and observations didn't write lyrical and lovely narratives. Flip back centuries. Daniel Defoe wrote about notorious criminals. Henry Mayhew wrote about an 8-year-old girl selling watercress. Stephen Crane wrote about a mob scene. Jack London wrote about the grinding poverty of East London. But it wasn't until the middle of the 20th century that narratives based on external research became a genre in their own right, starting with novelist John Hersey's "Hiroshima," a narrative that explored the lives of six people who survived the bombing of Hiroshima and ran in The New Yorker in August 1946 on the first anniversary of the bombing. Hersey told their stories from their point of view, gathering the content through exhaustive interviewing and research, and writing it as a novel, with a narrative arc, or a tension line, with a clear beginning, middle, and end. Readers were captivated. What followed was an explosion of narrative nonfiction writing based on reporting, from Gay Talese's profiles in Esquire ("Frank Sinatra has a Cold") to Joan Didion's essays in The Saturday Evening Post ("Some Dreamers of the Golden Dream") to Truman Capote's "In Cold Blood," which was first serialized in The New Yorker. While Capote called his creation a "nonfiction novel," Tom Wolfe trumpeted this breed of writing as "New Journalism," defining it as fact-based narratives written with the tools of fiction. They employed four key literary devices: scene-by-scene construction, dialogue, third person point of view, and rich detail. Wolfe called the latter "status life," or the use of detail to illustrate character, economics, and lifestyle.

Soon, all sorts of narratives based on all sorts of reporting filled magazine pages. Instead of what many readers considered traditional journalism, facts delivered by a distant omniscient narrator in a balanced, neutral way, you could hear the author's voice in the storytelling and feel his prose guiding one to a conclusion. In Tracy Kidder's "Among School Children," the scenes of a year in the life of a fifth-grade class in Holyoke, Massachusetts, reveal the challenges teachers face as they try to instruct children of financially and emotionally challenged families. Kidder's sympathies are clearly with Chris Zajac, the teacher he observed and interviewed for 10 months.

While many readers would be predisposed to condemn Bronx drug dealers and the women who loved them, few would not feel empathy toward these characters after reading "Random Family." Adrian Nicole LeBlanc spent over a decade immersed in the lives of drug dealers and their women and families, spending days and nights and weeks with them in their Bronx apartments, chauffeuring loved ones to prison visits, attending children's summer camp events, observing, and listening. By showing rather than telling why these young women so firmly attached themselves to the men who loved and mistreated them, to drug runners and dealers and murderers, "Random Family" did what all the academic articles and news stories crammed with facts and stats couldn't do: hit the reader on a visceral level:

> *Freed from school one afternoon, Coco and Dorcas headed for the bodega on Andrews Avenue. Coco had her black hair pulled up severely, with a dollop of Vaseline on her bangs to tame the curl, and two lollipops stuck in her ponytail. Her skin shone. She used Vaseline as a moisturizer, but also to protect her from scarring if she got into a fight. Conspicuous signs of wear were shaming in the ghetto, which was partly why Coco liked her clothes neat and new. "That was one thing, my mother always tried to keep us in style," Coco recalled. She preferred shirts that exposed her midriff, and tight pants of short shorts that showed off her thighs. The pants in style were called chewing gum because they stretched. Foxy bought Coco a pair in every color — blue, red, green, yellow, black, and pink .... That day, Coco wore a turquoise Spandex pair. She swished her way in the bodega. The cleats on her tiny feet clacked against the floor.*

> *"Yo, what's up with that girl?" Cesar asked.*

> *"Yo, what's up with your friend?" B.J. asked Dorcas. "My friend thinks she's nice."*

> *Coco returned to the sidewalk, and Dorcas filled her in. "Why can't he talk for himself?" Coco said pertly.*

> *"I can talk for myself," Cesar said.*

Through LeBlanc's indefatigable reporting, this scene pulses with sensory detail and dialogue, providing us insight into character, not just situation. A newspaper report might focus on teenage pregnancy in the Bronx or the numbers of juvenile drug dealers. But LeBlanc turns statistics and facts into a human story, a narrative throbbing with love and heartbreak, even humor, amid the drug deals and fights.

One could say that the author's voice and arrangement of material — the selection and phrasing — reveals the internal in a story that focuses on the external. In many cases, however, it isn't only the author's voice, but also the author's physical presence in the story that guides you to his or her point of view. By spending 11 years in the Bronx, LeBlanc developed a relationship with the men and women she observed. That relationship led to an understanding of why they often made disastrous choices — poverty, neglect, lack of education, insularity — and that understanding bred empathy. LeBlanc has no answers, but through portraying the lives of her characters, she tries to guide the reader to her sympathetic point of view, or at least to see the faces behind the urban world of drugs and guns and prison and single moms. We finish "Random Family" stunned by our ignorance and acutely aware of other lives lived.

Because of their immersion, the time invested into the research, narrative journalists such as LeBlanc have accumulated the ammunition, the content, to justify their strong points of view. Who would argue that 11 years isn't long enough to know a subject? Or the 5 years that Neil Swidey spent investigating and writing "Trapped Under the Sea," a harrowing tale of five divers sent into an airless, lightless, 10-mile tunnel deep under Boston harbor to complete a task that the engineers had overlooked? Two divers perished. To understand what went wrong, Swidey spent thousands of hours interviewing participants in the Deer Island Sewage Treatment project — the goal of which was to clean the polluted waters of the harbor by treating the raw sewage and sending it deep into the sea — from engineers to divers, as well as NASA officials to learn more about running high-risk missions. From his exhaustive reporting, Swidey deduced that the fault lay with multiple people and dismal communication. His narrative illuminates not just a singular tragedy, but also what can happen when multiple parties in a joint venture focus only on their role.

Some topics require not years but weeks, or perhaps just days, of total immersion. To understand why the country was in upheaval that cold, wet spring of 1967, why cities and towns were steeped in drugs and murders and bankruptcy notices, Joan Didion headed to the epicenter of the chaos, San Francisco, a mecca for teen runaways. She spent weeks roaming the streets of Haight Ashbury, talking to the police and peyote dealers and the missing children who called themselves hippies. She attended concerts in Golden Gate Park, drank green tea with Max, who hoped to start a commune in Nevada, and sat in an overheated room observing a group of teens tripping on acid for 4 hours, during which "a window banged in Barbara's room and about five-thirty some children had a fight in the street. A curtain billowed in the afternoon wind. A cat scratched a beagle in Sharon's lap. Except for the sitar music on the stereo there was no other sound or movement until seven-thirty, when Max said, 'Wow.'" She wrote "Slouching Towards Bethlehem" in first person, painting the social hemorrhaging scene-by-scene, concluding with moments that involve children:

> *When I finally find Otto he says "I got something at my place that'll blow your mind," and when we get there I see a child on the living room floor, wearing a reefer coat, reading a comic book. She keeps licking her lips in concentration and the only off thing about her is that she's wearing white lipstick.*
>
> *"Five years old," Otto says. "On acid."*
>
> *The five-year-old's name is Susan, and she tells me she is in High Kindergarten. She lives with her mother and some other people, just got over the measles, wants a bicycle for Christmas, and particularly likes Coca-Cola, ice cream, Marty in the Jefferson Airplane, Bob in the Grateful Dead and the beach ...*

For a year now her mother has given her both acid and peyote. Susan describes it as getting stoned.

I start to ask if any of the other children in High Kindergarten get stoned, but I falter at the key words.

"She means do other kids in your class turn on, get stoned," says a friend of her mother's who brought her to Otto's.

"Only Sally and Anne," Susan says.

"What about Lia?" her mother's friend prompts.

"Lia," Susan says, "is not in High Kindergarten."

Didion is clearly unnerved by the sight of this child on acid, yet she doesn't have to say she's unnerved. Her inability to articulate "High Kindergarten" and the facts of the scene reflect her unease. Didion is not the story; for the most part the camera is pointed out, at the characters tripping and baking bread and searching for hash in the floorboards. Instead, Didion's presence is the vehicle through which the reader experiences the drugs and sex and danger of 1967.

The author as vehicle is a popular tool. It allows the author to establish a point of view but keep the camera fixed on the subject, not the author. In "Encounters with the Archdruid," John McPhee uses his presence in a raft as a means to explore whether a developer and an environmentalist can find common ground as they tear down the Colorado River debating a proposed dam. In "Difficult Decisions," Lee Gutkind, the so-called "Godfather of Creative Nonfiction," shadows a veterinarian who travels the countryside treating farm animals. Gutkind states that he's working on a book about veterinarians and how they interact with animals and people. We know that he sits in the truck beside this veterinarian, a woman. But for the most part, the narrative spotlight shines on Wendy Freeman as she shoulders the weighty responsibility of euthanasia, a decision she must often make when an animal is ill or hurt.

In other essays, the writer launches an external exploration based on his or her own experience. Unmarried at 38, Kate Bolick framed "All The Single Ladies" around her dating life while devoting thousands and thousands of words to historical, sociological, and economic studies, along with the thoughts and experiences of other women. When another Kate — Katie Campbell — needed money, she began the process of donating her eggs to an infertility clinic. "The Egg & I" takes the reader on Campbell's personal journey, providing not only action (scenes portraying discussions about donation, Katie actively pursuing donation), but also her reflections on whether she could go through with it (her children would be walking the planet and she wouldn't know them) and facts and stats and background on the psychological and emotional impact of egg donation. Because the latter are woven into scenes, spooned to the reader in digestible chunks, the reader doesn't veer far from the narrative tension line: will she or won't she donate her eggs?

In "Please Don't Bury Soul," John Jeremiah Sullivan uses his fascination with the obscure music from the 1930s of two blues artists to trace the history of not only Elvie Thomas and Geeshie Wiley, but also that of "race records," and how these two African-American women were recorded in the first place. Sullivan is the explorer, the storyteller intent on uncovering the facts of these women artists and their music. We follow him on his journey, sitting with him at 2 a.m. in the Houston home of an octogenarian who, too, had been fascinated by Thomas and Wiley. We hear him on the phone talking to a 21-year-old researching the blues. We are with him when he hits pay dirt — transcripts of interviews 60-years-old that provide him with the details he sought — and we are with him when he interviews relatives and friends of the women. Present, he acts as the camera, recording what he sees and hears:

> *We sat up for several hours drinking screwdrivers. There was a black-and-white movie on, something from the '40s. He had a fat little dog named Charles, who has since died, that he loved very much. Charles would drink your screwdriver, if you set it on the floor, and McCormick kept having to remind me to put my notepad or a book on top of the glass, so Charles couldn't get to the drink. Now and then McCormick would pause and send me to locate a binder or folder. Mostly he talked, not tediously but spellbindingly. His recall was encyclopedic, though he frequently cursed his memory, saying he had suffered a small stroke. Yet he roamed through the years and names, stopping to ask if you had heard of some person, carrying on heedlessly whether you said yes or no.*

Through Sullivan, we study Robert McCormick, wait for the 80-year-old to share the tidbits for which Sullivan yearns. When he admits that he interviewed Geeshie and Elvie, we are elated. When he cancels communication with Sullivan, we are crestfallen. Sullivan's curiosity and drive is infectious; the reader, too, wants to solve the mystery. Sullivan is the engine but the camera is always facing out. The ultimate blend of internal and external.

SHORT ESSAY? KINDLE SINGLE? FULL-FLEDGED BOOK?

If writers approached every idea as if they were launching a book project, nothing would ever get written. Books are daunting. They start out fun and end up consuming your days, your nights, your dreams. They take *a lot* of time. As Winston Churchill said, a book begins as an adventure, a toy, then turns into a mistress, then a master, then a tyrant. Still, there are ideas that deserve the attention and sweat that books demand. On the flip side, there are plenty of subjects that *don't* deserve 70,000 words that are better off in a shorter form, perhaps a

TRY THIS

1. What is a problem you have resolved? A problem you can't resolve? No problem is too little (learning to say no to requests for your time) or too big (an inability to maintain close relationships). Free-write 500-words about this problem and how you solved or haven't solved it. Now turn your attention to other. Who else has this problem? How have they solved it? Why have some people not solved it? What do experts say? If the problem is time-sensitive (heroin dealers moving into your neighborhood) research the history of drugs in your town and surprising users. If the problem is medical, research the condition. Write an essay using your experience as the binding narrative thread as you weave in the other external material.

2. This time, start with the external. From the news briefs listed in a local newspaper or media site, select three items and identify ways that your experience, your insights, your observations would add meaning to the facts. For instance, if the news brief details rising gas prices, analyze how this change will impact you. Has impacted you? And if it impacts you, how will it impact others? Choose one and write a 250-word story, using the facts as the narrative spine and your insights as the supportive material. How might this short piece be expanded with more reflection and research?

3,000-word feature, or a 20,000-word Kindle Single, or perhaps as short as a 750-word essay for Brevity.

Often, an idea begins life with a modest goal. Acknowledging that all writing is challenging — as Anna Quindlen once said at a conference I attended, "I hate writing, but I love having written" — sometimes it is best to launch a project thinking in terms of a short commitment, or at least shorter than the number of years that a book usurps. Amy Ellis Nutt, a writer for the Washington Post, stumbled on the story of Jon Sarkin, a chiropractor known for his calm and discipline, who had suffered a stroke and emerged exuberantly obsessive, driven to create art. He wrote poems and letters to himself, but his true passion was painting. For hours and hours he would paint, creating art that began to attract a lot of attention and admirers. Diagnosed with bipolar disease in graduate school, Nutt had a keen interest in neurological science and was deeply intrigued by Sarkin's transformation. She dove into the research, wrote a series for the Newark, New Jersey Star-Ledger, where she worked at the time, called "The Accidental Artist," and was thrilled that the project was named a Pulitzer finalist that year. But she wasn't done. There are some stories that beg for more thought, more research, more exploration, and this was one. Nutt and Jon Sarkin kept up a correspondence in which she learned more about his creative genius, his memories, his present, and the impact his transformation had on Sarkin and his family. She delved more deeply into the science of the brain. She wrote a book proposal about Sarkin's experience and what it tells us about brain function. "Shadows Bright as Glass" was published in April 2011.

The national bestselling "Born to Run" began as a question — Why does my foot hurt? — that propelled the author into researching the long distance running greats of the Tarahumara tribe. Initially writing an article for Men's Health, Christopher McDougall recognized early on the book potential in the tribe's running secrets. In addition to the standard observation and reporting involved in any nonfiction research, McDougall decided to also insert himself and train with the tribe, the culmination of which was a 50-mile race. He wrote the magazine article, but kept researching, learning enough about the physiology of running, the psychology of long distance runners, and his own evolution as a runner that he had a book.

Not all subjects, of course, deserve expansion. They have a single theme, a single focus, and can be told thoroughly and engagingly in 4,000 words or less. Yet as Amy Ellis Nutt discovered, there are times when a subject surprises you and pulls you down different paths that could build the narrative into a book. Where one theme surfaced in the shorter piece, multiple themes run through a book. In the years following her mother's death, Cheryl Strayed attempted to make sense of her behavior and her grief in different essays. One essay explored her addiction to heroin and men ("Heroin/e"). Another, her mother's influence ("The Love of My Life"). In the years of reflection, other themes emerged, which Strayed pulled together in her memoir "Wild." Chronicling her 1,100 mile journey on the Pacific Crest Trail, Strayed explored not only her grief and self-destruction, but also family, isolation, community, and self-respect.

Fiction writers have always had the novella — that cross between a short novel and a long short story — but until recently, nonfiction writers found the market limited to either the traditional magazine length — between 3,000 and 10,000 words (if you're lucky) — and books (60,000 words plus). Digital publishing changed all that. Kindle Singles, an Amazon creation, publishes digital narratives from 5,000 to 30,000 words. Atavist seeks what it calls long magazine articles or short books for its multimedia format, a lengthy text complemented by illustrations, videos, photos, audio, and timelines. When a renowned author such as Buzz Bissinger writes a sequel to his bestseller "Friday Night Lights" but the sequel, which focuses on a main character in the earlier book, fills less than 50 pages, the sequel is published on Byliner, an online aggregator of longform nonfiction, and other digital formats. Cost: $2.99.

When students ask me how long a story should be, my first response is to say however long it takes to tell it thoroughly. Often, as we write, more questions surface, and those questions deserve answers. A writer's goal is to anticipate what the reader yearns to know and what the reader needs to know. Don Murray, the writing coach and author, gauged a narrative's completion when whatever scene or explanation he thought to add seemed repetitious. Ben Montgomery monitors his own excitement. "I try and stay in tune with my own feelings about a story," he says. If he's entertained by the tale, or finds himself in hot pursuit of more answers to more questions, then he keeps writing, hoping that the reader will be as engaged as he is. But as soon as his fascination wanes, when the key moments seem more boring than riveting, he stops. "If I don't find moments when I'm excited," he says, "then that will be a shorter story."

Montgomery is a pro; he will interview and observe and dig through archives until he has ferreted out every scene and factual scrap he needs to build a narrative. He knows the story is completed when he has run out of the good stuff, when the material he has left is dull. In contrast, the narratives of less experienced writers may lack verve because they do lack content. What they need is more research and reflection. It is up to the writer, then, to ask more questions and find the content to answer those questions. With stronger scenes and more specific facts, the writer can best assess how long the piece deserves to be.

CHALLENGING CHOICES

Facing Rejection From Traditional Print, Joshuah Bearman Finds an Alternative

Joshuah Bearman may be best known for writing the Wired article on which the movie "Argo" was based, but his byline appears on narratives in many of the nation's major publications, from Rolling Stone to Harper's to McSweeney's. As a freelancer, he knows he must navigate between forms, and also contributes essays to NPR's "This American Life." Yet when he stumbled upon a story about a guy who opened a bar in the Green Zone in Baghdad, a dry city in a country in which alcohol is forbidden, he encountered Iraq fatigue in all of his usual media outlets. He'd spent 5 months researching and writing what he thought was a fascinating tale of social and recreational life in a war zone, and was determined to publish it. Fortunately for Bearman, Atavist took it. But this digital publication required Bearman to think about form in a new way as he and the editors put together "Baghdad Country Club," a romp of a story that opens with illustrations and the main character, James, a British national, explaining in a voiceover how he became involved in international bootlegging. The narrative, told in text from Chapter Two on, is complemented with maps, time lines, photos, illustrations, and sidebars offering more details on specific characters, places, and events. As with all Atavist

(Continued)

(Continued)

publications, "Baghdad Country Club" can be read straight through, or the reader can stop at each icon and study a photo of the Green Zone's exterior wall or find Amman on a map.

While Bearman wasn't responsible for creating or installing these digital additions to his narrative, he was part of the team that brainstormed what audio and visuals would work with his story. The process was, he says, pretty fun:

Magazine writers like to appear in print and Atavist is like a mini book publisher. Length is no object. But you have to make a trailer of some kind, a little video. When Evan (Evan Ratliff is one of the founders of Atavist) and I were talking the multimedia thing, we talked animation because there wasn't anything existing. In other stories, traditional stories, you can present media embedded in the story. In a story about a jewelry heist in Scandinavia, they had footage of the robbery that they embedded. In my case, there was no media. We had to make it up.

In the lead of "Baghdad Country Club" we used voice and illustrations instead of text. But we made the text available if you wanted to read it.

I worked together with the person who does the multimedia. What maps do we need? What photos? How do we track down more imagery? In one case, we used a Google map with a pin on it. It has to be easy for the reader to click.

They have a professional radio lab produce the items. I've done radio for This American Life and could have done the recording myself, but they added a pro who cleaned up the sound.

It was very collaborative, a very smooth process.

Since then, I've gone in the reverse direction. I'm writing a book, a memoir based on a piece I did on "This American Life" about my mom who is a career alcoholic and my brother who is an aspiring rapper. They live together in a retirement community in Florida. Yet I still maintain my online presence. I'm really into this idea of the Atavist and Byliner, new ways to interact with longform nonfiction.

Multimedia options

Few writers would argue with New Yorker editor David Remnick's statement that language is man's greatest invention. Yet that statement, uttered at a forum at the New School in New York City in March of 2011 titled "Longform Storytelling in a Short Attention Span World," was sandwiched in the middle of a discussion on blending text with other mediums, of how best to use sound, video, interactive graphics, slideshows, and hyperlinks to lead the reader deeper into the narrative. On Remnick's left was Ira Glass, host and producer of National Public Radio's "This American Life." On his right was Stephen Engelberg, managing editor of ProPublica, an online newsroom dedicated to investigative journalism. Next to Engelberg was Raney Aronson-Rath, a senior producer at "Frontline." All renowned storytellers of fact, each representing a different medium.

While it is no surprise that the four couldn't agree on the point when technology teetered over the edge from enhancement to distraction, they did agree that the success of narratives depended on not just language, but also on employing digital tools. Recognizing that as e-books and online magazines, newspapers, and literary journals proliferate, as readers are as likely to scroll through a story on their iPad as well as flip the pages of The Atlantic, they agreed that fact-based storytellers are challenged to consider not just the proper words and metaphors, but also images (both moving and still), sounds, graphics, and links, mediums that can help lead the reader deeper into the text.

Just how much a narrative writer is responsible for depends on the publication and the writer. Daily journalists entering the job market are expected to wield an iPhone as well as a notebook and return to the newsroom to post a short video or audio clip to accompany a print news story. And while some of their long-form colleagues are competent photographers and are capable of producing a short video side bar, many are not. Or not capable of providing the kind of quality sought for the narratives of which we speak. Evan Ratliff, one of the founders of Atavist, is thrilled when a writer volunteers to provide some audio, video, or still photos, but he also understands that not all writers' talents extend to the visual, and that for a 20,000-word Atavist selection, the reader expects nothing less than professional. And that requires hiring seasoned photographers, videographers, and graphic artists. As Amy O'Leary, a multimedia producer-turned print reporter at The New York Times, says, "Everything requires a different skill." For a print journalist to produce professional-quality videos, or learn code, or build interactive graphics requires an enormous investment of time and concentrated effort. "They know the craft to write well," O'Leary says of her colleagues on the print side. "There is equal craft in other formats."

O'Leary may be one of the few narrative storytellers eager — and capable — of switching mediums successfully. Other writers may provide the text and an iPhone-shot video, but rely on the technically skilled to edit and produce the digital piece. Essayist Dinty W. Moore, for instance, is an elegant writer with a passion for photography. While visiting Edinburgh, Scotland, one year, he found himself taking lots photos of elderly men. White-haired men, their faces creased with lines, smoking pipes, smiling, chatting, thinking. Why was he so fascinated with these men? He started writing. What he crafted was an essay he called "History," which flowed from his interest in these men into an exploration of identity. Unlike the ancient city of Edinburgh, rich in antiquity, Moore wrote that his own family's history, riddled with early deaths and secrets, was paltry. His great-grandfather James was an unknown. In his essay, Moore ponders the details of this missing relative — who he was, what he looked like, why he's buried in a Protestant cemetery while his wife and children occupy the family plot in a Catholic cemetery nearby — and ruminates about how to understand oneself when one's foundation is porous. In the faces of the elderly

Scotsmen he shoots, he tries to find the image of his great-grandfather, the man who might explain the Moore past.

While in Scotland, he also shot videos of Edinburgh street life, the famous Edinburgh castle, traffic. He didn't have a specific purpose, only a thought that he'd like to try to tackle a video essay some day and perhaps these scenes might prove useful. It wasn't until he identified the story beneath the still shots of aged Scottish men, that he knew he had all the components for a video essay. But he also realized he didn't have the skill to put it together. He made some notes on how the images might connect with the words, and then handed everything to his collaborators, George Stoichev and John Bresland, who did the actual video editing. "They have skills, expertise, and software that I can only dream of," Moore says.

While writers may not have the software or expertise to produce award-winning videos, it is key in this digital age that they think in multimedia terms. They must think about how their narrative will read on a tablet or a computer screen. They must think about how to harness technology to their advantage, what kind of links should be imbedded in the text, what kind of graphics could add the detail words cannot, what kind of sound will strike a visceral chord in the reader.

In the early days, editors mulled what kind of video or graphic would enhance the reader's experience once the piece was written, sort of as an afterthought. But as digital storytelling flourished with the explosion of online journals and media sites, writers began collaborating with photographers and artists at the story's inception. Often that means that the visual artist will work in concert with the writer during the research phase, bringing in the other members of the team — photographers, page designers, graphic artists, mapmakers — as the material takes shape. "Collaboration, collaboration, collaboration," says Andrew DeVigal, an Emmy-award winning interactive media strategist. With a résumé listing posts from New York Times multimedia editor to creative director of Second Story, an Oregon-based center for interactive storytelling, DeVigal suggests that writers think in terms of questions. What is missing? What is difficult to convey in words? What could a video provide that words cannot? Could a map add understanding? Could a recorded interview? Does a character have a quirky mannerism or speech pattern that would best be conveyed in audio? Video? At what stage in the research would a photographer capture the most significant moments?

Visuals

When Rich and Carolynne St. Pierre invited Concord Monitor reporter Chelsea Conaboy to document for their three children Carolynne's effort to prolong her life despite the liver cancer that was ravaging her body, Conaboy thought she would write a one-time feature illustrated by a few photos for the Concord

WEB CHOICES

Are Rolling Seas Worth the Detail?

Amy Ellis Nutt on the power and peril of video

Jose Arias was the only survivor. In the days, weeks, and months that followed treading water in the frigid Atlantic off of Cape May, New Jersey, in the predawn hours of that March day, clutching the 8-foot board he had picked up on the dock, yearning to hear the voices of his fishing mates, so traumatized was he that speaking of the tragedy was difficult. He was always polite to Amy Ellis Nutt, then a narrative writer for New Jersey's Star-Ledger, when she asked him questions, but between his PTSD and his limited English, despite the translator, she wasn't getting the detail she needed about what happened on board the scallop vessel Lady Mary on March 24, 2009. She had reams of material from marine experts, meteorological experts, other fisherman, and family members, but she still didn't know what it felt like to be on the boat as it rolled in the monstrous waves and why Arias, or any of the other six crewman for that matter, didn't see or hear the enormous container ship barreling toward the scalloper at full-speed.

So Amy Ellis Nutt and Andre Malok, a Star-Ledger videographer, decided to recreate for the reader on a video the scene of the demise of Lady Mary by venturing out onto the ocean in a fishing boat about the same size on a night featuring similar wind and waves. If Nutt knew what she was in for, she may have never stepped foot on the boat. But in the end it was worth it; the trip delivered the specifics sought.

We work very closely together. Andre has an amazing talent. He began at the newspaper as graphic artist then branched out and became a videographer. He did the video, graphics, and photos for the series "The Wreck of the Lady Mary." Regarding working with him for video, he would show me pieces and I would help with the script. We were everywhere together. I would do an interview. He would sit down with a person while I was there, and he would do additional questions. He had questions that I didn't think of or forgot. I'm someone who spent 9 years at Sports Illustrated; I'm keenly aware of the value of the visual. Some writers are dismissive. It's an extra thing that they won't be bothered with. I'm not so vain to not realize that people will read a story because of a photo and not because of the fabulous lead.

Andre takes his cue from how I see how the story will develop, how I lay out the parts, how I lay out the story. I will let him and the video editors see the rough draft. He came to me and said that we needed to go out on a scallop boat. I knew that was important for me but critical for him.

The night we went out, it was similar conditions to the night the Lady Mary sank. You can read about 6-foot waves, but it is something different to see them, and experience them. It didn't bother these fishermen in the least; they worked right through it. When I say I've never been as sick in my life, I mean it. When we got back 14 hours later I told the captain, "I went through 18 months of chemo for breast cancer and I'd go through that again before I did this again."

I was sick over the side of the boat. The captain told me, "Amy, we'll have to tie you to the rail or we'll lose you."

(Continued)

(Continued)

"Just let me go," I said.

Fortunately, Andre didn't get sick until an hour after I did. He got most of his video. Then he got sick, too. It was brutal, but it was essential for him and critical for me.

A lot of people ask how could they not see the container ship? You don't realize that until you are out there that it makes sense that they couldn't. (Arias) was in the deepest part of boat. They work all night. They are fixing machinery, or shucking. If you were at the back of the scallop boat, the noise — the droning of the winch — is extremely loud and you can't see beyond the deck because of the bright lights. They are like theatre lights. You can't see beyond them. The night we were out, less than a quarter mile away a container ship went by, but I thought it was much farther. I couldn't tell the size and wouldn't have noticed it unless it was pointed out to me. It is so dark out there, so noisy that you won't hear it until it is past you. You'll be hit by the bow before you hear it coming. All those things helped me realize how easy it would have been not to see the ship.

Monitor's print and online issues. Conaboy was no stranger to shooting her own videos and photos, but it became clear that as her reporting deepened and she saw the potential in a series of stories, not just one, that the art needed to match the writing in its complexity and richness. Monitor photographer Preston Gannaway joined the project, and together she and Conaboy followed the family through the treatments, the preparation for her death, and the aftermath, documenting an experience that was both universal and individual. Their collaboration produced a series of five illustrated stories that ran over a period of 14 months, taking the reader on the family's journey as Rich and the three children learn to navigate through their grief to survive life without their wife and mother.

So moving was the series, that Conaboy and Gannaway collaborated and created an audio slideshow called "Remember Me." It is difficult to listen to the voice of Carolynne describe her fear that her 4-year-old son Elijah will not remember her as you view a shot of Carolynne, clad in a white bathrobe and turban that protects her bare head, at the beach waving to Elijah. Or watch photos of the teenage daughter braiding her hair in the bathroom next to the room where her mother lay dying as Rich's voice ponders how he will raise the children alone. The power of the slideshow and photos in the newspaper series earned Gannaway the Pulitzer Prize in photography that year.

Videos, too, are a powerful storytelling tool. Just ask Neil Swidey of The Boston Globe. On a recent June day in the Globe's multimedia center, a windowless set of rooms that is home to the video team, Neil Swidey edits a video that will accompany his story in this Sunday's Boston Globe Magazine on people who write inflammatory comments on news sites. Swidey grew weary of photographers producing videos of his print stories — he didn't like the loss of control — and so he worked with the photographers to gain the skills necessary to capture an angle of his story on film for the Globe's website. What he found was that videos operated on the same principle as his written narratives; they must have plot, a tension line that lures the reader from beginning to end, and they must have a message, a central theme. Like his text narratives, his videos have characters and interviews. But unlike writing, creating a video is not an isolated effort, but a group project. Today he works with the video editor trying to find the right moment in the interview to start the piece. As in text, you want to open with a moment that will capture the reader. They settle on a shot of the main character, a 64-year-old man with a hawk nose, typing his first response of the morning. We see his computer screen, we hear the click of the keys, we hear his voice summarizing his routine. Key images. Key sounds. Just enough to hook us.

Writers must ask themselves — and their photographers — what could moving images and sound do that words can't? In Swidey's text, we read the words the angry commentators post on websites. On his video, we see them in action, typing, and hear their voices justifying their rants. By hitting the reader's multiple senses through multiple mediums, Swidey provides an experience unattainable through text alone. Likewise, Amy Ellis Nutt knew that while her narrative text was strong, a video of a fishing boat going out at night in conditions similar to the ones the crew of the Lady Mary experienced the night it capsized was critical to the reader understanding why the crew might not have seen the container ship heading its way. The darkness, the wind, the waves, the machinery noise — all there on the screen for the viewer to absorb sensually as well as intellectually.

Audio

In her years as a multimedia producer, Amy O'Leary has found that audio is an appealing introduction to the digital arts for writers because, as she says, it is simple. Record. Edit. Upload. Done. Adding the voice of a character in the narrative brings authenticity. Life. Describing a Southern gentleman guffawing as he rocks back and forth on a porch swing can strike an emotion that print can't. "Paraphrasing him in print would be a disservice," O'Leary says.

As would paraphrasing the conversation between Joan Didion and Terry Gross, when Gross, NPR's veteran interviewer, asked Didion if she were afraid of dying. Didion was discussing her book "Year of Magical Thinking," which chronicled the year following the death of her husband and fellow writer John Gregory Dunne, a year of grief and a year of caring for her daughter who had suffered life-threatening infections and a cerebral hemorrhage. Several weeks before "Magical Thinking" was published her daughter died. "No, I'm not worried about my own death," Didion said, "I think I'm less worried. One of the things that worries us about dying always is that we are afraid that we're leaving people behind. They won't be able to take care of themselves. We have to take care of them. You see, in fact, I'm not leaving anyone behind." Her voice cracks, she stifles a sob.

Telling stories through sound is as old as radio, of course. But the ease of digital recorders and smart phones that capture children giggling and owls hooting with the touch of a key enable all of us, even the most techno-phobic, to become Ira Glass wannabes. With that technology, sound is easily added to a digital narrative. Sometimes that addition is as theatrical as a fog horn blowing or doorbell ringing at key moments in the text ("Mother, Stranger" by Cris Beam, an Atavist publication) or an interview with a key character. Or sometimes it is as simple as music in the background.

Interactive features

Tell me, and I will forget
Show me, and I may remember
Involve me, and I will understand

Chinese Proverb

Such is the power and philosophy behind interactive features. If a reader can press a link to learn detailed information — say on a map of Japan showing the tsunami destruction each click reveals statistics and data, perhaps photos and illustrations of various regions — then perhaps the physical act will help the reader better retain, or at least enjoy, the material. Take, for instance, the online New York Times profile about Kuk Harrell, a vocal producer for stars such as Justin Bieber, Rihanna, and Jennifer Lopez. Harrell's job is to build a whole song in the studio out of parts, several lines sung with different inflections and emphases, combining the bars he likes best to create the whole that we hear on the radio. A sidebar on the story was an interactive feature that prompted readers to test their skills as recording editors by choosing audio selections from the song "Right Now" by the group Calvillo and then check if their selections match those of Kuk Harrell.

"Beyond the Barrel: Following where your refuse and recyclables go on collection day" from the Arizona Daily Star combines illustration of trucks and conveyor belts, videos of people sorting trash, and text explaining the details of where the 254 million tons of trash Americans generate each year goes. Press on a number on the map of "Products of Slavery" and you get the name of the country circled by drawings of the products harvested or produced by children or forced labor. Mexico has 11 products, ranging from watermelon to pornography. Press on one of the items, say coffee, and a link to dozens of facts and stories about coffee (one child earns $1.50 a day, another was recruited to join the militia). Press on one of the stories and it expands. Each touch adds more detail, more depth.

Often, graphic designers will consult with writers about possible interactive features, but most writers, whose skills may not extend to software and programming to create a feature that changes with a keystroke, are happy to allow the experts to create the graphics.

TRY THIS

1. Listen to an audio narrative, say Joshuah Bearman's "Duty Calls" on "This American Life," or one of the essays of personal reflection from around the globe on bendingborders.org. Note how the writer uses sound, different voices, to enhance the narrative. Take one of your own narratives and make a list of sounds and voices that would intensify the meaning and impact.

2. Make a timeline for one of your longer pieces, highlighting every major event, every major character, every major place. For each item listed on the timeline, identify one way technology could amplify or better explain it. What still or moving photos could illuminate characters? Which places could be served as a map? What event could be explained through an interactive graphic? Pretend money and software are no objects — you have everything you need at your disposal — and let your imagination fly.

3. Using a smart phone or digital camera, spend two hours trolling through your downtown, shooting stills and moving images that capture you. In a quiet place, study these images. What stands out? Any patterns? What questions arise? Think of a personal experience or experience of others that somehow connect with an image or images. How could you pursue the meaning of this connection on the page? How could the images help tell the story?

3

What's the Content?

> **Overview**
>
> In this chapter we dive into the kinds of content different narratives demand and how to go about gathering the goods. By dividing the quest into three parts — determining what you already know, determining what you need to know, and figuring out where to go to find the material you need — content collecting follows a logical, sometimes surprising, and always enlightening sequence.

IT TOOK CHERYL STRAYED 15 YEARS of ruminating about her 1,100-mile hike along the Pacific Crest Trail when she was 26 before she committed to writing about the experience. Memoir to Strayed, as it is to most writers, is not just about what happened, but the meaning of what happened. In her case it was finding her way through grief (her mother's death and the end of her marriage to a man she loved) and destructive choices (too many men, too much heroin) to a more balanced, peaceful life as she lumbered with ill-fitting boots and an over-stuffed backpack through the mountains of California and Oregon. Yes, she had her memories of the bleeding and blistered feet, the lost toenails, the aching back, the snow, the bears, the dry hot wind. But details blur over time and memory is elusive. To resurrect the sounds, the tastes, the feeling of hair as parched as a burlap bag to write the book that eventually became the bestseller "Wild," she reread her journals and talked to others who had hiked the trail. She researched the facts about the hike and the geography that she no longer remembered or had not known in the first place.

While memoir is based on just that — memory — and the weight of the narrative lies in the strength of personal reflections, memoir also benefits from collecting external material, which can add credibility, dimension, and substance. As memoirist Mimi Schwartz says on the blog "The Art and Craft of Creative Nonfiction," "Research is essential, whether telling a coming-of-age story, investigating a family secret, or recreating the legacy of several generations. Whether we write about a world we know intimately or are just discovering, research leads to more layered and authentic narratives."

Unlike the fiction writer, scribes of all narrative nonfiction forms, from memoir to literary journalism, can't rely on imagination for content. Instead, true stories require content collecting, whether that content comes from resurrecting one's own memories to searching for facts, quotes, statistics, scenes, history — pretty much everything that is not based on one's own experience — from outside sources. This means that every storyteller of fact, be that writer Cheryl Strayed racking her frontal lobe for the image of the Pacific Crest Trail resupply box at the Kennedy Meadows General Store to Tom Bissell researching the history of Vietnam for his book "The Father of All Things" to Kate Bolick flying around the country to interview young women about their views on marriage for an essay in The Atlantic, seeks material from a breadth of sources.

How much material you need from any of the above depends on what kind of narrative you're writing. If you are researching a biography of Louisa May Alcott, chances are that unless you are a time traveler, you wouldn't have observed Ms. Alcott penning "Little Women" at the half moon desk built between two windows in her room at Orchard House. The content for your narrative will be gleaned from archives and historians. Likewise, if you're Mary Karr and you are recounting a turbulent childhood for the book you'll call "The Liar's Club," the detail your memory can't provide will come from other family members, perhaps old newspaper stories and neighbors' recollections. Or if you are Cynthia Gorney on assignment in Northern India for National Geographic, you will immerse yourself in village culture to understand why children as young as 5 are married. And you will pore over databases, magazine articles, and books, accumulating facts and statistics and background. You will interview experts on Northern India. Experts on village culture. You will talk to people in the village. You will talk to your interpreter. You will observe the village, the people, the ceremonies. You will let your curiosity point you to sources that you hope will have the answers.

For many of us, the research is the fun part, the stage where we explore the world, meet new people, acquire new insights. Research draws us out of ourselves before the writing pulls us back in. True, the prospect of unearthing all those stats and facts and scenes and insights can feel overwhelming. Yet by breaking the excavation into three parts — What do you know? What do you need to know? Where do you find it? — the Big Dig should not only loom less daunting, but also provide a sturdy framework.

WHAT DO YOU KNOW?

Donald Murray was a master at plumbing his life experience for both personal narratives and stories about other. While reflecting on the death of his 20-year-old daughter, he contemplated the importance of friends. Years later, when his wife Minnie Mae succumbed to Parkinson's disease and dementia, he wrote about the universal fear of nursing homes. His memories of World War II combat launched an exploration in another essay of the feelings of young men and women fighting contemporary battles in Iraq and Afghanistan.

A writer's experience not only can lead to story ideas, but also to content, and resources for content. Murray's experience moving his wife to a full-care facility not only provided him with his own understanding of the heartbreaking task, but also sparked an interest in the Big Picture. How do others deal with this choice? What percentage of people suffering from Parkinson's end life in a nursing home? What experts would have insights into the impact on spouses? As Kate Bolick approached her 39th birthday without any sign of a spouse, The Atlantic asked her to look into how men's worsening economic prospects influenced dating, marriage, and families, suggesting that she draw on her own experiences and write in first person. Once she began her research, she found herself more interested in flipping that question and examining how women's increased earning potential and decreased financial dependence on men were inspiring many women — herself included — to question whether they even wanted to be married in the first place. "All the Single Ladies" caused such a stir that Kate became a staple on media talk shows and the lecture circuit. Art imitates life indeed.

What one knows about a topic not only is based on experience, but also on observation and reading. We need not have fought in Iraq to understand the horrors of war; by reading accounts of IEDs bursting under Humvee caravans or having met vets still roiling with post-traumatic stress disorder we have the seeds to launch a writing project about returning soldiers assimilating back to civilian life. We know enough to form questions, to share observations, to identify people who do have firsthand understanding.

It's been a few decades since Todd Balf took the Scholastic Aptitude Tests (SAT), but when assigned a story for The New York Times Magazine about changes afoot at the College Board, he looked first to his high-school age children, their friends, and their classmates to study the emotional, intellectual, and financial stresses of preparing for the test. Formal interviews and data collecting would come later; in the beginning he had only to observe and hear about the kids studying their SAT flashcards, heading off to their Kaplan SAT-prep classes, bent over their SAT workbooks assigned by special SAT tutors.

During our days on this planet, we learn a lot about a lot of things. We learn about human error and motivation. We learn about sorrow and resilience. We learn about conflicts in Ukraine and drug deals downtown. Not all is absorbed and not all will be useful in future writing projects. But plenty might be. If a scene calls for Second Empire architectural detail, perhaps all you need do is cull out photos of the Louvre from your last trip to Paris or from the magazine article you just read. For a profile on a Paralympic skier, reflect on either your own physical limitations or those of people you know. How are you and/or they impacted? How are the challenges hurdled? What a writer has experienced, observed, and read may provide scenes and background, or it may simply provide a framework of knowledge on which to launch the rest of the research. From there, the question then is what other material do you need?

WHAT DO YOU NEED TO KNOW?

If Todd Balf were writing an essay about his son's SAT stress, he might seek some stats and facts about the number of students working with tutors, the number of

TRY THIS

1. Think back to the worst moment of your first job. Pouring scalding coffee over an elderly man? Swamping the boat? List every detail you remember of that moment. Sights. Sounds. Tastes. Dialogue. Movement. Stats and facts. Write the scene based on what you recall. What's missing? Make a list of the details and facts you need to complete the scene.

2. Write down everything you know either directly or indirectly about a story in yesterday's New York Times. For instance, for a headline about a possible kidnapping attempt — a fifth grader en route to school ran when a stranger offered him a ride — you could write down what you remember about being 10 years old. What were you afraid of? What had you been taught about potential abductors? How did it feel to run while carrying a backpack full of books and snacks? If you're familiar with the area where the child was solicited, describe the setting, the town, the kinds of people who live in the town. If not, describe the setting around your elementary or middle school. If you know someone who was once approached by a stranger, write what you remember about the encounter. What do you know off the top of your head about childhood abductions? Now write a scene based on the headline, weaving in the child's perspective, the setting, and any background facts you know about kidnappings. Yes, this is conjecture. But conjecture can inform and help articulate avenues to explore. If you were to write a story about this possible abduction, how do your own childhood reflections inform the kinds of questions that you would ask the child? His parents? His school principal? The police?

students in SAT prep courses, the amount of money parents pay for both. The bulk of the content, however, would focus on his son and the Balf family.

In contrast, for The New York Times Magazine piece on the SAT overhaul, Balf devoted months to learning everything he could about the SAT, the people behind the SAT, and the people and institutions impacted by the SAT. He traveled to the Manhattan headquarters of the College Board, which administers the SATs, and spent hours with the organization's new president, learning not only of his plans to make the SAT less daunting and more meritocratic, but also about the president's educational and professional background that contributed to his SAT thoughts. To understand the proposed changes to a test taken by 3 million high school students each year, Balf had also to understand the man behind the changes. In addition, Balf talked to teachers, parents, university presidents, university admissions officers, and high school college counselors. He researched the history of the SAT, the history of the SAT prep industry, the studies correlating SAT scores and academic success, and the rise of the SAT's main competition, the ACT (American College Testing). He researched the legacy of charges against the SAT, that the test that was created to equal the playing field — one test for all — but proved not democratic at all; those without means had no access to the extra test prep and tutoring available to those with more disposable income. He read books about college admissions and test score discrimination and surveys of high school teachers assessing whether the test reflected secondary curriculum. He talked to College Board staffers who worked for 2 years on the new SAT, which will return to the 1,600-point system in 2016, scoring an optional essay separately. Vocabulary words will be less obscure. Test questions will focus on students proving their answers rather than learning tricks from a tutor to eliminate the wrong answers.

Phew. That's a lot of research. But to understand this complicated topic and the myriad of people and institutions the SAT impacts, Balf knew he had to cast a wide — and deep — net. Some stories are like that. Stories that involve multiple people confronting multiple issues or perhaps just one very large and complex issue. To write a profile of Dr. Paul Farmer, cofounder of Partners In Health, Tracy Kidder knew he would have to travel to Haiti, where Farmer devotes much of his time, and also to Russia and Cuba and any other country that Farmer would visit to attend patients and promote public health. Kidder knew he would have to learn not only every detail he could about Farmer's past and his present by talking to and observing Farmer, but also talking to and observing people who knew Farmer, worked with Farmer. He would have to learn about the organizations to which Farmer was affiliated, including Partners In Health, the World Health Organization, Harvard Medical School, and the hospitals where Farmer practiced. Writing about one man sounds easy enough, but one man with as many tentacles as Paul Farmer requires the writer to gain an understanding of many issues.

More personal stories would, most likely, demand less external research. Much of the content may be gleaned from one's own experience. What is needed is supporting detail and context. Bonnie Rough was well aware of the rare condition the women in her family carried, a condition that struck primarily males, leaving them with an unusual facial structure, sparse hair, few teeth, and in inability to sweat. On the surface the afflictions don't sound life threatening until you live with someone who has *hypohidrotic ectodermal dysplasia* (HED). Rough's younger brother Luke was limited in physical activity because his body would overheat. He had to avoid sunlight. But his trials were minimal compared to her mother's father, who couldn't work his family farm alongside his siblings. Her grandfather grew up lonely and incapable of developing close relationships. An inventor as an adult, he couldn't sustain a marriage or close connection to his daughter, Rough's mother. He died penniless, alone, and drug addicted at age 49.

Rough knew a little of her grandfather, who died years before she was born, but not enough to tell his story in the book she hoped to write about this condition that plagued her family, a condition that she carried and could pass on to her future sons. To understand HED she had to delve into medical journals and talk to experts. To understand her family's past and her grandfather's legacy, she had to interview her family members and visit the communities where her grandfather lived and worked. She read his letters and his records of his business transactions. Only after she had collected enough material to tell his story from his point of view could she stop researching and start writing.

What kind of material one needs to gather depends, of course, on the subject. But it is safe to say that the following ingredients will strengthen most any true narrative.

Stats & facts content

In the summer travel writing class I teach in Cambridge, England, the students are more than eager to write about their adventures punting and pub-crawling, chronicling the tippy boat, quoting the feckless bartender. They are adept at describing the place, the moment. What doesn't come so naturally is providing the context, the background, the history, the numbers that would provide layers to the action, adding heft and depth.

Concrete facts and stats, woven in gracefully, not only educate the reader, but also deliver much-needed specifics that provide support, the mortar to the narrative's bricks. Instead of saying that Lost Springs, Wyoming, is one of the least-populated towns in the United States, why not state its exact population (one)? To place that startling stat in context, add fact. When it was founded. When people began leaving. How much land the town covers. Instead of saying a lot of your family members have been treated for breast cancer, state how many. Provide facts about the family medical history in general and individual members specifically. Adjectives are vague. Statistics and facts add life.

Yet it is a delicate dance to weave them in seamlessly so that they don't shriek. Take for instance John Jeremiah Sullivan's essay on his visit to Cuba, "A Prison, a Paradise," in which he shows through his own travels Cuba's complexity in general and the tension between Cubans and Cuban Americans in particular. In one section he describes a scene in a taxi in which his wife asks the taxi driver to explain the Cuban currency. A lesser writer would either quote the taxi driver directly or offer a sweeping statement about the convoluted money system that once accepted U.S. dollars. But Sullivan provides just enough factual background and numbers with such elegance that the reader barely knows that she has swallowed cold, hard fact:

> But in 2004, Castro decided — partly as a gesture of contempt for the U.S. embargo — that he would abolish the use of U.S. dollars on the island and enforce the use of CUCs, pegged to the U.S. dollar but distinct from it. This coexisted alongside the original currency, which would remain pegged to the spirit of the revolution. For obvious reasons, the actual Cuban peso is worth much less than the other, dollar-equivalent Cuban peso, something on the order of 25 to 1. But the driver said simply, "No, they are equal."

The details slip in so smoothly that it sounds like Sullivan flicked them off the top of his head, that these numbers and this history was stored in his own mental database. Perhaps he is a factoid machine, capable of retaining massive amounts of material that he can summon at will, but most likely, he spent hours, perhaps days, or more, researching the history of Cuba, the revolution, and how currency was impacted.

Background content

Every subject has a history. It could be short — yesterday's hurricane — or it could span decades — the SAT. Whether the piece is personal reflection or journalistic immersion, there is a past. An immersion piece on other people, other situations, calls for a deep investigation into their pasts, their choices. If the piece is more personal, say it is about your uncle's battle with Parkinson's, you need to understand the disease and your uncle's health history. If you write about coping with depression, learning outside facts will place your experience in perspective. "Research inspires curiosity, helps you break out of self-absorption and understand that you are not the only one who has passed down this road," says essayist Phillip Lopate in a column for Creative Nonfiction magazine. "You begin to see your experience as part of a larger pattern, be it sociological, historical, psychological, anthropological, cultural, political, or theological – disciplines useful in supplying new lenses to your private tale."

When Michael Steinberg expanded his essay "Trading Off," a personal reflection about his struggles as a Jewish boy playing high school baseball for an anti-Semite coach, into a book about coming of age in the 1940s and 1950s in New York City (often referred to by sport historians as the "Golden Age of New York Baseball") he devoted hundreds of hours to reading histories of New York and baseball as well as poring over videos and library microfiche, newspaper clippings, and magazine articles. To be a boy in New York at that time was to live and breathe the Dodgers, the Giants, the Yankees, even if the boy preferred reading Tennyson to talking RBIs. To understand New York in general during that time, and baseball in particular, he needed details and context, history and human perspectives. For the latter, he talked to sport historians, sport writers, friends, and family, anyone who could offer insight and anecdotes about baseball in New York during his childhood. The result was his memoir "Still Pitching."

For Steinberg, the history of baseball and New York was the backdrop for his tale of yearning to belong and excel — at something, which at that moment was baseball. For other writers, research is needed to tell a larger story, or at least a larger part of the story. For instance, while Tom Bissell's relationship with his father, a Vietnam vet, is the dominant thread of his essay "War Wounds" and his memoir "The Father of All Things," much like Steinberg's hunger for success is the arc of "Still Pitching," Vietnam for Bissell is as much a character in these narratives as are he and his dad. To understand his father, a complicated man who was as loving as he was harsh, Bissell knew that he would have to understand what happened to his father as a Marine in Vietnam. To understand what happened to his father during the Vietnam War, they would have to travel to Southeast Asia. In both the essay and the memoir, Bissell's narrative camera not only zooms in on his father and his father's reflections of the fighting, the terrain, his fellow Marines, but also widens to encompass the history of the conflict, the Vietnamese people, the landscape — the rice paddies, the jungle, Saigon's streets. The reader, like the author, needs that content to understand the country and the wartime horror that lay beneath the older Bissell's volatile rage and perpetual sadness.

Content from other perspectives

Katy Butler's "What Broke My Father's Heart" is a tale of the personal — her father's dementia, the pacemaker that kept him going, and her mother's wish to let her beloved spouse die with dignity — and the larger public issue of a medical system focused on prolonging life, regardless of quality. In addition to exercising her memoir skills by spinning scenes that illustrated her family's struggle to cope with her father's frailty, Butler also proved an indefatigable researcher. A journalist, she knew that to best understand end-of-life medical decisions she would need to talk to people beyond her family circle. And so she interviewed doctors and bioethicists, patients and caregivers. She learned the history of the pacemaker and how it worked. The people she spoke with steered her to documents and websites and science journals devoted to the controversy of end-of-life care. Her mission was to provide the Big Picture without overwhelming her family's drama. While much of what she learned didn't make it in to the narrative, what did provided a confidence in the subject that resonated in her narrator's voice.

> *My father's medical conservatism, I have since learned, is not unusual. According-ing to an analysis by the Dartmouth Atlas medical-research group, patients are far more likely than their doctors to reject aggressive treatments when fully informed of pros, cons, and alternatives — information, one study suggests, that nearly half of patients say they don't get. And although many doctors assume that people want to extend their lives, many do not. In a 1997 study in The Journal of the American Geriatrics Society, 30 percent of seriously ill people surveyed in a hospital said they would "rather die" than live permanently in a nursing home. In a 2008 study in The Journal of the American College of Cardiology, 28 percent of patients with advanced heart failure said they would trade one day of excellent health for another two years in their current state.*

No reader would dare question her authority.

Action content

Narratives require action. Action requires setting. Setting requires sensory detail. For all scenes recreated from the past, only research will provide the sounds, smells, and visuals necessary to create an image in the reader's mind. Even if the scene is based on personal experience or observation, specifics often blur with time and a little legwork is needed to flesh out the moment.

The question narrative storytellers face is what needs to be shown in scene vs. told in exposition? To make her grandfather vivid to the reader, Bonnie Rough knew that she wanted to portray him in scenes told from his point of view for her memoir "Carrier." Since he had died years before she was born, she collected the details needed to show him playing alone in the family barn or setting up his first invention or meeting his wife-to-be through interviews with family members, friends, and acquaintances of her grandfather. She visited the places he lived and worked, saw the fields, the dirt roads, and many of the buildings he would have known. She pored over books to understand the setting then. Here's a sample of the story through her grandfather's eyes:

> *After school when the sun screamed, I shot hoops on the barn, perfecting. I kept a shirt floating in a bucket of water, and I swapped when the one I wore*

burned dry. Sometimes at sunset the wind changed and puffed light and cold, and I could shoot hoops with a dry shirt on as long as I wanted, the stars finding their needle holes and the cows shifting on their feet and breathing on their babies, home for sleep ...

In the house in the cellar. Preserves jars red and blue, applesauce and peaches. Pickles and tomatoes and cold hard dirt to relax the soles of my feet. There was nothing to look at, but it didn't matter when I went down there so blazing white-eyed from the sun that I couldn't see and I was just lucky not to squash my toes on the dead deer mice.

To understand Earl's loneliness we need to see him shooting hoops by himself after school. To understand his discomfort, his physical challenges, we need to see him finding refuge in the cool of the basement. By recreating these moments, Rough shows rather than explains the plight of the character. The result is a deeper understanding, empathy.

Just how Rough and other scribes of true stories find the material to build these rich narratives comes next.

TRY THIS

1. Add five new statistics to a narrative you've already written. How many students were in your ninth-grade biology class? What's the distance between home plate and first base? How fast was the 17-year-old driving when he hit the Jersey barrier? What was the wind velocity when the boat capsized? How many pumpkins line the streets of Keene, New Hampshire, at Halloween? How many pounds of pasta feed the marathoners?

2. Read through a narrative and highlight: (1) the setting, (2) the main characters, (3) the central problem or issue. For each of these three elements list at least three people who could add perspective. For instance, for a piece on a cousin's struggle with depression, what three people could offer insights and facts about the culture of your cousin's home or school or office or any setting that might have influenced your cousin's mental health? What three people could offer insights into your cousin? What three experts could illuminate facts about mental illness in general and depression in particular?

3. Recreate a scene that you didn't witness by interviewing participants. Ask them what they did, what they said, what they noticed about the setting and actions of others. Collect from these interviews at least two examples of each sense and the history that led to this scene. Write the scene. What's missing? What other questions do you need to ask to complete the scene?

WHERE DO YOU FIND CONTENT?

When we need information the first instinct is often to head to the computer. That's fine. No one will argue with the power and reach of Google. But as helpful as Google and its online brethren are in helping storytellers find odd facts and connections, they cannot provide everything we need to tell a tale like "Carrier" or "What Broke My Father's Heart."

One of the most valuable skills gleaned from this line of work is learning to be resourceful, learning to find the info you need from a variety of sources. Having trouble with renewing your driver's license? A seasoned researcher will figure out whom to talk to at the Registry of Motor Vehicles or how to navigate online to find the resolution. Need to determine if assisted living is the right fit for an aging parent? Those trained to gather content will know how to find the local facilities and what to ask when they get there.

But let's forget the RMV for now and get back to our literary mission. Where does a storyteller seek content? I find the best approach is to divide the possibilities into five categories: people, observation, online resources, traditional media, and institutions.

People as resources: To whom do you talk?

For journalists, interviewing strangers is as natural as drawing lines is to an architect; it is a fundamental part of the job. By definition, journalists report on the outside world, gathering input from a range of sources to tell a story to an audience. One of the first skills they acquire is how to engage someone in a conversation that will produce the thoughts, opinions, and facts that will help build a story. Yet memoirists and essayists benefit also from seeking input from other people. Fresh (and probably conflicting) perspectives and insights can't help but add texture and depth to nonfiction narratives.

Whom you talk to depends on what you need to know. When Rebecca Skloot's beloved mutt Bonny was mauled nearly to death by a pack of junkyard dogs, Skloot talked to animal law experts, health department officials, police, and neighbors. The bulk of her essay "The Truth about Cops and Dogs" is her experience trying to understand how an elderly Greek man could collect wild dogs in midtown Manhattan and let them loose at will.

Dave Eggers spent hundreds of hours interviewing Abdulrahman Zeitoun and his wife Kathy for his book "Zeitoun" about their experience in New Orleans during and after Hurricane Katrina, as well as interviewing a large cast of supporting players who provided background, contrasting experiences, and opinions that added context and detail. Chris Jones talked to 101 people, from family members to soldiers to gravediggers for his Esquire story that followed an American soldier's body's journey home. Cynthia Gorney profiles many young athletes, most of who express their brilliance through their sport, not their speech. Besides, athletic luminaries, such as swimmer Natalie Coughlin or tennis star Rafael Nadal, don't give writers much time. To collect the content she needs to understand the athlete enough to write a profile, Gorney talks to coaches, parents, friends, teammates, competitors, critics, and fans.

Who do you talk to? Whoever can answer the questions you have. If all you seek is the color of your neighbor's house 20 years ago, call the family who lived across the street. If you seek to learn the kind of trees that line the main street of Fort Collins, Colorado, contact the city arborist. If you need to recreate a scene that you didn't observe, talk to everyone who witnessed or participated in the event. If you are writing about a town's reaction to a medical marijuana dispensary, talk to people representing all perspectives — patients with pot prescriptions, doctors who prescribe it, parents who fear their teens will have easier access, police who deal with easier access, drug counselors, bioethicists, marijuana growers — anyone who has knowledge or may be impacted by the dispensary and the product it distributes.

I'm a huge fan of lists and compile rows of names divided by category: expert, pro, con, observer, participant, major players, not so major players. Beside each name is a list of whatever info is available — a phone number, e-mail address, website, blogs, links to Facebook, LinkedIn, Twitter. We live in an age of interconnection, and it's rare to find someone without a variety of digital pages and means of contact.

How do you find experts and participants?

Writers researching a familiar topic know whom to talk to. Political reporters are in regular contact with the legislators and aides on their beat. Food writers have a stable of chefs and restaurants and food purveyors to call. Yet writing projects often start off from scratch, which means that to find someone to provide fresh perspectives and background requires investigating. The Web has made that chore so easy. Need a San Francisco forensic scientist? Go online and Google your request. Names and links to names will appear. Facebook and Twitter and other social mediums can also provide contacts and a means of messaging.

Another vehicle is online chat rooms or discussion boards. Seeking input from Midwest meteorologists specializing in tornadoes? State your request to the Kansas Tornado Chasers page. Need details on Lincoln's Gettysburg Address? Log on to the American Civil War Message Board. When I wrote for House Beautiful I routinely sought the names of expert finish carpenters and historic preservationists through online organizations, both formal and informal. Almost every topic you can drum up has chat rooms and discussion boards, groups of people who converse by computer.

What do you ask in an interview?

Some writers I know choose to enter interviews having not learned much of anything about the person they are meeting. This way they feel that their questions are original, heartfelt, and earnest. While all that may be true, most of us who have spent our careers interviewing everyone from pedophiles to pop stars believe with every cell that it is always, always, always best to enter an interview prepared. You are asking for someone's time, and it is only courteous to not waste that time asking questions to which you could have gleaned the answers elsewhere. Besides, the more you know the better questions you will ask.

Often, the best way to prepare is to find articles written about the person or the skill, issue, or place about which you will interview the person. If you are interviewing a celebrity gardener, go online and see what's written about him. Visit his website. Google his name and see who is talking about him — either nicely or not so nicely. To be extra prepared, talk to others about him, gather opinions and anecdotes. Profiles require outside opinions of the subject, so you might as well gather some outside views. Once the conversation gets rolling, you can ask your interviewee to comment on those opinions. A master of this technique is Terry Gross of NPR's "All Things Considered." By the time she turns on her mic, she has researched her subject so intensively, that when she asks Fox commentator Bill O'Reilly about his reputation for exaggeration she has ammunition for his rebuttal.

The first interviews are the hardest. You have the least amount of information and are grappling for an angle. You need to get background before you get the specifics. Later interviews are more fun because you have gobs of foundation facts and have the luxury of digging for nuggets of detail and the personal anecdotes that will make the story sing. Much more interesting to ask a winter surfer to recreate his best moment in January waves than to name his first swimming instructor.

The tone of the interview is dependent on the subject — asking your great aunt how the death of her son impacted the extended family would not call for a slap-on-the-knee cheeriness — yet the common goal for most interviews is to have a conversation. You have questions. The person sitting across from you has answers, or at least opinions and some history. If the person across from you is a friend or relative, you could probably jump straight into questions about Uncle Al's volatile temper or a neighbor's renowned hospitality. Occasionally a formal interview can begin successfully with a hard-charging question by catching the interviewee off-guard (Playwright Arthur Miller was notoriously adept at dodging questions about his failed marriage to Marilyn Monroe, but Miller opened up when CBS legend Mike Wallace opened with: "You know that people said at the time that you were together, what in the world is Arthur doing this for? Arthur is an innocent. What in the world — Arthur Miller and Marilyn Monroe?"), but in most cases interviews with people you've never met before require a gentler start.

Your goal is to have a conversation and to make your interviewee comfortable. Weather chatter is mundane but safe. Noting the wild boar photo or the unusual weave of the Oriental rug may be more original. In truth, any topic that breaks the tension and allows the defenses to relax is worthy. Veteran television interviewer Shana Alexander once said that it is much easier to be the interviewer than the interviewee because the interviewer is in control. So use that control to soothe that initial awkwardness.

When my students first start interviewing, they are likely to enter the conversation with a long list of questions. Rarely does the talk veer far from the list in front of them. Like the interviewee, they are nervous. But after a while they learn that they don't need a finite list, and when the last question is answered it is time to go. They learn that it is best to have a few general questions and ask more questions based on the answers. For instance, they might first ask a survivor of the Haiti earthquake to tell what they were doing when the quake hit.

"Well, I was working at my job in the hospital," the survivor answers.

"Tell me about your job," an interviewer would say. "And what were you doing for your job when you first felt the tremors."

The first response is vague so the interviewer returns with a question requesting more detail, more explanation. Writers new to interviewing learn quickly from exchanges like this that the most important ingredient, the ONE thing they must do if the conversation will prove fruitful, is:

Listen.

Listen to what the fishery guy is saying. Listen to your aunt remembering your dad's childhood fears. Listen to the Trinity College porter chatter about the famous students who have walked through his gate, and then pick his brain for specific anecdotes. What did Prince Charles say as he entered the porter's lodge? Did he tip his hat? Nod? Stare straight ahead? The two most useful phrases in an interview are "Please, go on" or "Please elaborate."

Interviews are guided by the interviewer's curiosity. She has a few core things she must learn — perhaps some background, some statistics, an order of events — but the bulk of the conversation will flow from topics hit in the questions and answers. The most unproductive interviews are the ones in which the interviewer has a fixed idea of what he will learn and steers the conversation to the point he wants the subject to make, regardless if the conversation rushes off in another, more interesting direction. For instance, while NPR reporter Elizabeth Blair was interviewing people for a biography of Billie Holiday, she learned that the writer behind the lyrics of one of Holiday's most famous songs, "Strange Fruit," adopted the two sons of Ethel and Julius Rosenberg after the couple was executed in 1953 for conspiring to give atomic secrets to the Soviet Union. Suddenly the story she thought was about Billie Holiday took a strange but fascinating turn and led to a "Morning Edition" feature called "The Strange Story of the 'Man Behind Strange Fruit.'"

Interviews are like stories in that they have a beginning, middle, and end. The arc may be a straight curve, or as Elizabeth Blair experienced, a curlicue. Even if you think you have all the material you need, keep in mind more questions will surface when you begin writing. To ensure that the gate is open for further discussion, end the interview by asking if it would be okay to contact him or her again if you have more questions. In the decades that I've queried this, no one has ever said no.

Well, that's not entirely true. After one grueling session, the third of three multiple-hour talks, the woman I was interviewing for a Boston Magazine profile grimaced, her mouth forming a perfect square. She'd been lovely, generous with her time, but the body language said it all: no more 3-hour chats.

Not a problem. While in-person interviews are always the best (face-to-face meetings allow a connection and comfort that is hard to duplicate), and phone interviews are second best (the human voice provides almost as strong a connection as eye contact), e-mail is an excellent vehicle for follow-up questions. You've observed, you've talked, you've connected, and for the niggling details that you need to bring the story to life (What color was your corsage? What did your passenger say when your car hit the guard rail?), an e-mail exchange will suffice.

The problem with relying only on e-mail interviews is that they don't allow for spontaneous follow-up questions and digressions. The writer poses the list of questions. The subject answers them. If an answer calls for more questions, that's another line of e-mail and the person can always ignore the message.

It's much harder to ignore the person in front of you.

Observation: What do you see? Hear? Smell?

As the writer Tom French says, the world is made of details, not generalities. In turn, our stories depend on detail to take us beyond fact and into someone else's world where the wind blows softly through the linen curtains and teacups clink, to make us see, feel, hear, smell, and taste, not just think. And to gather the detail that turns a story from bland to blazing, we must flex the muscle of observation. As writers, we are insanely curious, and that curiosity drives us to watch, to notice, to spot that fleck of red amid the green foliage, the frown that erased the smirk, the pantyhose that bag at the ankle.

Take for instance, the difference between a news story chronicling the search for Caballo Blanco–the real life hero of the book "Born to Run" who had disappeared into the New Mexico mountains for a run and hadn't been seen since — and a lengthy narrative by a writer who had participated in the hunt for the renowned runner. In the news story the location where the body was eventually discovered was described as "mountainous New Mexico wilderness." Yet in

TRY THIS

1. Every family has a secret or a problem that threads through generations. Perhaps it's a disease. Or extra sensory perception. Or inertia, a reluctance to change a bad situation. Identify what you believe is your clan's mystery and interview relatives about its origins, how it has impacted family members, what the future holds. Grandparents love to reminisce, maybe settle an old score. Plus they have the wisdom and context that comes with age. Parents, too, might be so thrilled that their child wants to engage in a lengthy conversation that they'll tell all that they know. Interview for background on the issue, details to recreate scenes, and for opinions and insights.

2. Identify an issue in your hometown about which you'd like to learn more (e.g., How will the community combat an increase in teenagers overdosing on the drug Ecstasy? Why is a proposed historic district controversial? Why is a proposed playground controversial?).

   • First, make a list of sources representing differing points of view and expertise (e.g., teens who have overdosed, their parents, their friends, medical staffers who treat overdose victims, addiction experts, school counselors, teachers, police who monitor drug sales).
   • Second, using Google, social media, and people, find two sources and their contact info for each category.
   • Third, contact two of the sources by phone or e-mail and set up an interview either in person or on the phone.
   • Prepare for the interview by researching the person and his or her area of expertise if appropriate. List five broad questions you want to cover (e.g., the person's background, a timeline of events, the person's opinions, pivotal moments recreated, what the future holds).
   • Interview the two sources.
   • Feel great? Do it all over again with the rest of the sources.

the hands of writer Barry Bearak, the reader experienced that wilderness with specifics in his narrative:

> For three days, rescue teams had fanned out for 50 yards on each side of the marked trail. Riders on horseback ventured through the gnarly brush, pushing past the felled branches of pinyon-juniper and ponderosa pine. An airplane and a helicopter circled in the sky, their pilots squinting above the ridges, woodlands, river canyons, and meadows.

The details ground the reader in the scene, allowing the imagination to conjure up a picture of the pines and the squinting pilots. Call it the case against sentimentality, but the more a writer settles in, the more the writer will observe, the more details, including flaws, will surface, the more honest a portrait will evolve. Adjectives are easy. Detail collecting requires time and patience. Thanks to technology, all you need is a smart phone to record what you see and hear. The video and audio may aid in selecting just the right words to describe the canyon or the sound of the waterfall. Or if you've collected enough quality clips, you can create your own video or podcast to complement the text. Either way, you'll be rewarded for hunkering down.

Gay Talese calls it the art of hanging around, and it is practiced by a myriad of writers in a myriad of settings. Adrian Nicole LeBlanc hung around the projects in the Bronx to write with authority and stark realism the lives of the women and men caught in the web of drugs and love. Tracy Kidder has built a career quietly watching his subjects — which have ranged from the globe hopping Dr. Paul Farmer to a computer engineer to a Burundi refugee — for months, sometimes years. For her book "Behind the Beautiful Forevers," Katherine Boo spent 3 years in a Mumbai slum that rose in the shadow of the city's international airport and luxury hotels, talking to residents, watching residents, capturing their squabbles, their dreams, their efforts to maneuver around corrupt police. She watched children leave school to support their families selling trash. She watched residents sleep and cook and raise children in shacks made of scrap metal, plywood, and plastic tarps. She witnessed unspeakable violence and discrimination as she sought to illustrate the plight of the very poor in a developing country, her goal to illuminate the individual through detail and careful observation rather than painting a broad canvas.

"When I start a project, I follow as many people as I can — go where they go, do what they do, whether they're teaching kindergarten or stealing metal scrap or running a household," says Boo on her website. "The larger the pool of people I get to know, the better I can distinguish between anomalous experiences and shared ones. As a writer I'm not looking to tell the most flamboyant tales, nor to describe only the most virtuous and super-talented people. I'm looking for resonant stories — stories that might illuminate something about the structure of a society. And it's difficult to predict in the beginning which individuals' experiences, months or years later, will come to shed that light."

Hanging around requires time and patience, factors most often associated with long-term book projects. Yet magazines, newspapers, and literary journals with space (and cash) often encourage their writers to devote a chunk of time to learning a subject by just being there.

Until my trip to New York City to interview the writer Dominick Dunne, my concept of collecting content for profiles involved asking a lot of questions in a sit-down interview, researching the person's background, talking to others about the person, and observing the person doing what he or she did that made him or her worth writing about in the first place. But during the

2 days I spent in New York talking to Dunne, I learned the power of Talese's "hanging around."

A former Hollywood producer, Dominick Dunne had just emerged from seclusion in the Oregon woods to recover from a broken marriage and alcoholism. He had reinvented himself as a novelist and journalist, becoming a national sensation with a Vanity Fair story about the murder of his 22-year-old daughter Dominique and the trial of the man, her boyfriend, who had strangled her. Because the Dunne family was originally from Hartford, Connecticut, and I was a feature writer for The Hartford Courant, profiling Dunne was a natural.

He was a reluctant interview. Still adjusting to his new career as a journalist, he wasn't sure why he was worthy of a profile. Besides, he was busy. He told me to call back in 2 months, when he would have finished his second novel, "The Two Mrs. Grenvilles." He thought — he hoped — that I'd forget about him. I didn't. Between phone calls, I read his first novel and every Vanity Fair piece he had written. When next we chatted, I asked questions about specific passages in both his fiction and nonfiction. He bit. What writer wouldn't grab a chance to expound on his work? Engaged, or perhaps just worn down, he agreed to meet me for lunch at a restaurant near his studio apartment in Greenwich Village. That way, he could escape quickly if he didn't like the way the interview was going.

Yet over Caesar salads and soup in a setting of linen, flowers, and delicate china, a setting where the wait staff knew his preference for bottled water and no dessert, we connected. Once he sensed that I wasn't out to sensationalize or ridicule, that I was really truly intrigued by his rise and fall in Hollywood and his New York literary life, he opened up. He talked about Beverly Hill parties, about movie sets, celebrities. He talked about his drive to become a respected journalist. He was so engrossed in his storytelling that after our 3-hour lunch he suggested we take a walk. As we strolled past the stables-turned-houses of MacDougal Alley and the Georgian Revival brick mansions on Barrow Street, he chattered. Over lunch, I had learned the facts of his life, the timeline. During our saunter, I absorbed his reflections and anecdotes, the thoughtful analysis of what those life facts meant.

The next day we met again at his studio apartment, his choice of venue to be photographed. While the Courant photographer clicked the shutter, he showed me his albums of photos taken during his Hollywood years. Gregory Peck, Shirley MacLaine, Elizabeth Montgomery. He shared stories about them, stories about himself. Accustomed to my presence, he was relaxed, chatty. "I'm okay now," he said as if to justify his candor.

And because of that candor, I was okay, too. Hanging out had paid off.

TRY THIS

Select a person whose job intrigues you. Stem cell researcher? Professional snow-boarder? Pole dancing instructor? Ask to shadow the person for a chunk of a day. If declined, move on to another person until someone says yes. Once you're in the pole dancing studio or stem cell lab, stand back and observe, absorb the moment. Take notes on all the sensory details, dialogue, and action. Ask for explanations and background when the time is right, and when it isn't, write down questions to ask later. Write the scene.

CHALLENGING CHOICES

Cynthia Gorney on Chasing Content

Cynthia Gorney is renowned for her indefatigable curiosity and thorough research. There is no such thing as a one-source story in her world, nor in the world of her students at the University of California Berkeley's Graduate School of Journalism where she teaches every fall semester. The rest of the year she travels the world reporting and writing stories for National Geographic, The New York Times Magazine, The New Yorker, and other publications. Author of "Articles of Faith: A History of the Abortion Wars" and former Washington Post Style writer, she was driven to report and write nonfiction narratives because she wanted to hear "the stories of everyone in the world." Among those who have told their stories to her are Dr. Seuss, Robert Kennedy's assassin Sirhan Sirhan, tennis phenom Rafael Nadal, and a circle of Missouri mothers whose sons have served in the military. She has written about estrogen treatments, Sarah Palin's abortion views, child brides in India, the Tarahumara's relationship with modern Mexico, and the Calaveras County Jumping Frog Contest.

"I've always wanted to be everybody," she says. "Experience everybody's life and point of view." Here are a few ways that the prolific writer attempts to achieve that goal:

On Curiosity

My confidence comes from horrible over-reporting. My biggest strength and weakness is the same thing: when I get a chance to get into a new story, I go crazy learning about it. Editors always say, "You've over done this." The good thing about this is that I really know what I'm talking about. The joke that my husband and I tell was that when I was working on the abortion book, the place he stopped me was when in all seriousness I came home and said, "One of the problems is that the Humanae Vitae (the encyclical

(Continued)

(Continued)

letter by Pope Paul VI on human life, contraception, and marriage) is in Latin. I need to learn Latin."

"No," my husband said. "You don't need to learn Latin."

On Questions

I don't ask tricky questions. They're very basic. What did that feel like? Tell me more. The thing that made the Dr. Seuss story work was that I articulated all the questions everyone has. How did you do that? Show me how you did that? (She watched him draw Yertle the Turtle) How did it feel? Explain yourself. Most people are pleased and enthusiastic when you are genuinely interested in them and what they do.

My willingness to ask questions is based on my own ignorance. When I'm in new territory, I ask to point me to books, which signals to people that I will put effort into this. I will call people back, and say this is what I see, is that right? My most complicated scientific story was the hormone story ("The Estrogen Dilemma," New York Times Magazine, April 14, 2010). There was so much new science. I read all these studies and ways that were and were not relevant to my situation. I called experts to see if I had it right. If you carry yourself courteously and work really hard at not being arrogant, people are generally willing to be helpful if they have time.

On Listening

The sacred task of listening is the most valuable thing we do. The biggest sin reporters commit is not listening, or listening with a selective ear, going for the hatchet quote.

My approach is to go out and try to hear from all sides. We all know stories have multiple sides. I try to understand the way people think when they have colliding views before them. As a northern California person who had gone to Berkeley and then gone to Washington, DC, I found the perspective of people who genuinely believed that abortion was taking human life as foreign. People of my demographic, young professional women, were the most hostile. That made me more interested in learning about the right-to-life people in communities, and how ill informed the stereotypes were.

On Reluctant Subjects

Athletes don't tend to be articulate. Their brilliance is expressed in other ways, and you, the writer, are an annoyance to them.

The Natalie Coughlin piece ("A Feel for Water," The New Yorker, July 5, 2004) started way in advance — a year before the 2004 Olympics. Access was going to become extremely limited. I got to hang out with her team and her coach and learned about distance swimming during a summer when not much attention was paid. I learned what that world was about. I went to the World Swimming Championships and used that material.

Clearly her genius was in her relationship with water so the piece was about her relationship with water. Most of the interviews were not so much about tell me about

Natalie, but tell me what it is like to be a swimmer, how to handle this, what it is that makes a person go faster in water.

I got a little more time with Rafael Nadal ("Ripped. Or Torn Up?" New York Times Magazine, June 17, 2009) because I spoke Spanish. I hung around a lot and had three conversations with him. Like with Natalie, I knew I wouldn't get much. Young athletes don't open up. They have a set of things that they say. The thoughtful comment comes from people around and who know them. I apologized when I called and they indulged me. I would ask them really dumb questions that they found interesting. What does it mean that a tennis player is tenacious? What does it mean for one player to be more tenacious than other? I use my ignorance and curiosity to guide me.

Online Resources

Whenever you hear someone complain about information overload — too many newspapers, too many e-mail messages, too many videos, blogs, and newscasts — just smile and nod. While there is no question that a quick quest to learn the results of an election debate, or dog-friendly resorts, or the fertility rate of Uzbekistan, can reap a crushing avalanche of opinions, facts, articles, videos, blogs, podcasts, online comments, books, radio shows, Tumblr posts, and Facebook friends, there is also no question that this is a fine time indeed for those of us seeking content for our storytelling. The issue is not so much whether the history, statistics, background, and people you seek are out there; rather the issue is where do you head first and how do you weigh your options?

Search engines and databases: Google and beyond.

If you ask a theater full of writers how they seek information on the Web, a chunk would say Bing, a few would claim Yahoo, but the overwhelming majority would say Google.

There's a reason Google has become a verb and is defined by Urban Dictionary as "the mother of all search engines." Google is an information beast that within seconds will spew tens of thousands of links that somehow relate to the term you queried. That's a good thing, a really good thing. We all use it. We all depend on it, for everything from locating the dermatologist's phone number to the history of Arlington National Cemetery. If we're savvy, we'll winnow down the options and use a Google Advanced Search, narrowing the field by geography, dates, and language. With Google we can research our topic by maps and images and videos. We can call up audio interviews to hear not just what our profile subject answered but how he answered, the inflection of his voice, the sadness, the joy. We can Google videos of the Rocky Mountains to enhance our understanding of place. We can Google blogs to see what other writers are thinking about John D'Agata's liberty with facts in his book "About a Mountain."

Yet as all-encompassing as Google is, there are other options. While all search engines operate under the same premise — they search billions of websites and create a database, or index, of relevant sites — the difference lies in their lists of websites (not even Google's index includes every website in the stratosphere) and how they list the findings. Some filter out unreliable sites. Others list a wider range, while others narrow the search. A quick search using the phrase "bike friendly communities" brings many of the same sites but one engine may post the AARP's Bike-Friendly Communities as the top find while another opens with the League of American Bicyclists Bicycle Friendly Community Program.

And then there are the meta search engines. My favorite is Dogpile (just because I like the name) but it operates just like Metacrawler and Pandia and the other metas, which is to say that it doesn't have its own library of websites to offer you but instead rifles through the indexes of other search engines and, voila, send to you what they think are the most relevant sites. Think of meta search engines as an aggregator, providing you with a selected list culled from the contents of other search engines.

The drawback of all these search engines is that their indexes include sites that are open, that don't require a password. And for research that requires something specific, say a legal case involving gay rights, or current multiple sclerosis treatments, you need databases that will provide you with the *Lancet* article about new drugs for multiple sclerosis or the case study of *Boy Scouts of America v. Dale*. The only catch is that most databases require a connection to a library or university or other institution that can afford the hefty price of contracts with Lexis-Nexis and JStor.

When asked what has kept me teaching at the University of New Hampshire for so long, I say my students, my writing colleagues, and am only half-kidding when I add Lexis-Nexis. Most of my writing projects begin with a search of newspaper, magazine, and legal documents available through this full-text database. If I need more options, I'll peruse Academic Search Premier on EBSCO-*host*. If I need specific medical or legal journal articles, I go to JStor. And that's only three of the hundreds of databases available to me through UNH.

But the beauty of our digital world is that public libraries, too, offer databases to their clients. You don't have to have a university connection — only a library card.

Traditional media.

Much of what we define as traditional media — newspapers, movies, magazines, TV, books, radio — is available online. Some of it is free, and some of it costs. I don't mind paying; how else will writers and print journalists and broadcast reporters earn salaries? The point is that so much of what we need for context and facts and stats is available from past media stories that to overlook them is like skipping the entire menu when you're so hungry you'd eat bark. The media provides sustenance to narratives.

Assigned to write a story about the resilience of a couple who had lost two of their three sons (their oldest son Josh at age 19 to brain cancer and their youngest son Nate, a Navy SEAL, at 29 in Iraq as he tried to evacuate his fatally wounded partner during a raid), I combed the Internet for newspaper stories on Nate, his work, and his death, and also stories on other Navy SEALs. Nate did not work alone, and through understanding SEALs as a group, I might better understand Nate. In addition, media stories fed me details about the fundraisers the parents had created to raise money for scholarships in both their boys' names. I read a book about the Spartans, Nate's military idols, and I read "Lone Survivor," a Navy SEAL's account of an Afghanistan ambush in which all his comrades but him were killed. I read stories and watched a video about Arlington National Cemetery, where Nate is buried. I read magazine articles about brain cancer. Even though most of what I learned from this media research isn't visible in the story, it provided background and a deeper understanding of the setting, the characters, and the challenges the characters faced.

For almost every subject, traditional media offers something. For an essay about loneliness, a search through NPR will unearth dozens of audio stories and interviews about loneliness-themed movies and books and therapy and organizations. Need to relive your family's vacation to the Gettysburg battlefields? There's no shortage of public television documentaries on the Civil War in general and Gettysburg in particular. For raging social issues, such as the heroin epidemic, dive into news shows such as "Frontline." Network TV, too, offers footage and background on all kinds of issues and people and events. Writing about campus efforts to increase diversity? Search local networks for coverage of protests demanding more faculty and students of color.

If we dig far and deep enough we will uncover little known facts and anecdotes that will add layers and texture to our narratives. And if we're lucky, will surprise the reader.

Social media.

Facebook may link you to your best friend's weekend plans or your cousin's wedding photos, but for the intrepid researcher, the digital network is so much more. Social media — LinkedIn, YouTube, Pinterest, Tumblr, Vimeo, and probably hundreds more by the time you read this — provide storytellers with infinite resources. First, these sites offer lots of contacts. Need to talk to someone about surfing in Costa Rica? Roam the social media world for Facebook pages, Tumblr posts, and YouTube videos and contact the host. While working on an essay about biking in England, I searched LinkedIn and Facebook for names of British bikers, and administrators of British biking groups and transportation agencies. If e-mail or phone numbers weren't available, I sent messages to them via the social network.

And there's more. Writing a travel piece about hiking in Quebec? Check out photos on Instagram. Need experts to provide background and opinions on Bangladesh child labor? Post a question on Quora and wait for the response. Tangled in your own emotions about a turbulent childhood and would relish outside perspectives by those who have shared similar experiences? Try Twitter. #Badchildhood. See who posts.

Writers and reporters use social media for all sorts of content, and in some cases, the social media becomes the story. A few years ago, Washington Post reporter Ian Shapira was trolling through Facebook and landed on the page of Shana Swers, a woman who worked with his wife. An enthusiastic poster, Swers had shared her pregnancy with her Facebook friends over the past months and had just given birth. The post announcing the arrival of Isaac Lawrence Swers was ebullient. But within hours of delivery she developed postpartum cardiac myopathy; the following chain of posts over the next few weeks grew bleaker. At the end was one by Shana's husband announcing her death. As a husband and father, Shapira was stunned. As a journalist who had written before about sharing public stories on social media, he was struck by how this tragedy had unfolded on Facebook. Shana Swers' voice tells the story through her posts. Her husband's entry at the end is a cold, hard slap. With the blessing of Swers' family and Facebook friends, Shapira began work on pulling together a story. Using Swers' Facebook page as the framework, Shapira wove in background information and context to explain the posts. He added details about Swers and her medical condition. He added explanations of the friends who posted responses. The result — "A Facebook Story: A Mother's Joy and a Family's Sorrow" — was a moving account that garnered pages of online comments.

WEB CHOICES

The Washington Post's Ian Shapira wrestles with ethics and humanity in a Facebook story

With an English degree from Princeton and a master's in interactive journalism from American University, Ian Shapira shapes many of his narratives for The Washington Post with content gleaned from social media. Facebook, in particular, he finds a revolutionary tool for his work. He scrolls through Facebook to learn more about the people who populate his stories. He'll use Facebook to find the names of people involved in an event. Sometimes Facebook pages themselves become the story. "Infertile Couples Cope with Prolific Facebook Friends" sprouted from a conversation with a couple he knew who had dropped out of Facebook because photos of sonograms and joyous birth announcements were too painful as they confronted their own inability to conceive. The Facebook postings by the crew of the HMS Bounty on its final journey during Hurricane Sandy formed the spine of "HMS Bounty: A Tall Ship's Final Hours in Hurricane-Ravaged Seas." But the story that used online postings to the most dramatic effect was "A Facebook Story: A Mother's Joy and a Family's Sorrow," which told the story of Shana Swers' pregnancy, delivery, postnatal illness, and ultimate death through her Facebook page's status updates.

A revolutionary storytelling tool it may be, but using Facebook to help tell stories poses its own breed of demands. Says Shapira:

I've been using Facebook especially since its earliest days for stories. I've always operated with the sense that if the page is public, and the people know that I'm reporting for a story, there are no surprises, no playing gotcha. If people decline to talk, I don't mention them (or their page) in the story.

I use Facebook in cooperation with them. For the infertile couples story, I sat at the kitchen table while the couple showed me posts of friends and relatives and their new babies, walking me through how tough it was for them.

My wife was a colleague of Shana Swers. We were in the airport in Chicago, headed back to Washington. My wife was checking her news feed when she saw that someone had posted on Shana's page that Shana had died. I said I'm so sorry. Then I went on her Facebook page. There was this incredible narrative that Shana had authored herself. Getting pregnant. Going on date night with her husband.

The question was how we would use this material. I went to my editor and said we could do a traditional story and use status updates as a thread. The editor, Marc Fisher, said let's just use status updates and offer annotations as explanation.

The big hurdle was going through her page and then choosing the right status updates. If she said she was going out for date night and a friend replied "Where are you going?" I'd have to track down the friend. Or she'd have a status update on what's going on in the hospital and 30 people would respond. We would have to select which responses we'd use and then find the people and make sure that it was okay to use their comments. Shana's page was open for me to use with her family's permission, but the friends didn't give me their permission. So I tracked them down, and asked their age, a little about them. I had them explain abbreviated comments, which I clarified in the annotations.

The story got a lot of feedback. Some people felt that we had given short shrift to why the woman had died, the possible hospital mistakes (We could have solved that with more annotations). Other people thought it was gimmicky. But the vast majority of responses were positive. They thought it was an innovative, respectful way for Shana to tell her own story. It was a way to show that we all write stories on Facebook but that we just don't know it. She didn't know it.

Crowdsourcing.

Breaking news has benefited for years from videos, photos, and stories posted on social media sites by electricians and kindergarten teachers and meandering teenagers, citizen journalists if you will. Think observers describing the December 2008 Mumbai massacre on Twitter. Think following the Arab Spring of

2011 on YouTube, the Asian tsunami on Flickr. But longer projects that require not just immediate reaction and observation, but thoughtful experience and analysis, are also employing input from the public. In The New York Times blog "At War; Notes from the Front Line," the editors asked readers to help identify a weapon found on a Libyan battlefield for its feature. In an effort to learn how much money nonprofit groups and Super PACs spent on TV ads during the 2012 election, ProPublica requested public participation through Facebook, asking for volunteers to visit network affiliates, request to see the contribution documents, and report back their findings. For its patient safety series, Pro-Publica's Facebook page asked for patients and providers to share their stories of health care quality.

On a side note, writers also crowdsource to finance their work. My friend Joel Brown used Kickstarter to help cover the research costs of his latest book, a non-fiction narrative about a local scenic byway that weaves through 13 towns on Boston's North Shore. His reward was generous: he promised that whoever donated the most would be a character killed off in his next novel.

Brick & mortar institutions

When Eli Sanders sought to learn exactly what happened on that July night in 2009 when two women were assaulted in their Seattle home, he attended the trial of the accused assailant. He studied court documents and transcripts. He learned from the survivor's testimony how the perpetrator had beaten the women, raped the women, and then killed her partner. From court and police records he learned of the accused's troubled mental health history. From the coroner's report he learned of the dead woman's injuries. From the crime lab reports he learned of bloody footprints and fingerprints. The product of all this research was the Pulitzer Prize winning narrative, "The Bravest Woman in Seattle."

TRY THIS

1. On a map stick a pin in a town in a country you'd like to visit. Research that town using Instagram, YouTube, Dogpile, Facebook, EBSCO*host*, or any other online resource. Write a 500-word mini profile of the place citing odd little facts that make this spot distinctive.

2. Scroll through five social media sites and find 10 different people to contact for a story on how social media can promote social change.

When Katherine Boo needed to verify the arrests and criminal proceedings of the people she followed in the Annawadi slum, she hung out at the local police station. Amy Harmon of The New York Times knows her way around hospital hallways and research labs for her prize-winning narratives about the impact of science and technology on our culture.

As wonderful as the Internet is for providing facts, stats, and background, do not overlook more tangible resources. Hospitals have records. Town halls have shelves filled with historic documents. Schools, churches, libraries, health departments — name an institution that performs a service and that institution may have just the numbers and historical perspective you seek.

What Would Don Suggest?

Donald Murray, who devoted his later years to writing about writing, began his career as a journalist, winning a Pulitzer Prize along the way for his Boston Herald editorials. Although he retired from UNH shortly after I arrived there to teach, he kept in touch, often dropping off a new book or an article he just wrote. One of my favorites was a list he compiled pre-Internet of places writers should seek content for their stories:

- 10 people
- 10 books
- 10 movies
- 10 television shows
- 10 radio broadcasts
- 10 magazine articles
- 10 trade journals
- 10 institutions (e.g., school, town hall, hospital, fire station, business, courts)
- 10 photos

Had Don, who died in 2006 from heart failure at age 82, decided to update this list to include digital resources, the updated version might add:

- 10 websites
- 10 databases
- 10 social networks
- 10 videos
- 10 podcasts
- 10 RSS feeds
- 10 Google Alerts

The point, Don would say, is that not one kind of information source will provide you with the variety of content you need, not even for a short essay.

TRY THIS

Visit a local cemetery and find a grave that dates back at least 50 years. Now write a profile of that person using content gleaned from databases and interviews. If the cemetery feels too impersonal, dig through your hometown's real estate files, find someone who lived in your home or apartment decades ago and write a profile. (Hint: talk to historians, locals, and if you can find them, family members.)

Let the information come to you

Instead of launching new searches each time you log on to your laptop, you have the option of directing the news to come to you. Type in key words and Google Alerts will send you blog posts, news stories, websites, videos, and any other kind of post that included those key words. For instance, I have "creative nonfiction" as a Google Alert, and several times a day, Google sends me fresh postings that involve creative nonfiction, from syllabi to essays to new books. RSS (Really Simple Syndication) feeds on news sites and blogs will send you content based on topics you'd like to track. While my graduate student Larry worked on his creative thesis about adoption in the age of social media, he arranged for RSS feeds to ship him updates on adoption topics. While I made sense of my youngest son's college search by writing about it, I had an RSS feed that provided links to any new columns posted on The New York Times college blog "The Choice." So much information available *is* overwhelming, but with thought and tools we can reel in just what we need.

4

What's the Focus?

Overview

A former student once said that only one word will appear on my tombstone: Focus. True enough. I am a fiend for focus. In the following pages, we explore how to find meaning, the narrative's soul, amid the chaos of memory and mass of notes and tapes, observations and interviews. We ask the tough questions and seek clues for that central message in place, character, and detail, as well as in research and reflection.

THE NUMBERS MATCHED. What Katie Campbell needed to pay for grad school was exactly the same amount the donor agency would pay for her eggs. She was 27, healthy, a runner and writer and photographer. Why not? Some bloating, some discomfort, a few needles and she wouldn't have to take out a student loan. So she started the process, collecting facts about the long-term effects (unknown), the daily injections (do-it-yourself syringes), the procedure itself (not too bad). The more she researched, the more remote the dangers seemed, the more comfortable she felt. She could give something of herself to others and go on to live a happy, healthy life. She didn't see how donating her eggs would alter that dream. Her boyfriend, though, did.

He feared for her health, and he feared for their future. How would it feel to know that your child wandered the planet? He worried how this shadow might affect their relationship, their future marriage. What would happen if the child sought her out one day? And what about the ethics? Was egg donation a means to prevent undesirable traits? An exercise in eugenics?

Like most writers, Katie thinks best with a pen in her hand. Torn by her drive to donate her eggs and respect for her boyfriend's concerns, she shifted her note taking from listing facts to chronicling conversations with her boyfriend and her reaction to their debates. The more she wrote about it, the more she talked about it. The more she talked about it, the more her friends wanted to know. She's found over the course of her career that how her friends react to a subject is often an indicator of a story's viability. If friends ask a lot of questions, she's golden. If their eyes wander, she has a clunker. With this subject, she struck platinum. How are you selected, they asked. Will there be side effects? How will the procedure impact your fertility? Could the parents sue you over birth defects?

She envisioned a global piece, an essay that weighed the Big Picture of egg donation, using her experience as a vehicle to explore whether donating one's eggs is a wise choice. The bulk of the story would emphasize the choices of other women, background facts and stats, and the thoughts of ethicists and medical experts. In cinematic terms, the camera would focus on others, not herself.

Yet as she began crafting the essay, the camera angle kept pivoting back to her, and ultimately to the moment she decided not to go through with it. Through many drafts she discovered the meaning behind the experience, and the resulting essay "The Egg and I," which was first published in Etude and later in the "Best Creative Nonfiction" (Volume II). Turns out, the focus wasn't the Big Picture, the pros and cons of egg harvesting, but the human connection, transitioning from "me" to "we." Her last paragraphs:

> *My frustration is morphing into anger, and I turn on my side away from him, seeking space to understand my feelings. They are my eggs. It's my body. Why can't it be just my decision?*
>
> *He eases his arm through the gap between my neck and the pillow and slides close. As I let myself lean against him, I suddenly understand that this is not about asserting my independence. This is about deciding to be a couple and make what could be a life-altering decision as we should make all important decisions — together. My eggs don't belong to him, but our futures are inter-twined. And ignoring that would be disregarding the partnership we've created.*
>
> *My tears surprise us both. I didn't realize until that moment how attached I'd become to donating my eggs. I'm filled with a sense of loss, but at the same time, I realize what's at stake here: our relationship, the life we intend to share with one another, our future. I turn to him.*

Finding focus. Meaning. The universal message. The one thing you want to say. The one point to which all the content adheres. For most writers, figuring out that central point is one of the hardest parts of the writing process. We spend days, weeks, months, sometimes years researching and reflecting. When the memories are unearthed and the notebooks overflow, we face the daunting task of making sense of all those observations and facts and opinions and recollections. Often, we'll just start writing, crafting scenes, tossing in supporting background, perhaps weaving in some facts and stats. Yet the whole exercise feels like we're in a rudderless boat zigzagging across the bay. Without that rudder, we can't control the destination. Without the destination, who wants to share the ride?

Focus drives the narrative. It determines content and provides the narrative arc, the beginning, middle, and end. Without focus, readers wonder where even the most riveting scenes and fascinating facts are taking them, what they are supposed to understand. After a while, they'll move on to empty the dishwasher or choose another essay that they hope will share a slice of wisdom, an insight. Without focus all they have is — to borrow a phrase from Robin Hemley, author, essayist, and former director of the University of Iowa's nonfiction writing program — a "prose blob."

If I received a free dinner for every time a student said the meaning behind a block of facts or a sequence of scenes was "It is about the aftermath of the hurricane" or "It is about the deer ramming my sister's car," I would never, ever have to cook an evening meal again. For these emerging writers, it is enough to deliver the anecdote or information. They would paint scenes of a home destroyed by water and wind, a mother frantically searching for a photo album. They would explain step-by-step how on a rainy August night a deer bolted from the woods and into their sister's car as she was headed home on I-95 from her waitressing job. Yet in essayist Vivian Gornick's terms, all they've relayed is the situation. What the writer wants to say and the reader will learn about the deer ramming and hurricane flooding is the story, the angle, the focus, the message the writer has chosen. "Every work of literature has both a situation and a story," Gornick writes in her book called — what else? — "The Situation and the Story." "The situation is the context or circumstance, sometimes the plot; the story is the emotional experience that preoccupies the writer; the thing one has come to say."

The situation for Katie Campbell's essay was egg donation. The story was whether or not it was the path for her. The narrative arc led us from one scene to another, from her awareness of the option, to exploring the pros and cons, to scenes of her actively weighing the choice. The final moment illuminates the central message: while egg donation may be fine for others, it was not right for her. In another writer's hand, the focus may have been on the ethical or moral dilemma of selling body parts for people to use. "But for me," Campbell says, "it was learning to make a decision that not only affects me but also my (now) husband. I don't have the luxury to decide on my own anymore. That's a good but sad realization."

And a powerful focus.

Whether the situation is the writer's experience (internal) or the experience of others (external), or a combination of both ("The Egg & I"), tellers of true stories must search to find the meaning behind the action. Michael Steinberg seeks in his personal essays to chronicle the inner story beneath the literal story of his experience, to understand why, for instance, his childhood baseball coach still haunts him. Narrative journalist Tom French strives to detect the theme beneath the surface of the murder he has researched or the zoo he has observed. Countless people have played baseball and visited zoos, but it is the writer's mission to think through the situation and find the story, the one thing the writer alone wants to say.

Faith Adiele shares universal messages about race and identity and failure in her memoir of her year as a Buddhist nun in Thailand. The situation: a biracial 21-year-old on academic probation from Harvard who found herself in a Thai forest with a shaved head and eyebrows, meditating for 19-hour stretches. Exotic as it was, the experience alone, however, was not enough to carry a narrative. Her mission was to tell a larger story than just the scenes and thoughts that filled her journals.

Or, in her words, to write a book that "someone besides my mother would want to read." Through reflection and writing, she found that the focus of her memoir was on finding her core, her sense of self. Hence the title: "Meeting Faith."

HOW DO YOU FIND FOCUS?

In a perfect world, during the research and reflection or early writing stage we would be struck by a thunderbolt of epiphany. Aha! That's what all this means! And, like John Irving, who knows the last line of his novels before he writes the first, we would mold the material to the point we want to make.

But writing is rarely that easy (who knows how many years John Irving mulled the options before he arrived at that last line), and the art of finding meaning hinges on ruthless self-interrogation. And because there is not just one possible focus for each subject, there is not just one question we can ask ourselves to find meaning. Instead, narratives demand deep thinking and multiple inquiries to unearth the message one wants to share. Still, some general inquiries can help lead the way toward figuring out just what in the Sam Hill we're trying to say.

What question launched the project?

A narrative's focus is often the answer to the question that launched the project in the first place. Take the work of Montaigne; his essays are based on issues that vexed him — How should children be raised? What's the value of the study of philosophy? Is drunkenness a "brutish vice"? — and then he twists and turns and attacks the question from every angle, weaving in his own observations, historical references, and reflection. The focus of his essays — the universal message he leaves the reader — is the answer to the queries that sparked the literary exploration.

Katie Campbell sought to learn if donating one's eggs to another woman is an ethically and medically sound choice. The answer: For some women, maybe, but not for her. With that central point in mind, she could create a structure and select the content to build the narrative arc.

As he does with most projects, Tom French launched "Zoo Story; Life in the Garden of Captives," with a broad, sweeping question: what is life like at a zoo, for both man and beast? And, as he does with most projects, he immersed himself in his subject, in this case Tampa's Lowry Park Zoo, observing and interviewing, researching and reflecting. That one question launched multiple explorations — How do the people inside the zoo grapple with complex moral and ethical questions about captivity? What do those questions mean for the animals? What's the relationship between the animals and their human keepers? Should they have a relationship? — and the resulting focus hinged on his conclusions about captivity, extinction, and conservation.

Perhaps the best example lies with the writer Richard Ben Cramer. For "What It Takes: The Way to the White House," a chronicle of the 1988 presidential election, Cramer was driven by a single query: what kind of life would lead a man to think that he ought to be president of the United States? He devoted years to researching the candidates' lives before the election, as well as chronicling them during the election. He talked to staffers and uncles and grandparents, sons, daughters, wives, friends, and foes. He observed others interviewing the candidates. In fact, he observed the candidates for so long, he never had to ask them a question. Instead, they were so comfortable with him, they just confided. The result was a 1,047-page profile of ambition.

What's the conflict?

All stories have conflict. There's a central conflict — Will Cheryl Strayed overcome her demons and her grief on the Pacific Crest Trail? — and there are often multiple sub-conflicts — Will Cheryl's bruised feet ever heal? How will she deal with unpredicted snow cover? How will she avoid being eaten by a bear? Will she use that one condom? The longer the narrative, the more conflicts.

Katherine Boo has spent her career telling stories of poverty, social injustice, and economic policy, subjects with inherent conflicts. Her approach — telling a larger story through characters — requires total immersion, living, breathing, observing the people she writes about, plus interviewing armies of experts and digging deep into political documents.

"In my kind of work, you don't parachute in after some big, terrible event, which is important and has to be covered, but offers only a glimpse," Boo said in an interview with Guernica, an online magazine of art and politics. "It's the kind of work in which you ask, what is my understanding of how the world works, and where can I go to see these questions get worked out in individuals' lives?"

To understand public treatment of the mentally disabled, she immersed herself in government-run group homes for the mentally handicapped. To understand the impact of government intervention into marriage, she spent months in Oklahoma with women participating in state-sponsored classes on marriage, the goal of which was to help the students escape poverty. Through focusing on a few people in her book "Behind the Beautiful Forevers" — a teenager who sells trash to support his family of 11, a woman who sets herself on fire to attract attention, a mother who seeks economic gain for her family through affairs with powerful men — and the crises they endure (death, disease, rats, arrests, violence, abuse), she explores the question: with so much working against them, how do the 3,000 residents of the Annawadi slum move out of their scrap metal homes covered in tarps and participate in India's expanding economy?

Conflict, too, can be subtle. Conflict is Ryan Van Meter recognizing at age 5 that something is wrong when he states that he wants to marry his friend Ben. His essay "First" captures the confusion and pain of a child yearning for something his parents — and culture — aren't ready to accept. Conflict is Gabriel Gomez, a political neophyte, running road races to connect with the electorate in his campaign for a U.S. Senate seat. Will this unorthodox approach succeed? The Boston Globe story "On the Run for Votes" shows in scene how the candidates' efforts conflict with the runners' attention to pace rather than politics.

Conflict is a collision of forces. Sometimes the collision is person vs. person (Ryan Van Meter's yearning for closeness with another boy collides with his parents' discouragement of such intimacy), and sometimes it is person vs. nature (Jon Krakauer attempts to climb Mt. Everest in "Into Thin Air"). Or it could be person vs. the system (Abdul, an Annawadi teenager, seeks justice from corrupt Mumbai politicians and police) or person vs. self (Cheryl Strayed attempting to save herself by walking 1,100 miles).

In the end, a story's focus, the glue that holds all the narrative pieces together, is that collision and what the writer perceives as the outcome of that collision. Ryan Van Meter loses innocence. Jon Krakauer gains profound respect for nature's power and man's limitations. Abdul learns justice is elusive. And Cheryl Strayed finds stability through her journey. The central question is answered.

What's the most important thing you learned?

During one of my first feature writing jobs, I would seek my editor's advice when I became overwhelmed by a story. I would approach his desk, wringing my hands, fretting over the piles of notes I'd collected, whining that I just couldn't figure out the story's center. He'd put down his pen, swivel his chair to face me, and ask, "What's the most important thing you learned?" And then he'd wait for my answer.

What crept out of my mouth was less plot and more theme. "That a man can hit bottom but still learn to thrive." "Testing one's limits may not be such a good thing." "Compromise is key." When facing the notes brimming with descriptions and dialogue and thoughts on the people I met and the situation in which they found themselves, I struggled to see past the action. But when asked to reflect on what all that action meant, out popped universal themes. Themes that illuminate the human condition. Themes that resonate with a reader. Themes that provide the central meaning, the focus.

The challenge, of course, is how to illustrate those themes in a fresh, new way, a way that will surprise and engage the reader. The key, as veterans will tell you, is in the specifics. Through detail Krakauer makes us feel the raging wind of Everest, the fierce cold, the breathlessness that thwarts the climbers' progress. Through detail, Katherine Boo wakes the reader to the horrors of classism and government corruption by making us care about the Annawadi residents. She doesn't portray the residents as character studies, but rather as characters. We know what they think, feel. We know what they say and how they interact with their peers and the police. We see them cook dinner in a makeshift kitchen of sheet metal and cardboard. We feel their despair:

Although Manju attributed her mother's grief entirely to a secret heartache, Asha's heart at forty was stubborn and knowing. Her brain was the trouble-some thing. When not reflecting on the cause of past failures, she brooded on the smallest of slights: a police officer who no longer returned her phone calls; a Shiv Sena colleague who had a special puja and failed to invite her. The nor-mal Asha would have been happy not to visit Reena, who was grumpy and had the face of a cow. But in her current mood, small affronts were bundled with larger disappointments and became a body of evidence. Something bright in her had been eclipsed.

Through intimate detail we learn what Boo has learned. The focus is clear.

What do you want readers to know when they finish the book, the essay, the story?

When writers pitch an idea to literary agent David Black, he'll often open the discussion with the question, "What will the reader learn when he or she finishes the book?" On a tale of abuse, neglect, and isolation, the answer was "How one survives the unthinkable." For Melissa Fay Greene's first book, "Praying for Sheetrock," the reply was "How idealism and bravery and a slow awakening to justice brought the civil rights movement to rural Georgia." For "Tuesdays with Morrie," readers learn ways to live contented and productive lives through the wisdom of a dying professor, shared during weekly visits with a former student.

Often that message, that one thing the writer wants the reader to learn, is called "The Elevator Pitch" — the way one would state the heart of a narrative to someone between floors. While visiting Random House, writer Jonathan Harr bumped into the publisher's executive editor on the elevator. In greeting, the editor asked what Harr's book-in-progress was about. Harr launched into a lengthy diatribe about a lawsuit involving tainted water, leukemia clusters, dead children, professional hubris, and corporate greed. In the middle of his description, the elevator stopped, the door opened, and the editor walked out. "Interesting," he said, his eyes forward. Fortunately for both the editor and Harr, "A Civil Action" sold millions of copies, was made into a movie starring John Travolta, and won the National Book Critics Circle Award. Still, Harr advised a group of student writers during a visit to UNH, the memory of that elevator ride stung. Lesson learned: whittle the point to a sentence or two.

What would make a good title and subtitle?

While listening to writers suggest story ideas, David Rosenbaum, former editor of Boston Magazine, would close his eyes, rub his hands together, and try to think of a title and subtitle. If he could, the writer got the assignment. If he couldn't, the writer could either move on to another idea or collect more content to make a stronger pitch.

For my Boston Magazine story on day care, the headline he wrote was "Who Cares for the Child?" and the lengthy subhead was "If we all care so much about our kids, why are child-care providers so poorly paid? Why do so few employers offer child-care assistance? The truth is to be found not in what we say but in what we do. And we don't do much." The headline aroused curiosity and the subhead stated the focus — not much is done to ensure quality child care. The story, then, illustrated through scene and exposition why and how the state of child care is so woeful.

TRY THIS

1. State your narrative's focus in six words, which must include a specific subject and active verb. Do NOT include the word "about."

2. Put your notes away and write. And write. Do not let the internal editor stop you. Keep writing until you have piles of pages. Where did all that writing lead? What insights? Summarize the point in one sentence. Remember that what one might consider "fluff" might turn out to be essential foundation. Don't skimp!

Examples of powerful titles are on every magazine and literary journal's table of contents. An Atlantic title: "Dirty Sexy Money; Is Porn Recession Proof?" The subject: questionable money. The focus: how does pornography fare in an economic downturn? From The New Yorker: "The Prism; A Secret History of Privacy." The title provides an image of refracted transparency and the subtitle states the story's heart centers on privacy policy. From Creative Nonfiction: "An Insider's Guide to Jailhouse Cuisine: Dining In." The combined title and subtitle let the reader know the piece will focus on a jail stint.

While an editor's job description may include writing headlines, writers benefit from crafting their own. First, writing a title and subtitle articulates focus. If the title is fuzzy, so is the meaning. Second, a clever title can go a long way to selling a freelance narrative. No title, or a lame title, could jettison the piece to the trash without so much as an editorial scan. Capture the editor's interest with an intriguing title and that editor will start reading. And reading is the first step toward acceptance.

TRY THIS

1. Leaf through three narratives you've written and identify the universal themes that run through each. Resilience? Power of love? Persistence? Once clear on the theme and thus the focus, cull out the material that doesn't support the focus and weave in more scenes and facts and background that do support the focus.

2. A strong title and subtitle will state the focus and highlight the question the reader will pursue in the piece. For example: "Lost in the Meritocracy: How I Traded an Education for a Ticket to the Ruling Class," the title for an Atlantic story Walter Kirn wrote about academic achievers, the promise of aptitude, and where it will lead. Write five titles and five subtitles for a writing project. Eliminate all that don't articulate the focus.

WEB CHOICES

Travel Writer Rolf Potts Finds That
Video Works Best When Time is Tight

To write a travel narrative with insight and meaning requires time. Time to observe. Time to research. Time to reflect. Rolf Potts has built a career writing about place, travelling

(Continued)

(Continued)

around the world writing essays and travel narratives for publications from National Geo-graphic Traveler to The Believer to Worldhum.com. He's written two books, hosted docu-mentaries on the Travel Channel, and shared his accrued wisdom in workshops from Australia to Paris to Yale. If anyone knows about what's required to capture the essence of a locale, it is Potts.

Forever seeking ways to explore his belief that travel is about the experience, not the accouterments, he developed a few years ago a project that would entail traveling around the world without luggage. No suitcase. No backpack. No man purse. All the items he carried would be stowed in his clothes. For the "No Baggage Challenge" he recruited a video camera-man, Justin Glow, to accompany him on this 6-week journey to five continents and 12 countries. Because their time in each place would be brief — they were in London for hours — Potts knew that he wouldn't have time to really learn the pulse of the sites to write with much meaning. Instead, he channeled most of his attention to the videos Glow shot and they both edited. Their mission was to find that one element at each stop on which to focus a 5- to 8-minute cinematic story. Potts says:

Video was the best strategy for "No Baggage Challenge" because we didn't have the time to discover the places in a meaningful way. Spending so little time in places made it impossible to find the deeper meaning that goes into narrative. If Anthony Bourdain spent months and months in a place, his TV show ("No Reservations") wouldn't be any better.

I was the director and Justin was the producer, cinematographer.

He's from Missouri. I'm from Kansas. We worked well as team. I couldn't do this by myself.

In almost every situation we ended up performing our travels, creating our own set ups that lent themselves to visual narrative. In Egypt, when you go to the pyra-mids in Giza, you are surrounded by tourists and touts. In your mind's eye you think that you'll commune with ancient history when in fact the present is forcefully pressing in on your face. I spent a whole day trying to capture this experience by setting the scene for the touts. You see me being hassled by these guys six times in a condensed period. In another shot you see me walk in amid a bunch of overweight tourists. There were moments that we didn't have swarms of tourists, but we sought out the moments when we would. We manipulated like a documentary film crew would do.

In South Africa I was on safari a lot. The narrative arose from the footage. In Morocco, we were lost a lot. We had this classic misadventure. We asked the taxi driver to take us to Chefchaouen and he took us to Tetouan. We mispronounced it. Tetouan turned out to be more interesting. It was market day so the town was very colorful. We were befriended by a teenage kid, who after ten minutes we learned was not a random teenager but a kid who steered tourists to certain vendors. We ended up in a carpet shop, as all westerners do in Morocco. We filmed it. This guy could have been on Home Shopping Network. In the end, we created a very charming video without a whole lot of narrative manipulation.

WHERE DO YOU FIND FOCUS?

The story's soul may rest in an individual narrative element. Somehow a character, or the setting, or an image, or perhaps a quote personifies the insight gained from the reflection and research. When Susan Faludi was researching "Where did Randy Go Wrong," a profile on the antiabortion crusader Randall Terry, she visited his hometown in upstate New York, an area renowned for launching religious and political upheavals, including the suffragette movement. During her research, Faludi became convinced that Terry's motivation to organize crowds to blockade abortion clinics stemmed from fear of independent women seeking equal rights, in this case reproductive rights. By opening with a description of northern New York's landscape — *The city of Rochester clings to the shore of Lake Ontario, a gritty urban speck lost between water and waves of rolling hills* — and its role in instigating political upheaval — abolition and, in particular, women's rights — Faludi uses place to state her point:

> *Susan B. Anthony and Elizabeth Cady Stanton launched the campaign for women's equality from these hills; the 1848 Woman's Rights Convention in Seneca Falls ignited the nation's suffrage movement.*
>
> *But to others, the distance from the state's prosperous southern end only feels like exile. Disenfranchisement has yielded religious and reactionary zealotry: Mormonism began here and evangelism has always thrived. And when the aggrieved went looking for a scapegoat in the last century, the upstate feminists provided a convenient one. "Anti-vice" crusader Anthony Comstock, a struggling New York salesman, led what became a national campaign against abortion and birth control. His efforts culminated in the 1873 federal Comstock Law, banning the distribution of all contraceptive devices. By the end of the 1800s, dozens of state legislatures would join the cause, criminalizing abortion for the first time in the nation's history.*
>
> *Now, at the close of the twentieth century, Comstock's campaign is threatening to repeat. This time, the drama unfolds not only in the same region but also inside a single family.*

Place, of course, is only one source that may reveal a narrative's focus. Writers find the central meaning in all sorts of ways.

Finding focus in characters

The people who populate narratives are not sources — those talking heads spewing quotes found in daily news stories — but characters, three-dimensional human beings with histories and feelings and conflicting thoughts. No human is perfectly good or perfectly bad, and the literary characters that stick with a reader are the ones brought to life on the page in all their contradictions and complexities. Often, those complexities and contradictions illuminate the central conflict of the tale.

When Rolf Potts set out to discover Beirut, he did what he always does in his travel writing research: he made himself accessible to locals. "I have an aura for attracting the weirdest person in every village," says Potts. "My Midwest good nature lets me get along and be nice to these oddballs." The oddball he met in Beirut was Mr. Ibrahim, a native who insisted on showing Potts his version of his native city, not the war-torn, bullet-riddled destination "war tourists" sought. He took him to elegant restaurants, ancient castles, Roman ruins, prosperous shopping malls, and luxury hotels. He fed Potts lamb and kibbeh. He spoke rhapsodically of his country's history, of his respect for the American soldiers who patrolled his childhood streets. He thundered against Potts' plans to view the parts of the city ravaged by Muslim-Christian discord as well as international feuds featuring Syria, Israel, Iran, and the United States. In "My Beirut Hostage Crisis," Potts illustrates in scene and dialogue how Mr. Ibrahim symbolizes Lebanon's campaign to promote its cultural riches, not war-weary past:

> "THE GREEN LINE IS NOT FOR TOURISTS!" Mr. Ibrahim yelled, shaking his finger at me. For the first time since I'd met him, Mr. Ibrahim was not grinning, and this gave me a chill.
> "What?" I stammered.
> "The Green Line has only bullets and old buildings. Why would you want to see that?"

Instead, day after day, Mr. Ibrahim told him of the city's successes, his own success selling European detergents and soaps in Lebanon, his aversion to tobacco and alcohol, and to women.

> "I've had thirty different women who wanted to do sex with me,
> AND I TOLD THEM ALL 'NO!'" Mr. Ibrahim bellowed, startling a group of Sri Lankan Pilgrims as we spiraled our way up to the bronze Virgin. "Some of them rented hotel rooms for me! ONE OF THEM SHOWED ME HER PANTIES! But do you know what I told her?"
> "What did you tell her?" I asked wearily.
> "I TOLD HER 'NO!'"

"This story found me by accident, as often my best stories do," Potts says from his farm in Kansas, his home base when he's not in Andorra or Ecuador. "Mr. Ibrahim was initially an interesting guy who became annoying. I thought that I'd hang out with him then experience the city. Then I realized that he was the experience." The narrative conflict was not imbedded in the place but in the relationship between Potts and his tour guide, whose hospitality harbored a menacing thread. Their relationship echoed what Potts concluded about Beirut — darkness lurked beneath the weddings and Western developments.

CHALLENGING CHOICES

Katie Campbell on Soul Searching

To master any craft requires deep concentration and gobs of time and practice. While technology has produced lots of opportunities to tell stories on a variety of platforms, it is rare to find nonfiction storytellers who are as adept with visuals as they are with words. Amy O'Leary of The New York Times, who spent close to a decade as a multimedia and radio producer before switching to print, is one. Her Emmy-nominated videos on subjects such as private equity dealmakers are as thoughtful and thorough as her narratives on a 20-something YouTube star or sexual harassment in online video gaming.

Katie Campbell is another. The daughter of a professional photographer, she grew up expressing herself through capturing still and moving images. When she was introduced to longform narrative writing in college she thought, "Man, wouldn't it be wonderful to combine" her two skill sets. Unfortunately for Campbell, the editors she worked for preferred a separation of powers; for the first years of her newspaper career she was either shooting photos or writing stories, never combining both to tell a more textured tale. It wasn't until she landed a job with a PBS station in Seattle that she was allowed to exercise multiple muscles as she wrote, shot, and produced environmental documentaries. The result is a series of productions, which include "Undamming the Elwha" and "How We Got Into Such a Mess with Stormwater," which have earned her awards and accolades.

During her years at the University of Oregon earning her MFA in writing, Campbell recognized the commonalities between the storytelling forms, particularly when confronted with deciphering the story's soul. What's she's learned over the years is that the process of discovering the focus for both text and video is identical.

Storytelling is really the same in multimedia and text. Good storytelling always comes from finding great characters. You want to find the characters that embody something larger. They have to be the lens through which to look through a larger issue. In the case of the "Egg and I," I happen to be that person with experience that is emblematic of the larger issue of egg donation. Should we be doing this? What are the emotional and ethical concerns?

"Elwha" was the same thing. We found Adeline (an elderly member of the Lower Elwha Klallam Tribe), who grew up on the river. No one else could embody the larger issue (the dam devastated the salmon runs and other fish populations) who had a perspective of depending on the river, of watching the lifeblood of culture (fishing) die out over the course of her lifetime. The other character — Kevin Yancy (a dam employee) — embodied the idea of a dying generation of people as we enter an era in which we

(Continued)

(Continued)

depend less on dams. He's the last guy who operated this dam. These two characters helped us start the process of finding focus.

To find focus imagine either an airplane or a buzzard going round and round. The circle gets tighter and tighter until I can pinpoint what it is I want to share. Can I narrow it down to one central question? A yes or no question is best. Egg donation: should I donate my eggs or not? Is this a good idea for me or for the world? With the dam: can a river restore itself after 100 years of being dammed? Sometimes the answer is you don't know yet. In Stormwater we asked: Can we change course? Stormwater has been a problem for decades.

With "The Egg & I" I kept fighting it. While I was pursuing the central question, "Is this a good thing to do for society?" I started to feel a sense of obligation, that if the research indicated that yes, it was a legitimate thing to do, I would have to do it. But when I really recognized that Michael didn't want me to do it, I felt caught. If I don't do it, I'm telling people it isn't a good thing to do. It took a number of weeks of debating I-want-to but he-doesn't-want-me-to before I figured out that my personal decision didn't have to serve as the endorsement. I could write about it in a way that could make people understand that I was ready to do this, but in my particular relationship, it was not that easy. A light switched flipped on. For me, the decision wasn't affecting just one person, but instead it was a decision for our relationship. And that relationship was more important to me than the decision.

Sometimes the act of fingers on keyboard unlocks stuff. Sometimes it is incredibly frustrating and I feel like I don't have anything to say. If it is that much of a struggle, I shut down the laptop and do something else. That something else is often running or walking or cooking. Chop, chop, chop. My hands and body are active with something that I don't have to think about. I can let my mind wander. Or I run through Volunteer Park or the hills around Seattle. Running is the right pace. The scenery goes by fast enough that I can't pay attention to it.

Finding focus in images

In the body of content you've collected and drafted, an image may often materialize, an image so clear, so strong, so startling in the way it embodies the heart of the narrative conflict that it appears as a title. Jeannette Walls' alcoholic often-unemployed father spoke of building his family a magical glass castle, a shimmering, if fragile, architectural fortress. He was a scientist, a man intrigued by design and possibility. What better title than "The Glass Castle" could sum up the underlying conflict of a parent who encouraged her to dream big but also fed her butter for dinner, offered her to the winner of a pool game, and made her cook her own hot dogs at age three, and when she caught on fire, whisked her away from the hospital and put her back in front of the stove? Her father was a dreamer, incapable of providing stability, yet he also craved beauty and shelter for Walls and her three siblings.

In Joan Didion's much-anthologized essay about a murder in the San Bernardino Valley, "Some Dreamers of the Golden Dream," she burrows beneath the facts — husband dies in a flaming Volkswagen as wife runs up and down the empty road — and explores the California culture of the 1960s that she suspects fuelled Lucille Maxwell Miller's spousal incineration:

> *This is the California where it is easy to Dial-A-Devotion, but hard to buy a book. This is the country in which a belief in the literal interpretation of Genesis has slipped imperceptibly into a belief in the literal interpretation of Double Indemnity, the country of the teased hair and the Capris and the girls for whom all life's promise comes down to a waltz-length white wedding dress and the birth of a Kimberly or a Sherry or a Debbi and a Tijuana divorce and return to hairdressers' school. "We were just crazy kids," they say without regret, and look to the future. The future always looks good in the golden land, because no one remembers the past. Here is where the hot wind blows and the old ways do not seem relevant, where the divorce rate is double the national average and where one person in every thirty-eight lives in a trailer.*

The image is illusion, the perpetual search for something better. In Lucille Miller's case it was the illusion that her lover would leave his wife and marry her to elevate her above the mundane life she lived as a dentist's wife. Instead, she lived behind bars and her lover married his children's nanny. The last passage: *The bride wore a long white peau de soie dress and carried a shower bouquet of sweetheart roses with stephanotis streamers. A coronet of seed pearls held her illusion veil.*

Finding focus in language

Often a statement, a quote, crystallizes the meaning of all one has learned. I spent a year chronicling the events inside and outside an abortion clinic, and on the last day of my research I stood on the front steps with one of the young women who guided patients through the phalanx of protesters and into the clinic. Her name was Laura. It was quiet for a Saturday, with only a handful of protesters carrying signs of fetuses sucking thumbs and women bloodied from botched abortions. A far cry from other Saturdays when Laura had had to shield the young women from one crowd of protesters screaming, "Don't kill your baby!!" and another chanting, "My body! My choice!"

As Laura guided a patient inside, one of the elderly male picketers draped in rosary beads stopped praying and started lecturing on the Holocaust and its legacy of baby killing. Laura ignored him. But as she returned to her perch on the stairs, she pondered the past year of legislation and court orders coming down for and against the protesters, for and against reproductive choice. Nothing had been settled. With nothing settled, the battle of wills and posters and shouting continued every day the clinic offered abortions.

Surveying the scene before her — the cluster of hymn-singing men in their frayed wool coats and wood crosses, the cluster of NOW recruits in black jeans and Doc Martens linking arms to create a barrier — Laura wondered aloud: "Will I be doing this forever?"

And there was my hook. After a year of chronicling how the protests and politics on the outside affected the patients and staff on the inside of Preterm Health Services, Laura's statement made me realize that unless something drastic happened — *Roe v. Wade* was overturned or technology allowed women to safely terminate pregnancies in the shelter of their own home — this battle would go on, and on, and on.

If not a whole statement, a solitary word can summarize the narrative's core. Cheryl Strayed titled her memoir "Wild," not just to give meaning to the wilderness she walked, but also to the rawness of her present grief and her past childhood, to the father who abused and abandoned her. On a very literal level, "wild" also describes the route she followed into adultery and heroin addiction. For Tom French, the focus of "Zoo Story" is encapsulated in one word: Freedom.

Finding focus in time

Editors and workshop members often ask a writer to answer "So what?" about a proposed narrative. Why should we read this? What will we learn? The second question they might ask is "Why now?" What's new about this topic? What will I learn that I don't already know?

TRY THIS

1. In a narrative, select three images that you think may serve as symbols for what you're trying to say. For example, if the essay is about your family's efforts to stop your aunt's alcohol abuse, one image might be your parents emptying out her liquor cabinet, another the Alcoholics Anonymous intervention pamphlet, and the third might be her favorite beer mug. Figure out which image is the most powerful and revise the essay using the image as a recurring focal point.

2. Do the same with language. Find one word or a phrase that sums up the narrative's focus. Revise the story, building the narrative around the word or phrase. How would that word or phrase work in the beginning? The end? How would it serve the focus in the middle?

Tapping into that question of timeliness — why write this now? — is another route to fleshing out focus. What about this subject should a reader learn at this moment in history? What insights can a reader gain about the human condition, an institution, a culture that's unique to this particular time?

Although a character as colorful as Mr. Ibrahim makes for good reading any time, his passion for his native city was a particularly useful vehicle to illuminate the Beirut that Potts found in the spring of 2000. Devastated by decades of war, the city had been open to tourists only since 1997, and the effort to control the city's message was strong. Like Beirut itself, Mr. Ibrahim anguished over the violent past that had left much of the downtown a blackened shell. But also like his city, he celebrated its rebuilding and its cultural history with relentless enthusiasm. In another decade, both he and the city might have healed to the point where neither would require a forced cheerful façade and Rolf Potts would have had to find a different focus for a piece on Lebanon's capital.

Timely stories may also illuminate timeless themes. Terry Tempest Williams wrote "Refuge" as her mother was dying of cancer and the Great Salt Lake flooded one of her favorite spots, the Bear River Migratory Bear Refuge. She wove together the two events that focused on the links between family, loss, and the natural world. The events were timely but the message was eternal.

In January of 2009, novelist Melissa Pritchard found herself dressed in body armor and military-issued winter underwear on a U.S. base in Panjshir Province, Afghanistan. Reeling from divorce, death, and a house empty of the two grown daughters who had left for lives of their own, she writes that she "was drawn to places of suffering that surpassed my own." She was in the war zone to write about women in the Air Force delivering food and medical supplies to remote villages and working with the local women, one of her first attempts at immersion nonfiction. She spent several weeks with these service women, and grew especially close to one, 21-year-old Senior Airman Ashton Goodman. After she returned home to Arizona, she began to write what she envisioned would be a timely, journalistic piece about the war, and when that didn't work, she crafted profiles of the service women she met. Eventually, she discovered that she could best tell the story of the service women by focusing on one, Goodman. Yet the profile she envisioned imploded when she learned in the middle of writing that Goodman was dead, killed by an improvised explosive device. Instead of an external tale of one young woman involved in an ongoing war, an intimate angle to a top news story, Pritchard wrote about her relationship with Goodman, how she had run away to Afghanistan to find her own equilibrium but instead had found a young woman who offered a friendship she hadn't expected. Through pursing a timely piece about women servicemen in a controversial war, she unearthed the timeless theme of discovering oneself through connecting with another.

WHEN DO YOU FIND FOCUS?

From the start of every project, my antennae are up, on alert for a potential focus. When they pick up the signal depends on the subject and its complexity. For an essay about my mother's legacy, I knew from a life of observing her what I wanted to say about the source of her resilience, how a woman with osteoporosis so severe that her vertebrae broke with a hiccup, and an ejection fraction so weak that doctors wondered if her heart pumped any blood at all, survived day after day, month after month. Cheerfully. Answer: She focused on the moment. Each day. Every day. All I had to do was think of examples illustrating the point and the essay flowed, or at least didn't cause me to contemplate another career, which is what happens at some stage during most writing projects.

As a feature writer for newspapers I had, for the most part, weekly deadlines that allowed me some time to ponder the meaning of my reporting but not so much that I could loll about in a lounge chair for days, counting buds on the neighbor's maple tree. Taking a cue from the daily news reporters, whose frequent deadlines force them to think through each story's focus before their hands hit the keyboard, I sought the story's angle from the first interview. For a story about a young Hispanic woman who shot and killed her husband after suffering years of abuse, the obvious central question was why? What led her to fire bullets into her first and only love and how did she live with leaving her two sons fatherless? Through weeks of visits with her in prison, and interviews with her mother, friends, lawyers, supporters, and domestic violence experts, the focus of this tragedy's narrative took shape. Caught in a web of poverty and a culture that told her to stay by her man, she endured a decade of unfathomable physical and emotional cruelty (once her husband plunged a soda bottle up her vagina in front of her mother) until she snapped. She feared for her life and the lives of her sons. No one offered to protect her, not even her mother, who for years after his death carried a photo of her son-in-law in her wallet. The challenge once I sat down to write wasn't, then, what the heck do I want to say, but how do I want show how her culture and familial abuse had led to this tragedy? What scenes best told that tale? What opinions? Thoughts?

Yet for every time the focus surfaces during the research and/or reflection stage, there are many other times that it lies under wraps through draft after draft. Through writing, patterns emerge, surprise strikes, understanding evolves. Sometimes we just have to let the material guide us to the narrative's center.

Research reveals focus

Cynthia Gorney has been writing researched narratives for over three decades, and it still astounds her that every time she gets to the point where she has to articulate the main thing she wants to say, she is flummoxed. "It's so not fair," she says. "You figure that for a builder of beautiful houses, it gets easier by the 100th beautiful house. But writers are just as self-tortured and self-pitying on their 100th piece. Christ! Would this just get easier?"

Despite the angst, Gorney pulls off again and again deeply researched and beautifully written tales on topics ranging from hormone replacement therapy to feminism and Brazil's birth rate. For Gorney, the search for meaning starts gelling during the reporting phase. As she witnesses many scenes, talks to countless people, collects the reams of background and statistics that provide context, themes emerge. She hears the same anxieties interview after interview. The same justifications. In a rural Northern Indian village she heard villager after villager say that they marry off their 8-year-old daughters because they can't afford to feed them. Because it is tradition. Documents verified the statements. Indian officials concurred. International human rights workers concurred. The material she collected began to answer the question that launched the story: why do certain Indian villages marry children as young as 5?

Isabel Wilkerson devoted over 10 years of her life to researching and writing about the 55-year Great Migration of black Americans leaving the Jim Crow south for the Northeast, Midwest, and West. During her interviews of over 1,000 people, she wanted answers to dozens of questions — How did they get there? Why did they leave? What gave them the drive to leave the only place they knew for the unknown? What was life like in the Georgia? In Boston? Oklahoma? As she sifted through the answers for her book "The Warmth of Other Suns," her focus became clear, as she told an audience at Whitman College in 2012: "This was the only time in our country's history that American citizens were forced to or felt that they had no other choice but to leave the land of their birth merely to be recognized as the citizens which they had been born."

When the bolt strikes is as individual as the writer, and as the story.

CHALLENGING CHOICES

Mark Bowden on Ignorance and Keeping a Notebook

Mark Bowden likes challenging stories. For magazines such as The New Yorker and Rolling Stone, he's written about drug lords and computer worms and the killing of Osama Bin Laden. He is, though, perhaps best known for his book "Black Hawk Down," the story of the 1993 U.S. raid in Mogadishu. Figuring out the story's heart doesn't get easier, he has learned; each project harbors its own unique challenges. Below is an excerpt from Bowden's keynote address at the 2010 Mayborn Literary Nonfiction Conference about finding focus:

(Continued)

(Continued)

I generally begin working on a story in total ignorance, which I think is the ideal starting point for me, because only if you are truly ignorant can you ask the truly ignorant question. But I have only the foggiest idea of what the story is when I get started on it. And in fact, every story that I write, when I'm doing my reporting, I always come upon some information that completely destroys my concept for the story.

I think I know what the story is, and then I interview one more person, or I come across a document, or I see a video, or something, some piece of information that tells me, you know what, I'm wrong, I don't get this. The initial response that I have when that happens is "Oh god, I'm screwed now. I've just wasted my time. I don't get this at all. The story's gone all to hell." But on a few moments of reflection or sometimes waking up the next morning, inevitably, the realization is, "Wait a minute. No, this story just got better." Because my understanding of it has deepened. I have a much broader and different take on what happened than I had before. So to me that's the process.

And I can tell you it happened to me a number of times in writing "Black Hawk Down." In those early meetings at Fort Benning, those original eight interviews, the Rangers all told me these fantastic stories, but what I didn't know at the time was that the raid that is the center of the story of "Black Hawk Down" was a Delta Force raid, a special ops raid — a unit that the Army would not even acknowledge existed. It was totally a black ops unit, and so the Rangers whose job it was to set up a perimeter around the block where the Delta guys were doing their work were not allowed to mention the name of Delta Force. So they would try to tell me their stories, and they kept getting stuck. They would go out in the hall, and there would be a representative there from public affairs, and they'd huddle and confer. The soldier would come back in and say, "And then a soldier from another unit would did thus and so." And I would say, "What other unit?" "I'm not at liberty to discuss that, sir," he'd say.

So I left Fort Benning at the end of that that first day knowing that I had a great story, but knowing there was something essential about it that I wasn't going to be able to get at, that I didn't know. Well, the one question, and Kristen Hinman this morning in her talk said she always does this, and it's something I've always done — when I interview people for a story, the last question I always ask is "Who else should I talk to?" And of course each of these Rangers that day had lists of their buddies who had fought with them, and many of them had, in the years since this battle, left the Army. You would be amazed at how much more a guy will tell you with a beer in his hand in his basement in Cleveland, than a Ranger sitting next to a public affairs officer at Fort Benning. So I eventually got to learn a lot more about Black Hawk Down.

Now, just as I don't know what a story is going to be when I start out working on it, I have no idea how to write it, either. In fact, I try to preserve that state of mind. There's this teaching in Zen called "beginner mind," which says if you want to be original and creative, then you have to approach each new project as though you were an amateur, as though you had never done this before. And obviously, it's not completely possible — or Zen would be easy, but I try to approach a story without knowing how I'm going to — often I honestly don't know how I'm going to report it; I certainly don't know how I'm going to write it. But I have a trick that I learned as a daily newspaper reporter. And that is, you carry your reporter's notebook around with you, and you scribble notes when you interview people. Because I was writing for a daily newspaper, I was never certain in reporting a story when I had reached the end of the amount of information that I was going to get, or when an editor was going to call me and say, "You know that story you're planning to send me, you were planning to write it tomorrow? Well, I need it now, I need it this afternoon."

So I had begun the habit of taking that notebook and flipping it upside down, right from the beginning of the story and jotting a little outline of what the story would look like if I were writing it right now, on the basis of maybe just one interview and a little back story. And then I'd get another interview, and my knowledge of the story would be shot all to hell, and I'd have to redesign it, but I kept outlines always so that when I had to write I wasn't having to start from scratch. And the wonderful advantage of doing that was that as I grew older, and I began working on stories that were far more complex, that would take me weeks and months and years to report and write, that habit of keeping that outline constantly alive and constantly changing enabled me to focus my story far more intelligently than if I hadn't done that.

I knew in time what were the pieces of this story that I really needed to find out more about and focus my energies on, but even more important, what were the pieces of the story that I wasn't going to be writing about. I didn't have to waste any time gathering more information about this. So it focuses your efforts.

Writing reveals focus

Don Murray was a huge believer in writing to discover. Just sit down and write, he'd say, and eventually the memories and thoughts and facts will lead to meaning. This can be true for researched pieces — put the notes away and write, let the subconscious guide you to what you want to say — and it is particularly true for essays about one's own experiences, or Montaigne-like essays that seek answers to random questions. There's a reason free-writing is such a staple in writing courses.

Essayists such as Ryan Van Meter allow their minds to wander when they're writing. As Van Meter says in an interview with Brevity, "You have to bump into things, stumble over a forgotten memory or some aspect of the experience you didn't even know was there." An advocate of free-writing, Van Meter says that he'll write as fast as he can by hand, and after gathering a lot of pages, will find the opening section and the first sentence that will establish the voice and introduce the essay's problem. Then he'll move to the computer and start writing, asking himself "What is the focus here?"

"It's only after you have the structure and the direction and the details that you start discovering the insight that will surprise you," he says. "If there's nothing in your essay that surprises you, how could it ever surprise the reader?"

Even if the subject is external, about something other than one's own experiences and thoughts, and the material collected is a pile of interviews and database research, sometimes it is best to write to find the tension point, the line that will lure the reader from page to page. Write what you know. Explore what you don't know. Write a draft without looking at your notes. Write a draft without bothering to pause and reflect. Let the subconscious take over and see where it takes you.

Is this the right focus?

During almost every writing project I hit a point where I wonder if the focus I've chosen is right. Would another message work better, form a stronger narrative spine? I may play around with other options — scribble notes on how to support a new focus with the material before me — but eventually I'll realize that every subject harbors a myriad of angles to pursue and the "rightness" is based on how effectively the writer explores and builds the point she's making.

We each bring our own perspective to a topic, and those differing perspectives lead to different approaches and differing insights. Three people assigned to write about sexism and summer jobs would craft three distinctly different narratives. One woman might focus on the stress of fending off advances from male patrons at the resort where she waitressed. A guy might argue that men get the shaft, too, that his gender earned him the dishwashing job at the ice cream stand while his female peers were placed at the front window, earning all the tips from the customers they served. And the third writer might focus on the persistence of women who filed and won a sexism suit against their summer employer, the busiest lobster pound in Maine. Each approach would pivot on its own point for the reader to absorb.

A stellar example is when Chris Jones of Esquire and Chris Heath of GQ were both sent to Zanesville, Ohio, to write about Terry Thompson and the 50 exotic animals he let loose before he shot himself. They talked to many of the same Zanesville residents and neighbors of Thompson, the same exotic animal experts, the same police officers who spent a very long night chasing and killing Thompson's wild pets. They saw the same photographs of bloody carcasses, rows of dead tigers and lions and wolves and leopards and cougars and grizzly bears. They collected many of the same details, such as the tiger tumbling through the air after being shot, the neighbor hiding in his barn while a lion studied his corralled horse.

Yet Heath's story — "18 Tigers, 17 Lions, 8 Bears, 3 Cougars, 2 Wolves, 1 Baboon, 1 Macaque, and 1 Man Dead in Ohio" — and Jones' story — "Animals" — each had its own unique focus. Jones explored the story from the police point of view, what it was like to be a small-town Ohio cop driving around town, slogging through woods, shotgun in hand, in search of a lion. What it was like to be charged by a bear, to see only the flick of a tiger's ear in the tall grass, to watch through a rifle's scope a lion running through a hay field. The terror for your own life as you hunt the beasts and the terror for the residents if any lion or grizzly escapes capture.

Heath, too, chronicled the experience of the townspeople and police, but his piece veered off and explored more why and how did this happen. He delved into Terry Thompson's past and psyche, ferreting out possible motives why he would open the cages of his dangerous menagerie, place a gun in his mouth, cover himself with raw chicken, and end his life being eaten by his white tiger. In addition, Heath expanded the story's scope by discussing in one section the laws in certain states that allow citizens to raise exotic animals in their backyards. For this richly layered tale that explored both the microcosm (Thompson's defiant act and the repercussions) and the macrocosm (why laws allow people like Thompson to house dangerous animals), Heath was awarded the 2013 National Magazine Award for Reporting.

TRY THIS

In the movie "The Player," Tim Robbins plays a producer who sits behind his desk day after day, asking writer after writer, "What's the pitch?" The writers are expected to sum up their proposed script in a sentence. Movie people call that sentence a log line. Writers call it a hook line. Book editors call it a high-concept sentence. Whatever you want to call it, that all-important sentence condenses the major plot lines and high-concept ideas into a digestible sound bite to hook an audience.

A few examples:

- "Seabiscuit": The extraordinary story of a thoroughbred racehorse — from his humble beginnings as an underfed workhorse to his unlikely rise and triumphant victory over the Triple Crown winner.
- "Shakespeare in Love": A comedic portrayal of a young and broke Shakespeare who falls in love with a woman, inspiring him to write "Romeo and Juliet."
- "Into Thin Air": On assignment for Outside Magazine to report on the growing commercialization of the mountain, Jon Krakauer, an accomplished climber, went to the Himalayas as a client of Rob Hall, the most respected high-altitude guide in the world, and barely made it back alive from the deadliest season in the history of Everest.
- "A Heartbreaking Work of Staggering Genius": The memoir of Dave Eggers, who at the age of 22, became both an orphan and a "single mother" when his parents died within five months of one another of unrelated causes, leaving Eggers the appointed unofficial guardian of his 8-year-old brother, Christopher.

Now you try. Write 10 hook lines for a writing project. Done? Write 10 more for another project. Get the hang of it and perhaps you'll be recruited to star in another Hollywood movie about Hollywood pitches.

5

What's the Structure?

Overview

The ways to frame a story are infinite. But there are some basic guidelines and questions to consider, from targeting the source of tension to the balance of scene and summary. In this chapter we investigate how to build a compelling narrative that lures a reader from beginning to end. Among the structural options discussed are straight chronology, reverse chronology, circular, framed, braided, parallel, themed, and collage.

WHENEVER STRUCTURE COMES UP IN A conversation between nonfiction types, it is inevitable that someone will mention John McPhee. For over six decades, the master storyteller of over 30 books and countless essays has plotted narrative architectures so intricate and original that drawings don't do them justice. He has regaled audiences with his elaborate process of transcribing, annotating, copying, coding, slicing, filing, and indexing his notes onto 3x5 cards that he will arrange and rearrange until he finds the formation that will best lure the reader to the end. McPhee knows the end before he types the first word.

Yet for all the McPhee reverence, his disciples should also remember that behind every engaging narrative is a writer who built a structure from a mountain of notes and interviews or pages of reflections. McPhee's method is just one reed in a vast marsh. That's not to say that the strategy that created such gems as "The Search for Marvin Gardens" and "Travels in Georgia" isn't valuable and can't be emulated. The sheer concentration and material maneuvering required for McPhee's method demands scrutiny — and is in the pages that follow.

Yet the process to construct a narrative framework is as individual as the writer, and what may be most helpful to the discussion of structure is first talking about goals.

The main mission of any narrative structure is to engage the reader from beginning to end, to intrigue her somehow, some way to follow musings, scenes, observations, memories, stats and facts and background and arrive at a targeted destination, the central message or messages. It's one thing for a writer to chase an idea or series of events on the page, but another to chase them to an end in a way that others not only can follow but also *want to* follow.

The next mission is to construct a framework strong enough to support the material and divide it into digestible chunks. McPhee compares the process to cooking dinner. First you go to the grocery store to collect the ingredients. When you return home, you place the ingredients on the kitchen counter. You can't toss all the ingredients whole in the pot, so instead you select what you need, chop and sauté, careful to make sure that the red pepper doesn't overwhelm or that there's too little chicken. Proportion is everything.

The last is less concrete but critical. When we talk about building a structure we aren't talking Roman numeral outlines — although some may find comfort in reliving their high school composition days — but rather a skeleton on which the material will rest and expand. Some, like the writing coach Jack Hart, think of structure as an architectural blueprint that is more visual than logical, a pattern of parts that fit together in their own way. A goal, then, is to trust the right brain to help guide the construction, to let intuition as well as analysis choose the pattern.

While some emerging writers argue that all this talk about structure is too mechanical, too confining, a boa constrictor around their creative muscles, the truth is that a sturdy foundation allows the writer the freedom to concentrate on the writing. It is akin to building a house. Once the timbers are in place, firm in their footings, the framework solid, the carpenters can turn their attention to the individual rooms, the moldings, the arched doorways, the soft pine floors. The detail.

A cracked beam or ill-conceived frame will send all those lovely moldings and floorboards tumbling. Likewise with a narrative. Absent a firm skeleton, the string of scenes and thoughts collapse. Perhaps the McPhee message for which we should be most grateful is the importance of structure in the writing process, that it deserves sweat, thought, and innovation.

"To some extent the structure of a composition dictates itself, and to some extent it does not," wrote McPhee in a New Yorker article titled "Structure: Beyond the Picnic Table." "Where you have a free hand, you can make interesting choices."

Let's talk about those choices.

HOW DO YOU FIND THE STRUCTURE?

Ted Conover, a master of immersion research and storytelling, said in an interview published in "The New New Journalism" that in his early days of crafting narratives he would write and write until a structure emerged. Once he realized the inefficiency of this strategy, he began thinking through his experiences of driving across Africa with truckers or his months as a prison guard at Sing Sing. What are the main points he wants to make? What scenes did he observe that will illustrate those points? Illustrate conflict? Scenes that show how AIDS may be transmitted across sub-Saharan Africa or why prison is so dehumanizing for both inmates and guards? Which characters reveal the issue's complexities? What background facts and stats provide context for the action? He'll sift through hundreds of pages of typed notes, extracting key scenes, character description, facts, and insights, arranging them in an order that builds drama, that feeds the reader just enough action, just enough background to keep her engaged and reading to find out what happens next. By thinking, not writing, a structure emerges.

If Conover's cerebral approach is typical, and in my experience and that of all the writers in my circle it is, then in the balance of right versus left brain, the scales tip to the left in the initial stage of constructing a structure. There's no shortage of things to ponder (How best to tap into the reader's curiosity? Scene or exposition based? Does the targeted publication [if there is one] have a structural style?), but most nonfiction storytellers will tell you that the first area on which to focus laser-like concentration is also the most obvious — the material.

Know thy notes and thoughts

When I was a feature writer for The Hartford Courant one of the news reporters would mock me as I wandered through the maze of desks clutching stacks of notebooks, books, and folders stuffed with typed notes and thoughts and story clips. "You look like a high school student preparing a term paper," she would say. We all have our systems, and mine was to collect as much information as possible, then organize it by subject, surrounding my desk with cascading channels of content. I didn't have the space or filing system of McPhee, who types all his notes, annotating and adding his impressions and analysis, making a copy, filing one copy in a binder and chopping the other up by subject, placing the shards of content into subject-specific files. But like McPhee and unlike the news reporters who simply flipped open their skinny notebooks to write the latest city council vote, I had so much content, so many conflicting perspectives and histories and scenes, that not organizing my notes would have been structural Armageddon.

But to organize one's notes and ruminations, one has to study the material with the intensity of a scientist at a microscope. Sometimes that means highlighting insights and observations, jotting down thoughts in the margins. It may mean transcribing tapes, typing up hand-scribbled thoughts and interviews, selecting key moments on a video. By poring over the swath of observations and facts and reflections, a writer can identify the ripest scenes, the details that illuminate character and setting, the background that best explains motivation and events. Once the richest material is selected, the writer is in position to think through how each snippet of dialogue, each slice of history, each round of explanation will be used in the tale. Where it will fit. On what it will build. What the reader needs to know when.

Building a structure is aided, too, by a user-friendly filing system. Some writers prefer printing out their notes and scenes, observations and insights, separating them by subject into individual folders. For my abortion book, I surrounded my desk with crates containing files of my notes and supporting articles. One crate contained material on the history of abortion politics. Another on individual characters. Another was devoted to scenes from the year I spent observing what happened inside and outside Preterm Health Services. Another was filled with folders for each chapter. By separating the material by subject and events I could better envision an order that would build drama and cover the points I wanted to make about reproductive rights and responsibilities.

Now, however, I rarely print out notes, preferring instead to tuck my typed interviews and observations into electronic files. Like many writers, years with a laptop has increased my digital dexterity and I no longer need hard copy files splayed on the floor before me. Instead, I cut and paste on the screen, plugging similar content into separate electronic folders. When it is time to build a structure, I can quickly find the material I need to determine the order of the scenes and which character should be introduced when, arranging and rearranging the chunks of material on the screen.

For short pieces, the arranging can often be accomplished in one's head. Kate Bolick admits that she didn't think much about organizing her notes and meditations before she wrote "All The Single Ladies," a 13,000-word essay about why women, including herself, choose not to marry. The essays and stories she had written before were shorter, less complicated, about single subjects such as celebrating aunthood. But by the time she finished reflecting on her own experience, researching the social and sexual history of single women as well as the economic shifts of male and female wage earners, she realized that she needed a new method, that her intellectual bandwidth couldn't stretch far enough to keep all the material straight.

What's the mystery?

Like the research phase, constructing the narrative skeleton on which the content will rest and expand hinges on a question, a mystery, that the reader will pursue

CHALLENGING CHOICES

Kate Bolick on Shaping the Personal and Political

With only seven weeks to research and write how men's worsening economic prospects and women's improving financial stability impacted dating, marriage, and family, Kate Bolick needed a system to organize the piles of interviews she'd collected, the notes she'd culled from books and databases, as well as her own observations and thoughts on her singleness and her mother's marital choices. An indefatigable researcher, she had flown around the globe talking to women and men and experts (last stop: an all-woman housing complex in Amsterdam) for The Atlantic assignment. The mass of material was daunting. Yet she found that if she could divide her content into subject blocks, she could build the narrative that became "All the Single Ladies," one of the most discussed nonfiction pieces of 2011.

The Atlantic assignment was both specific and a huge ocean all at once. I started researching — interviewing, reading, gathering a bunch of stuff while having no idea where to go — and once I saw the statistics around single people, that there are more than ever before, I had that heart-racing journalistic feeling. This is the story! This is how I can write it in first person! Once that happened, things started congealing better. I wanted to get at larger issues from as many directions as possible. I was going anywhere that I could think of. But I couldn't start unless I had an outline. That's the first time I had done that. I needed to articulate myself to myself and to my editor. I was juggling so many aspects that I needed the outline just to make sense of it all and remember it all. What I was doing was amassing all this material, smooshing it into my head and finding an internal logic to it and then threading that through.

I can't do that thing where you write to figure out what you're thinking. I have to do all my thinking in advance. It's a very constipated way to do it. By the time I start writing, things are pretty clear to me.

I knew with "Single Ladies" that I would start with the break-up because everyone, men and women, can relate to that. It leaves a bit of a hook — we don't know what happens next. The outline that followed was more like plot points. I knew that I wanted to hit the African-American experience, the historical perspective, my personal anecdotes. Each piece was a building block.

Arranging the building blocks was intuitive. You needed this information to appreciate the next block. The outline I wrote 3 weeks into the research was pretty much what I followed.

Writing in first person made it easier. Once I figured out that the "single thing" was my Velcro to these ideas, I was able to inhabit the research personally. What does this mean for me? How do I fit into this larger story? I came to understand that I was part of this generation that was dealing with a lot of forces and influences that I hadn't thought about before. That was really exciting for me. Being single is something that I think about all the time, talk about to my friends, but I had never applied any intellectual rigor to it. I was so excited to be learning as I went.

I can't write about things unless I understand them on a personal level. I can only write about something if I feel like I own it. That intensive research, travel, and reporting process was essential to understanding it.

page after page in hope of finding the answer. That question, that mystery, forms the essential narrative tension, without which a tale falls flat. If a reader's curiosity isn't aroused, if there's nothing to learn, to solve, what's the point of continuing?

In personal essays, that central mystery is often neon-bold. Montaigne's literary legacy is based on his exploration of intellectual conundrums. What is the merit of lying, of idleness, of quick versus slow speech? Moving up a few centuries, in his essay "How I Met My Wife," Robert Boswell pursues why we are drawn to stories about people falling in love. Through detailing his romance with the woman who would later become his wife, employing the fictional tools of character, plot, and conflict, he explores the allure of love and its power. On a grimmer note, Steven Church ruminates about the connection between ears and barbaric behavior, the beast within us, in his essay "Speaking of Ears and Savagery," exploring different examples (Mike Tyson biting Evander Holyfield's ear; an ear in the grass in David Lynch's "Blue Velvet"; Travis the chimpanzee biting off every facial feature of a woman except her ears) and why we feel the urge to attack something so soft, so vulnerable.

In external research-based stories, the mystery that forms the narrative arc is often the same question that launched the writer's interviewing and fact collecting. For instance, why did a seemingly well-adjusted, happy teen immigrant from Russia plant a bomb at the Boston Marathon finish line? That question determined the direction of Janet Reitman's reporting and research as well as formed the central tension line of her Rolling Stone profile "Jahar's World" on the surviving brother accused of the 2013 Boston Marathon carnage. When gathering material for a story about adult children caring for both their parents and their own children, I sought to learn how those adult children managed. It didn't take much analysis to realize that that's exactly what a reader would want to know, too. So the story walked the reader through the lives of families balancing the needs of the very old and the very young, building the case that while some juggle the demands better than others, no one has it mastered.

Longer narratives comprise a chain of mysteries with each chunk raising a question that will eventually be answered. In Capote's "In Cold Blood," we yearn to know first how the Clutter family will connect with Dick and Perry, the two drifters introduced in the opening scenes. When we learn that Dick and Perry murder Herb and Bonnie Clutter and their teenage son and daughter, we want to know if the killers will be caught. When they're caught, we want to know how and why they murdered four innocents. When we learn that Perry snapped — that he decided to make the Clutter family pay for all the abuse and hardship he'd suffered at the hands of his alcoholic mother, negligent father, and abusive nuns — we want to know what will happen to the pair. Plot points. Thematically, each of the plot points feeds into Capote's central exploration of lost potential and tragic choices. When one mystery plot is resolved, another surfaces, keeping the reader flipping pages until all the mysteries are resolved. Dick and Perry die in the noose. The Kansas community has closure and moves on. The reader is satisfied.

J.R. Moehringer searched the country for the ferocious fighter Bob Satterfield, who seemed to find only trouble after his stellar career in the 1940s and 1950s. When the story opens, Moehringer is in a Columbus, Ohio, hotel room waiting to hear from a guy who may have information about Satterfield. Early on in his piece "Resurrecting the Champ," he provides the bait to hook the reader's interest:

> *Maybe it's fatigue, maybe it's caffeine, maybe it's the fog rolling in behind the rain, but I feel as though Satterfield has become my own 180-pound Moby Dick. Like Ahab's obsession, he casts a harsh light on his pursuer. Stalking him from town to town and decade to decade, I've learned almost everything there is to know about him, along with valuable lessons about boxing, courage and the eternal tension between fathers and sons. But I've learned more than I bargained for about myself, and for that I owe him a debt. I can't repay the debt unless the phone rings.*

In that single paragraph, Moehringer sets the reader up to pursue a multi-pronged adventure. Why is the author so obsessed with Satterfield? What has happened to Satterfield? Will he find Satterfield? And how has Satterfield taught the author about himself, and about father and sons? Later in the narrative, after Moehringer finds a homeless guy with huge hands who is known as "Champ," we wonder if this is The Champ? When we find out he may be an imposter, we wonder why the façade? And how will it impact the author? The little mysteries feed beautifully into the central mystery: What will Moehringer learn from an encounter with the mysterious Satterfield?

TRY THIS

1. Think of an image that haunts you. This image can be from your own past or perhaps an image you observed while researching a story. What does it say to you? What questions does it pose? How might a narrative be structured around the meaning behind the image? For example, Tom French taped on his computer a photo of Michelle Rogers, one of the women murdered in his tale "Angels & Demons." That photo helped him understand her character, which helped him build the structure around the complicated story.

2. Think thematically. First, identify the individual chunks, or sections, that will compose the narrative. There might be a history chunk. A personal reflection chunk. A scene chunk. Or multiple chunks of all the above. Then define each chunk by theme and pulse, the engine that drives the scene or exposition. How best to plot these sections to generate a forward flow toward resolution?

What is the target medium?

Often, the medium for which one writes will determine a story's structure. While journalists working for a daily media site have more storytelling opportunities than ever before, they often find that because of their publication's time constraints they are asked to follow a structural formula. Writers of breaking news follow the inverted pyramid, summing up the most important updated information in the lead, or opening paragraph. The rest of the facts follow in descending importance. Writers of less time-sensitive, more human-based features spell out the So what? Why now? in a "nut graph," a paragraph that follows a creative lead, such as a scene, anecdote, or one-liner. The body of the story may be all explanation, a collection of quotes and description and background, or a balance of exposition and scene. Narrative journalists writing for magazines may also follow a similar pattern, except that their opening scene or anecdote may be many paragraphs and the "nut graph" is more of a "nut chunk," a mini-chapter detailing why the subject is worthy of the reader's attention. The body is a balance of scene and explanation.

Find the Nut Graph

The Washington Post story below is breaking news and follows the inverted pyramid with the first paragraph answering the who, what, when, where and why:

> *A lawyer for Edward Snowden, who gave journalists secret documents describing the National Security Agency's surveillance operations, said Wednesday that the former contractor could soon leave the Moscow airport where he has been living for weeks.*

In contrast, the lead to The Boston Globe feature about the end of the fabled restaurant Anthony's Pier 4 is a scene followed by a nut graph that answers so what and why now?

> *Frank Meloski had just celebrated his daughter Elsa's birthday by devouring a baked stuffed filet of sole, and now the two were outside taking photos of each other.*
>
> *"I've been coming to Anthony's Pier 4 for years, and I always take pictures," said Meloski, a retiree who lives in Cambridge.*
>
> *But as he looked through the lens at his daughter, her hand gently rocking a baby carriage, the 66-year-old Meloski saw something unsettling. Crowding the frame were construction workers, a crew of hardhats standing around a gaping hole in the ground just 100 yards from the restaurant's front door.*
>
> *Soon a gleaming, 21-story apartment and retail tower will rise from the chasm along Northern Avenue, and, in a long-anticipated move, Anthony's Pier 4, once one of the busiest restaurants in the country and a local institution for a half-century, will close its doors, a vestige of a bygone Boston giving way to the new. Considered progress*

by some, to others the prospect of the South Boston waterfront without Pier 4's white tablecloths, popovers, and lobster à la Hawthorne is painful.

"Like a knife in the heart," said Meloski.

Likewise, magazine stories employ a similar structure, only each part is longer, crammed with more detail, more emotion. In Rolling Stone's "Jahar's World," for instance, the opening paragraph establishes tension by detailing how a high school wrestling coach reacts when he hears that one of his former wrestlers may be one of the Boston Marathon bombers:

> Peter Payack awoke around 4 a.m. on April 19th, 2013, and saw on his TV the grainy surveillance photo of the kid walking out of the minimart. The boy, identified as "Suspect #2" in the Boston bombing, looked familiar, thought Payack, a wrestling coach at the Cambridge Rindge and Latin School. On the other hand, there were a million skinny kids with vaguely ethnic features and light-gray hoodies in the Boston area, and half the city was probably thinking they recognized the suspect. Payack, who'd been near the marathon finish line on the day of the bombing and had lost half of his hearing from the blast, had hardly slept in four days. But he was too agitated to go back to bed. Later that morning, he received a telephone call from his son. The kid in the photo? "Dad, that's Jahar."

We are in his head, pondering whether this suspect is Jahar, feeling his agitation. The next seven paragraphs dig deeper into the coach's reaction ("I felt like a bullet went through my heart," the coach recalls. "To think that a kid we mentored and loved like a son could have been responsible for all this death. It was beyond shocking. It was like an alternative reality."), and the relationship of the Russian-born Dzhokhar "Jahar" Tsarnaev to Payack and other friends, teachers, and acquaintances in Cambridge, Massachusetts, where Tsarnaev had lived for over a decade. Described as shy, laid-back, a soccer player and wrestler who liked hip-hop, weed, and girls, Tsarnaev was like thousands of other teenagers roaming urban streets. We hear Payack speak on CNN, asking his former wrestler to turn himself in. We learn that Tsarnaev is holed up, bleeding from an overnight gun battle, in a boat parked in a back yard, and that he has covered the walls with jihadist screed, admitting to the bombings. "Fuck America," he wrote. We hear of his surrender and that he invoked Payack's name while speaking to the FBI negotiating team.

By the time we reach the paragraph that provides an overview of attacks on America by Americans since 9/11, we are anxious to know where this narrative is headed. Enter the "nut chunk," the section that establishes the central question the story will explore: How and why this ordinary Cambridge kid and his brother killed two and injured hundreds of others with their pressure cooker bombs and exploding shrapnel.

> Russian émigrés, [the Tsarnaev brothers] had lived in America for a decade — and in Cambridge, a city so progressive it had its own "peace commission" to promote social justice and diversity. Tamerlan, known to his American friends as "Tim," was

(Continued)

(Continued)

a talented boxer who'd once aspired to represent the United States in the Olympics. His little brother, Jahar, had earned a scholarship to the University of Massachusetts Dartmouth and was thinking about becoming an engineer, or a nurse, or maybe a dentist — his focus changed all the time. They were Muslim, yes, but they were also American — especially Jahar, who became a naturalized U.S. citizen on September 11th, 2012.

Since the bombing, friends and acquaintances of the Tsarnaevs, as well as the FBI and other law-enforcement officials, have tried to piece together a narrative of the brothers ... what emerges is a portrait of a boy who glided through life, showing virtually no signs of anger, let alone radical political ideology or any kind of deeply felt religious beliefs.

The narrative direction is established. From there, we dive deep into the Tsarnaev's history, family discord, and radicalization. The structure of a complex story like "Jahar's World" is like a symphony, with multiple layers, each building to the resolution. In this case, the resolution is the answer to the why: the teen had been abandoned by his parents, both of whom had returned to Russia, and was left in the care and under the influence of his older brother, a self-proclaimed jihadist.

A narrative structure, in contrast, has no nut graph. As Ben Montgomery, a narrative writer for the Tampa Bay Times, says, why give away the end at the beginning? Instead, a narrative structure, either explanatory (more explanation than scene) or cinematic (more scene than explanation) is a sequence of events or ideas, a deliberate arrangement that lures the reader from one paragraph to another to an eventual resolution or epiphany.

In Montaigne-like essays, the structure is based on ideas, and how those ideas build on each other to reach the writer's concluding insight. The writer takes the reader on an intellectual journey, a mystery based on connecting thoughts. Take for example Zadie Smith's essay "Joy." In this piece from the New York Review of Books, she pursues the difference between pleasure and joy, arguing that contrary to most people's definition, joy is not simply a more intense feeling of pleasure, a higher number on the pleasure scale. Instead, she finds that they are two separate emotions; pleasure arrives frequently from such treats as a pineapple Popsicle or an egg sandwich, but joy strikes rarely, and is often preceded by more turbulent emotions:

Occasionally the child, too, is a pleasure, though mostly she is a joy, which means in fact she gives us not much pleasure at all, but rather that strange admixture of terror, pain, and delight that I have come to recognize as joy, and now must find some way to live with daily. This is a new problem. Until quite recently I had known joy only five times in my life, perhaps six, and each time tried to forget it soon after it happened, out of the fear that the memory of it would dement and destroy everything else.

A complicated premise to be sure. We must hurt before we experience joy? But Smith untangles this knot of an idea by slowly and carefully explaining what she means by pleasure and then what she means by joy. Exposition dominates; her narrator tells us what she's thinking, using scene merely to support her theory. For example, while introducing this notion of rare joy, she summarizes her experiences of joy before stopping and showing one of the episodes in scene. She's in a London nightclub coming down from Ecstasy, without her handbag or her friends. She's panicked. But then the song "Can I Kick It?" began, a man grabbed her hand and she started to dance. "I took the man's hand. The top of my head flew away. We danced and danced. We gave ourselves to joy." The scene illustrates her point that pleasures can roll in and roll out but we cannot know joy without terror.

She concludes:

The writer Julian Barnes, considering mourning, once said, "It hurts just as much as it is worth." In fact, it was a friend of his who wrote the line in a letter of condolence, and Julian told it to my husband, who told it to me. For months afterward these words stuck with both of us, so clear and so brutal. It hurts just as much as it is worth. What an arrangement. Why would anyone accept such a crazy deal? Surely if we were sane and reasonable we would every time choose a pleasure over a joy, as animals themselves sensibly do. The end of a pleasure brings no great harm to anyone, after all, and can always be replaced with another of more or less equal worth.

We have followed her on this adventure, and while we may not agree that joy must follow unhappiness, we respect Smith's reasoning and conclusion.

A dramatic narrative structure, however, is the opposite; it is based on action rather than explanation. Like its fictional counterpart, a nonfiction narrative arc follows a pattern of rising and falling action, a chain of scenes that build to resolution. The character has a problem, the character struggles with the problem, the character either hurdles the problem, is beaten by the problem, or is changed in some way by the problem. The finale is the resolution, which in some cases is no resolution. Life is full of ambiguities, and the epiphany may be that there is no easy answer.

In all narratives, though, the structure is created to move the reader from one scene to another, chasing the answer to the question posed, either subtly or overtly, early in the story. Returning again to J.R. Moehringer's "Resurrecting the

Champ," note how he establishes the tension line in the first few paragraphs while employing a fiction writer's gift of storytelling:

> *I'm sitting in a hotel room in Columbus, Ohio, waiting for a call from a man who doesn't trust me, hoping he'll have answers about a man I don't trust, which may clear the name of a man no one gives a damn about. To distract myself from this uneasy vigil—and from the phone that never rings, and from the icy rain that never stops pelting the window—I light a cigar and open a 40-year-old newspaper.*
>
> *"Greatest puncher they ever seen," the paper says in praise of Bob Satterfield, a ferocious fighter of the 1940s and 1950s. "The man of hope—and the man who crushed hope like a cookie in his fist." Once again, I'm reminded of Satterfield's sorry luck, which dogged him throughout his life, as I'm dogging him now.*
>
> *I've searched high and low for Satterfield. I've searched the sour-smelling homeless shelters of Santa Ana. I've searched the ancient and venerable boxing gyms of Chicago. I've searched the eerily clear memory of one New York City fighter who touched Satterfield's push-button chin in 1946 and never forgot the panic on Satterfield's face as he fell. I've searched cemeteries, morgues, churches, museums, slums, jails, courts, libraries, police blotters, scrapbooks, phone books and record books. Now I'm searching this dreary, sleet-bound Midwestern city, where all the streets look like melting Edward Hopper paintings and the sky like a storm-whipped sea.*

He then takes us on his journey searching for Satterfield, finding a homeless man named Champ, who claims he is Satterfield, and then his quest to learn if Champ is the real deal or a confused imposter. When he learns that Champ is the latter, we don't know how to feel because of Moehringer's description of the guy; we like him. He's a sympathetic character. And we like how the author's character has evolved during the quest. The last paragraphs:

> *We watch the cars whizzing by, jets roaring overhead, strangers walking past.*
> *"Well, Champ," I say, slipping him $5. "I've got to get going."*
> *"Yeah, yeah," he says, stopping me. "Now, listen."*
> *He rests one of his heavy hands on my shoulder, a gesture that makes me swallow hard and blink for some reason. I look into his eyes, and from his uncommonly serious expression, I know he's getting ready to say something important.*
> *"I know you a long time," he says warmly, flashing that toothless smile, groping for the words. "Tell me your name again."*

What is the balance of scene vs. summary?

Action versus reflection. Cinematic versus exposition. Show versus tell. Fill in the blank on whatever you choose to call these two critical narrative components. For simplicity's sake, let's settle on scene versus summary.

In short, scene is the action, the setting, the characters moving, speaking, thinking, working, walking, feeling, plotting, observing. Scene provides the cinematic angle, bringing the reader in close to the subject and then expanding for a wider angle that encompasses more characters, more setting. In Ryan Van Meter's essay "First," the camera zooms in on two 5-year-old boys sitting in the way back of a station wagon holding hands then widens to encompass the reaction of the parents in the front seats to the little boys sitting so intimately. All in all, a pretty tightly shot scene. In contrast, Susan Faludi opens her story "Where Did Randy Go Wrong" with a sweeping shot of the farmland, lakes, and cities of upstate central New York complemented by some history before narrowing to a present-day scene of an abortion protest. In subsequent scenes, the angle remains tight on the characters, be they Randall Terry's aunts discussing him over coffee at a local café to Randall Terry berating his wife at dinner that the green beans were burnt. In scenes of crowds, either protests or Randall Terry speaking engagements, the camera spans the audience, capturing the Big Picture and not just isolating the individual. A scene of any kind expands a moment.

Summary, on the other hand, condenses time, providing the material needed to explain the scenes and link the scenes together. I often refer to the summary as the voiceover in a documentary. On the screen is the scene and the narrator's voice explains the meaning of what you are viewing. Where filmmakers must sprinkle that voiceover judiciously (let's face it: we watch films for the scenes, not so much the narrator), print writers have this narrative tool at their disposal; we can inject summary whenever we feel it is necessary.

The essayist Phillip Lopate was asked in an interview with Poets & Writers what he had against the "show don't tell" approach to the personal essay. He said that it wasn't so much he had anything against "showing," but rather that he honored the "great traditions of essay writing," which centered on the reflective voice, making sense of an event, an issue, a quandary. His goal as an essayist is to search for meaning. Unsure of where he's headed when he starts this search, he finds that reflection, or telling, is the path that leads to the wisdom the reader — and the writer — seek. For instance, in his essay "Against Joie de Vivre," he opens by explaining that over the years he's developed distaste for the spectacle of enjoying life, not because he disapproves of joy but because what should be a private condition its concept has turned into "a bullying social ritual." He then builds a case against, well, joie de vivre, by first providing the history of the French phrase then attacking experiences many would perceive to epitomize it.

Only in the section titled "The Houseboat" does he employ scene to show his disdain for the pleasure one is expected to feel. While he sprinkles mini scenes throughout (leading his young wife to the bedroom, unbuttoning her blouse), he devotes his prose to exposition, to explaining:

> *And for all that, depressives make the most rabid converts to joie de vivre. The reason for this is that joie de vivre and depressives are not opposites but relatives of the same family, practically twins. When I see joie de vivre rituals, I always notice, like a TV ghost, depression right alongside it. I knew a man, dominated by a powerful father, who thought he had come out of a long depression occasioned, in his mind, by his divorce. Whenever I met him he would say that his life was getting better and better. Now he could run long distances, he was putting healthy food into his system, he was more physically fit at forty than he had been at twenty-five; now he had dates, he was going out with three different women, he had a good therapist, he was looking forward to renting a bungalow in better woods than the previous summer ... I don't know whether it was his tone of voice when he said this, his sagging shoulders, or what but I always had an urge to burst into tears. If only he had admitted he was miserable I could have consoled him outright instead of being embarrassed to notice the deep hurt in him, like a swallowed razor cutting from inside.*

As Lopate explains in his book "To Show and To Tell" the adventure for him in reading nonfiction is to follow an "interesting, unpredictable mind struggling to entangle and disentangle itself in a thorny problem, or even a frivolous problem that is made complex through engagement with a sophisticated mind."

Other personal essayists, such as Ryan Van Meter, opt to explore the meaning of their experiences through scene-by-scene construction, as do narrative journalists. In "The Marriage Cure," Katherine Boo opens with a close shot of one woman getting dressed while her friend waits outside. As the now-dressed friend hops in the passenger seat, Boo slides in the reason for the trip. The first part of the opening paragraph is scene. The last sentence is summary. The following paragraph is scene and the next paragraph is summary, explaining the setting and the story's main problem, the question the reader will pursue for the rest of the narrative:

> *One July morning last year in Oklahoma City, in a public-housing project named Sooner Haven, twenty-two-year-old Kin Henderson pulled a pair of low-rider jeans over a high-rising gold lamé thong and declared herself ready for church. Her best friend in the project, Corean Brothers, was already in the parking lot, fanning away her hot flashes behind the wheel of a smoke-belching Dodge Shadow. "Car's raggedy, but it'll get us from pillar to post," Corean said when Kim climbed in. At Holy Temple Baptist Church, two miles down the*

road, the state of Oklahoma was offering the residents of Sooner Haven three days of instruction on how to get and stay married.

Kim marveled that Corean, who is forty-nine, seemed to know what to wear on such occasions. The older woman's lacquered fingernails were the same shade as her lipstick, pants suit, nylons, and pumps, which also happened to be the color of the red clay dust that settled on Sooner Haven every summer. The dust stained the sidewalks and gathered in the interstices of a high iron security perimeter that enclosed the project's hundred and fifty modest houses.

This forbidding fence, and the fact that most of the adults inside it were female, sometimes prompted unkind comparisons with the old maximum-security women's prison five minutes up the road. But Kim and Corean believed that they could escape Sooner Haven, and so were only mildly irked by what one of their neighbors called "our cage." Besides, other low-income areas had fierce border-lines, too. The distance between Sooner Haven and Holy Temple Baptist Church edged the territories of the street gangs Hoover Crip, Grape Street Crip, and Rolling Twenties. Kim's brother had been murdered by a gang, but she couldn't keep track of their ever-mutating names, boundaries, and affiliations. And Corean had refused to learn, even when Hoover Crip members started shooting at one of her five children. It was Corean's contention that you could be in the ghetto and not of it. Ignoring the stunts of heavily armed neighbors kept your mind free for more enriching pursuits, such as the marriage class for which Corean had roused her young friend from bed this morning.

Laurie Hertzel, an editor at the Minneapolis Star Tribune, spoke eloquently about scene and summary at a recent narrative storytelling conference at Boston University. She recommends thinking of scenes, not as a sidewalk but as stepping-stones, keying moments that move the narrative to its rightful conclusion. Scenes build suspense, making the reader ask questions about what will happen, why is character X behaving that way, why are certain choices made? Scenes serve as cliffhangers and foreshadow. In their sequence they provide rising and falling action, with the narrative's intensity rising to a climax, and ending with falling action.

Summary is the "truncated necessary stuff," Hertzel writes in her essay "Setting the Scene." Summary provides the backstory, the explanation, whatever information is necessary for the reader to understand the action of the scenes. In Cheryl Strayed's essay "The Love of My Life," the summary that follows the intimate scenes of her adultery and sexual relationship with her husband is critical for the reader to understand her erratic behavior:

We aren't supposed to want our mothers that way, with the pining intensity of sexual love, but I did, and if I couldn't have her, I couldn't have anything. Most of all I couldn't have pleasure, not even for a moment. I was bereft, in agony, destroyed over her death. To experience sexual joy, it seemed, would have been to negate that reality. And more, it would have been to betray my mother, to be disloyal to the person she had been to me: my hero, a single mother after she bravely left an unhealthy relationship with my father when I was five. She remarried when I was eleven. My stepfather had loved her and been a good husband to her for ten years, but shortly after she died, he'd fallen in love with someone else. His new girlfriend and her two daughters moved into my mother's house, took her photos off the walls, erased her. I needed my stepfather to be the kind of man who would suffer for my mother, unable to go on, who would carry a torch. And if he wouldn't do it, I would.

The rest of the essay is a mixture of scene and backstory, each building on each other to arrive at Strayed's final destination, the realization that her mother was the love of her life and she would always grieve her absence.

What are the key scenes and reflections?

Narrative structure evolves from this pattern of scenes and reflection. How they build on each other is a matter of intuition and logic. We rely on instinct to ferret out the most compelling scenes, the moments that best illustrate the story we

TRY THIS

1. Think visually and map the narrative. What's at the center? What's on the periphery? Where do events and insights intersect? Where do the characters fit? What's the role of setting?

2. During childhood we are often frightened. Choose an episode in which you were scared to your marrow. Was your fear justified? Why or why not? How did the episode change you? Write an essay first in a series of scenes, using only a tiny bit of exposition to explain the situation. Then write another more meditative essay, using scene only to explain your reflections. Which of the two best illustrates what you learned from the fright? Perhaps yet another version — a combination of equal parts scene and summary.

3. Try the same exercise with a researched topic. For instance, report both sides of a local controversy, say dog owners lobbying the city cemetery to not implement a proposed leash rule. Observe the dogs romping through the tombstones. Talk to the dog owners. Talk to the cemetery maintenance folks. Talk to cemetery visitors paying respects to graves of loved ones. Write a scene-based narrative that uses only enough reflection to explain the action. Next write a narrative in which the narrator explains the problem, using scene to prove a point.

want to tell. Logic informs how much and what kind of explanation we need to explain the scenes to the reader. To figure out the flow, the arrangement that creates the most tension on the march to resolution, writers of true tales often borrow from their fiction counterparts by storyboarding.

Storyboarding is a visual technique in which key scenes are identified on separate boards, or my preferred vehicle, 4x6-inch pieces of paper. Sometimes theme and other components of the scene (character, dialogue, setting) are included with the individual scenes. Once a writer has identified and isolated the key scenes on those pieces of paper, she can then begin arranging the scenes in various patterns to see how plot, theme, and characters can evolve. Intuition — which develops from reading and analyzing what works in the writing of others — is the guide as we feel our way to a structure that establishes suspense and meaning. Logic steps in to determine where to plant the background, reflection, stats, and facts necessary to provide context and author interpretation.

Joe Mackall spent years developing the friendship with his Amish neighbors that led him to write "Plain Secrets: An Outsider Among the Amish." Out of those years of dinners and conversations and working side by side, Joe had to cull out the scenes that best illustrated what he hoped to convey about the Amish. On one hand, he was troubled by the Amish view of women (their role is confined to tending the home and children), education (eighth grade maximum), and those who leave the insular community (permanently exiled). But on the other, he deeply admired their work ethic and devotion to family, the land, community, and simplicity. He loved and trusted his Amish friends. "We've gone through some serious shit together," Mackall says. Because of that friendship, because of his intimate knowledge of his Amish neighbors, he couldn't pretend to be objective. Instead, he opted to serve as the docent, the narrative guide into this culture, which like all cultures, is complicated. "I had to be the guide who cared about them, who loved parts of the culture and was skeptical about others," Mackall says. "You can't talk about them getting out of school in eighth grade and not have that bother you."

To construct a narrative pattern that reflected his conflicted feelings, Joe sought scenes that accomplished multiple tasks, that illustrated character as well as theme, that provided a segue to history and factual context, that showed the warmth of the community as well as the harshness. One of his favorites is the opening scene in which Samuel, his Amish neighbor, slaughters a pig. While Samuel approaches the task nonchalantly — how else would his family eat? — and his children slide their bare feet around in the blood, Joe is horrified. This portrait, he feels, illuminates the differences in background, motivation, and also provides drama.

In another, Joe describes helping Samuel, his children, and a neighbor boy clean and load pumpkins into a wagon to bring to market on a crisp autumn Saturday. Five years earlier, Samuel's 9-year-old daughter Sarah had died of a brain tumor, and this scene was a soft way to introduce the family tragedy, as well as discuss Amish children's clothing, Amish dating (the neighbor boy and one of Samuel's daughters were clearly flirting) and the Amish perspective on medicine. More important, the author experiences clarity about himself, his Amish friends, and the fragility of life:

> [B]ut suddenly I experience a paroxysm of joy — sheer, sharp unadulterated joy. I'm suspended between two worlds, an outsider in an outsider's world. I'm here with friends who consider themselves separate from the world but woven in the earth, while we all throw fruits of the earth to one another: seed planted, sown, produce reaped and cleaned, soon to be sold, bought and eaten. Toddlers play, teenagers laugh, a friend loses his hat, my back aches, and through it all the beauty and heartbreaking brevity of this life pierce me with their stunning certainty.

While another writer may have chosen to explain the complexities of Amish living through exposition, telling the reader what to think through the narrator's interpretation, Mackall chooses to show in scene the choices the Amish make, which allows readers to form their own conclusions.

WEB CHOICES

Phillip Toledano on The Importance of Intuition

Phillip Toledano doesn't think of himself as a photographer, although his photos have appeared in galleries around the world and in publications such as Vanity Fair, The New Yorker, and Le Monde. He doesn't think of himself as a writer, although he's published four books with a fifth on the way. Rather, he thinks of himself as a conceptual artist who lets the idea guide him to the medium.

He started shooting photos of his 96-year-old father the year after his mother died suddenly from an aneurism. An only child, he was the sun and the moon to his parents, the intensity of which he fought as a child and took for granted as an adult. But he found in the absence of his mother a mourning for what was lost, what was not said. By chronicling his days with his father, he could record for perpetuity his father's expressions, his mannerisms. And so he shot and shot and eventually put the whole thing together with text in what became "Days with My Father," an online photo essay that went viral. Millions have viewed it. Thousands have e-mailed him. MediaStorm, an interactive design studio that works with artists to create visual narratives, recruited him to produce "A Shadow Remains," a documentary about his family. None of the accolades he predicted; he wasn't sure from the start if anyone beyond his circle would be interested. Yet after reading the e-mail and talking to those touched by his work, he understands that his experience was universal, that the chord he struck was not about death, but about love, and aging, and celebrating family.

Structuring a photo essay on a topic so amorphous wasn't as challenging as one might think. He simply relied on his intuition.

My mother died so suddenly and there were so many things about her that I wanted to remember. Now that she was gone, so much was out of my reach — the help, the support — and I realized that everything she had said was true.

I took pictures of my father so that I could remember him, the jokes we shared, the love we had for each other. I wanted to record his face. A large source of his joy was my success in business. So I recorded how his face looked when I said I took a photo for The New Yorker.

I'd been taking photos for a while and thinking. Then I sat down and put it all together. I wrote the whole thing in a couple of days. Everything came out in one big vomity hairball. I revised, of course, and then put it up while he was still alive. It was like a blog. I'd amend it, add a photo.

It's not really chronological. It begins the year after my mother dies and ends when he dies, but the middle isn't linear. When you have dementia, time doesn't matter. My father existed in a nebulous haze. The moments and sentences and looks between us weren't about time-specific things. When the photos are exhibited, the order is changed, and it doesn't matter.

You put things where they feel right. It is hard to quantify why you put this photo and text here and not two pages later. When you're making art, you do what feels right. You let the compass within you direct you. The picture is good there, but not there.

Photos were not enough for "Days with My Father." It's very liberating to not say I'm a photographer; I'm not constrained. The medium can be anything. I let the idea take me in any direction.

It's hard to see out of that experience. Here's another photographer talking about his dying parent. Since I've done that, people have sent me projects about their parents. And now I sense why mine resonated with people. Most are unremittingly sad. Old people in terrible situations. They're unwell. They're in hospital. The thing about "Days" is that it reflects slightly more of what life is — the sadness, the beauty, the humor, and above all, the love. That is why people connect to it. Kids write to me that "Days" made them realize that their parents won't be around forever.

I felt "Days With My Father" was so personal that no one would understand it. I couldn't have been more wrong, and I couldn't be happier that I was more wrong.

WHAT ARE SOME STRUCTURE OPTIONS?

When a writer sits down to organize a narrative, the path of least resistance is to choose the tried and true, the structure that has worked before. For some that could be alternating chunks of scene and exposition. For others it could be a scene-based chronology. Writing is hard enough; who can blame anyone for selecting the path that promises the least amount of head banging? Yet here is where John McPhee is a role model. One would think that after over half a century of plotting the arrangement of factual tales, he would have exhausted structural possibilities. Yet as he says in his New Yorker columns on the writing life, every essay, every book provides a new opportunity to play with order.

In earlier days, he tinkered with what he called ABC/D, which he defined as three journeys and one common denominator. In "Encounters with the Arch-druid" that formula became David Brower, the Sierra Club executive director, as the common factor (D) and his journeys through the North Cascades with a mining geologist (A), on a Georgia island with a resort developer (B), and rafting down the Colorado River in the Grand Canyon with a dam builder (C).

For a profile on Thomas Hoving, director of the New York's Metropolitan Museum of Art, McPhee arranged the piece as a museum with each section representing a separate room by illustrating a different aspect of Hoving's life. The reader moves from one room to another and by the tale's end has a complete portrait of the man.

In his collection of personal essays "Silk Parachute," he experiments still, using repetition in the title essay, his grandchildren as a framework for an essay on the evolution of Britain's chalk cliffs, and a New Yorker fact checker as a vehicle to ponder accuracy in print. In "My Life List" he creates a patchwork of mini-essays about eccentric foods he has eaten, ending with an alphabetical list of 43 specific foods, from bee spit to witch-hazel tea. The takeaway is clear: like the architecture of buildings, story frameworks are infinite, limited only by the imagination.

Yet like the architects of housing developments and downtown skyscrapers, storytellers enjoy a range of standard structures. Here are a few:

Straight chronology

Chronology. Start at the beginning, move through the highs and lows, end at triumph, defeat, or a noted change by the events. This strategy works particularly well in memoirs, crime stories, and mysteries — tales that build tension through the passage of time. Characters start in Place A, which is usually a place of confusion or conflict, work their way through the confusion and conflict, and arrive at the resolution. Crime stories are perfect: start with the crime, work through the investigation, and end with the solution.

"Angela's Ashes" begins at the *very* beginning — when the parents of the author, Frank McCourt, meet — and spins forward, frame by frame through McCourt's impoverished childhood in Ireland, turbulent young adulthood in New York, ending as he settles into a teaching career on more stable footing. In "Caballo Blanco's Last Run," Barry Bearak opens with the mysterious disappearance of the long-distance running protagonist of "Born To Run" — *GILA HOT SPRINGS, N.M. — Micah True went off alone on a Tuesday morning to run through the rugged trails of the Gila Wilderness, and now it was already Saturday and he had not been seen again* — and ends with the discovery of his body by a wilderness stream, and its trip down the mountains and into a hearse. Why he died — a heart ailment — seemed almost an afterthought woven into the last paragraphs; the narrative pulse was the search.

As for crime writing, look no further than the captivating tales published regularly in Texas Monthly. One of my favorites, "The Last Ride of Cowboy Bob" by Skip Hollandsworth, opens with Peggy Jo Tallas dressing one May morning not in her usual khakis, blouse, and loafers, but in a pair of men's pants, a man's shirt, boots, beard, and cowboy hat. She then drives to the American Federal Bank just off West Airport Freeway in Irving, Texas, robs it, and then returns home to feed lunch to her ailing mother. From there the narrative chronicles the next bank robbery, and the next, and the next, following her through her crime career, ending — spoiler alert — with a shootout at her RV. The weapon police found in the dead woman's hand: a toy pistol. Why did she rob banks? To buy drugs for her mother initially. But then her mother died and her family — and police — could only speculate why a gray-haired woman who drove an RV would hold up banks then confront a swarm of FBI agents and police with a toy pistol. The mysteries of why she lived this double life and would she get caught keep the reader riveted. The end answers the second question. The answer to the first died with Peggy Jo.

Flashback chronology

Instead of following a straight timeline — A to B to C to D — another route is to start at the middle, or near the end, with a scene highlighting the major drama. *In medias res* is the Latin phrase for this literary technique that establishes character, setting, and conflict in an opening scene that takes place in the middle or end of the timeline. Repeat. Mary Karr employed this device in her first memoir "The Liar's Club" by opening with a scene of chaos at her family home that included the sheriff whisking away the young Mary and her older sister. High drama indeed. The narrative then flashes back to earlier, better times that deteriorate as her mother's instability flourishes. Eventually the narrative works its way to the moment of the opening scene, which is when her mother hovered over her children brandishing a knife, and then forward to the later years of family resolution.

John McPhee — him again — employs the same tactic in his well-anthologized essay "Travels in Georgia." The opening scene is of McPhee and his two road kill hunting compatriots stopping by the roadside to view a wounded snapping turtle, which is eventually shot by a sheriff who just happened to drive by. The scene, which occurred not on Day 1 but later in the 1,100-mile journey around the state, is dramatic, funny, establishing character, conflict, and setting. The piece then flashes back to the beginning, unfurling chronologically, as you will see in McPhee's structure illustration below, lighting on important road kill episodes that McPhee experienced during his adventure. In his New Yorker essay "Structure: Beyond the Picnic Table Crisis," McPhee writes: "As a nonfiction writer, you could not change the facts of the chronology, but with verb tenses and other forms of clear guidance to the reader you were free to do a flashback if you thought one made sense in presenting the story."

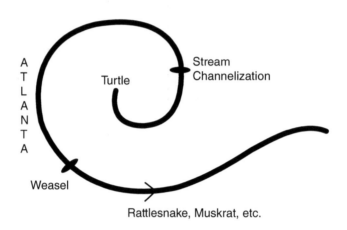

SOURCE: Princeton Weekly Bulletin, April 30, 2007.

The climax arrives at the end as McPhee and his companions escort then Georgia Governor Jimmy Carter in a canoe down a river that is threatened by a proposed sewer line. Carter is impressed enough by the wildlife and waters that he vows to try to protect the river. Yet nothing in life is that simple, which McPhee acknowledges in his concluding paragraph as he describes the four playing basketball at the governor's mansion:

> *The Governor had the ball and was dribbling in place, as if contemplating a property owner in front of him, one-on-one. He went to the basket, shot, and missed. Carol got the rebound and fed the ball to Sam. He shot. He missed, too.*

Reverse chronology

Another tactic is to start at the end (D) and work your way back to the beginning (A) step by reverse step. The tension derives from seeking the story's start rather than its end. When Chris Jones proposed the idea of following a soldier's corpse from Iraq to its final resting spot on home soil, his Esquire editor suggested writing the story backwards, starting at the funeral and working back through the body's journey home to the moment the soldier died. In this way, the narrative of "The Things that Carried Him" builds Sgt. Joe Montgomery's character, with each scene providing more background, more details, until we meet the living, breathing, joking, talking Sgt. Montgomery in the final scene, accompanying him on the fatal convoy. When Montgomery's Humvee rolls over an IED and explodes, the reader's loss is profound. We know from the beginning that he will die, but we don't know how, and we don't know the man that we are losing. By the final words, we do:

> *The last time the platoon saw Sergeant Montgomery was later that morning, at first light. It was Wednesday, May 23. They all came out of their barracks to see the helicopters land. And these sleepless young men, from Colorado, from Pennsylvania, from Washington, they took hold of the poles of the stretcher, three on each side, with their friend from Indiana between them, zipped up inside a black bag tucked under a green Army blanket, and they carried him into one of the Black Hawks, and they watched them lift off into the dawn and dust, and they saluted then, saluted the start of one journey and the end of another, holding their salutes all the while as the birds flew away, until they were gone over the horizon.*

Framed structure

Long before Tracy Kidder decided to frame his book "Soul of a New Machine" around the 9 months he spent observing a Data General team build a computer, nonfiction storytellers had used a specific event or a period of time as their narrative architecture. Stephen Crane used the scene of a mob gathering to gawk at

---

TRY THIS

1. Make a timeline of events. Cut up the timeline by event and play with chronology. Which event is the most dramatic? Most pivotal? Most revealing? Which event belongs at the beginning to lure in the reader or at the end to leave the reader with a finished taste in her mouth? Which events will play best as flashbacks?

2. Collect a pile of 4x6-inch cards or scraps of paper. On each card, write a key scene, key anecdote, and key piece of background, key insight, and key statistic. The more pieces of paper the better. Now arrange those pieces of paper in 10 different orders. Which order creates the most tension, builds the greatest suspense? Which order allows the scenes and summaries to build on each other? Which anecdote or scene would make the strongest lead?

a man convulsing on the streets of Manhattan in "When a Man Falls, A Crowd Gathers" to explore social responsibility. In "Portrait of Hemingway" Lillian Ross chronicled 2 days she spent in New York City with the legendary author, capturing him at his most exuberant (drinking champagne with Marlene Dietrich) and most churlish (buying a trench coat at Abercrombie).

Yet in fairness to Kidder, it was his list of best sellers that raised the visibility of this structural device so brilliant in its simplicity. A year in the life of a teacher and her fifth-grade class ("Among Schoolchildren") illustrates the personal and political challenges of engaging students and their families. A year in the life of two roommates in a nursing home ("Old Friends") explores aging and friendship and the financial and medical challenges of institutional care. Following the construction of a house ("House") from the perspective of all the players — architect, homeowners, sheetrock installers, plumbers, carpenters — helps us understand the dynamics of home building. Who can forget the scene when the builder debates whether or not to add windowsills, which weren't included in the architecture plans?

By isolating an event or time, by digging into the emotions of particular people participating in a particular event at a particular time, the writer can tell a much larger story. In her essay "Infernal Paradise," Barbara Kingsolver uses an early morning hike to Haleakala, the world's largest dormant volcano, to investigate not only her experience but also the human impact on nature in general and its role in endangering species specifically.

Circular structure

When I think of circular structure, I always think of the Quentin Tarantino movie "Pulp Fiction," which opens and ends with the scene of the two main characters, Jules (Samuel Jackson) and Vincent (John Travolta), eating breakfast in a diner. In between we follow them over several days, through their murders and drug heists and philosophizing, and watch as Vincent is shot to death on the toilet. If the movie were chronological that would be the last time we see Vincent. Instead, Tarantino ends the movie with a scene of Vincent and Jules walking out of the diner that first morning after breaking up an attempted robbery.

On the page, narratives, too, can work well if they begin and end in the same place. The bulk of the story, then, is like one long flashback, or backflash as my German grandmother called it. The advantage of this form is its neatness. Start at Point A, digress to Points B and C and D, and then return to Point A to wrap up. For an essay about Tuckerman's Ravine, I chose to open and end with my oldest son's struggle to climb Mt. Washington on a clear August day, using our hike as a metaphor for the story's focus: that the lure of Tuckerman's Ravine, the Northeast's alpine playground, is its challenge. The narrative tension rested on my 12-year-old son's misery and reluctance to keep going. In between, I wove in background, stats, facts, and insights from other Tuckerman experts and adventurers as well as the history of our own climb and my relationship with the mountain. At the end, the narrative returns to the tension point established at the beginning and moved toward resolution. Good news: he survived and made it to the summit.

Chris Jones employed the same tactic in his profile of movie critic Roger Ebert. He opens with a scene of Ebert settling into his seat at his 281st screening in 10 months and ends with him writing the review of "Broken Embraces," the movie he screened. In between we learn of Ebert's multiple surgeries that left him unable to eat or talk. We learn of his cancerous thyroid, his cancerous salivary glands, his near death experience from a burst carotid artery, and his long, slow climb back to his chair in the screening room. We learn more of his professional history, his partnership with Gene Siskel, his medical prognosis. We watch him in scenes as he drives around Chicago and attends a reception. We end with him settling down to write the review. We walk away from the story grounded in Ebert's resilience and vulnerability — exactly Jones' point.

Braided structure

Take two or more narrative strands, weave them together, in and out, in and out, and the result is a braided structure. One strand could be past events, one strand could be present, and a third could be background. Or one strand could be internal (personal experience) and one could be external (researched history and facts). Or the strands could be competing points of view, or images. The variations are limitless, but the goal is the same: to approach the subject from multiple angles, providing a richly textured tale that weaves together multiple fragments that, combined, illuminate a central message.

When Rebecca Skloot launched the research that would eventually become the best-selling "The Immortal Life of Henrietta Lacks," she was simply trying to learn how the cells of a poor black woman, Henrietta Lacks, could be taken without her knowledge in 1951 and then go on to be the foundation of major medical advancements, from polio to gene mapping to in vitro fertilization, without her or her family receiving any more recognition or benefit. Over the next 10 years she became involved with the family and their quest to learn more about Henrietta's cells. Eventually, Skloot realized that she had three distinct narrative threads: the life of Henrietta Lacks, the science behind the cells Lacks unwittingly donated, and the author's role in the Lacks family's understanding of their matriarch's contribution to science.

To figure out how to braid these threads together, she dissected novels with multiple storylines that also jumped around in time. And she watched movies, which often rely on a multiplot structure. The novel "Fried Green

Tomatoes at the Whistle Stop Café" helped her understand how to go back and forth between present and past with multiple characters. But the major inspiration came from the movie "Hurricane." Watching the tale of the boxer Hurricane Carter, his childhood, his brushes with the law, his murder charge, his imprisonment, and the three people who proved his innocence, Skloot saw how her book could unfold. She isolated each scene and created a storyboard of the movie. Then she took the color-coded notecards she created for her book — each color representing one of the three narrative lines — and placed them on the "Hurricane" storyboard. By moving the cards around, she found her structure.

Parallel construction

Parallel construction is two narrative lines chugging along a few feet apart. First we see what one person is doing. Then we see what the other person is doing. Tension builds as we wonder what will happen, what these two parties mean to each other. And then they intersect. The plot unfolds.

A cinematic device, parallel construction is portrayed at its finest in the opening chapters of "In Cold Blood." Truman Capote begins the book with the sweeping landscape of Kansas — *The village of Holcomb stands on the high wheat plains of western Kansas, a lonesome area that other Kansans call "out there"* — spinning a description of rural isolation. We then meet Herb Clutter, the 48-year-old rancher, as he begins his day as he walked his orchard, waved to one of his ranch hands and reminisced about his teenage daughter's performance the night before in "Tom Sawyer." The section ends with Clutter greeting a group of pheasant hunters and *"touching the brim of his cap, he headed for home and the day's work, unaware that it would be his last."*

Dum-de-dum-dum.

In the next passage, the reader is introduced to a short but thick man with tiny feet who waits in a café for his friend Dick, who has invited him on a "score." We don't know what the score is, but we do know that Perry intends to head to Mexico afterward. We know that he's in Kansas and that only 4 months earlier he had sworn to a parole board that he would never set foot in the state again. We know that he envisions a life of treasure hunting, reaping riches from the sea. The section ends when Dick drives up.

Back and forth the narrative flows between the Clutters on this day, their last, and Dick and Perry as they buy rope and drive. The Clutters watch TV. Dick and Perry stop for food. Bobby Rupp, the daughter's boyfriend, leaves the farm at 11 p.m. And then we follow Dick and Perry in their car as they head down the Clutter's lane.

The lines intersect. And the story unfolds.

Collage

In middle school art class, collage meant gluing all sorts of magazine images and photos on to a background. For writers, a collage means assembling shards of memory, scenes, research, history in a meaningful order. By that I mean an order that leads the reader to the insight(s) the writer hopes to impart. Like the braided structure, the collage allows the writer to approach the subject from multiple angles and perspectives. Collage is a favorite tool of memoirists, who arrange pieces of memory as a way to make sense of an experience or thought.

In "The Girls in My Town," for example, Angela Morales divides into numbered chunks scenes of her sun-bleached arid California town, miles inland from the glorious surf and beaches, and the local teenage girls who seek love and purpose through motherhood. In the first chunk she introduces the once-fertile land ravaged by drought, describing the abandoned homes, shuttered restaurants, the air that smells of pesticide and manure. Next we meet a beautiful boy in the narrator's high school classroom who represents all the boys who seduce young women and then leave once the baby arrives. And then we meet the narrator's neighbors and their teenage daughter, who one day walks onto the porch, her belly as big as a watermelon. Each chunk that follows shows a different angle into these young women and the town that breeds such hopelessness. We see the young mothers marching their babies in a stroller brigade, learn of the parenting classes they attend and then ignore. We're in the maternity ward with the narrator after she gives birth to her daughter, a thin curtain separating her from her 14-year-old roommate, her boyfriend, and their baby. We learn of dead babies and crazed mothers and the narrator's struggles to support these young women, her students, while not encouraging more babies. The essay ends with a scene of the narrator's daughter, now 13, happy and unburdened. How fared the daughter of her 14-year-old roommate in the maternity ward?

> *Would our daughters have anything in common? My roommate's daughter, according to county statistics (based on her mother's age and ethnicity), will very likely have a baby before she turns eighteen. Then the girl will most likely drop out of school and struggle to care for her child in this place of leached soil turned to clay. My roommate's daughter may never know about the migratory waterfowl such as Canadian geese and whistling swans that once stopped off in our valley marshlands — most of which have been drained to rechannel water for irrigation. And maybe the babies, in some weird way, reflect our need to find beauty once again in this landscape.*

By the essay's last lines, we have witnessed enough scenes, absorbed enough of the narrator's insights to see the connection between the land and these young women, and to ponder the fate of the generations to come.

Similarly, in his essay "36 Tattoos," David Shields explores the meaning of body decoration and ownership by creating a montage of research and observation. We learn the history of tattoos, that 35 percent of NBA players have tattoos, that slaves were tattooed for identification. Quotes on body art and image weave through the text ("The human body is always treated as an image of society." — Anthropologist Mary Douglas. "White folks are not going to come to see a bunch of guys with tattoos, with cornrows. I'm sorry, but anyone who thinks different, they're stupid." — Charles Barkley). Each chunk provides new facts, new insights, building the reader's appreciation and understanding of body art in our culture, particularly our professional sports culture. By the essay's final paragraphs, Shields has woven a rich quilt that asks the readers to ponder their reaction to basketball great Allen Iverson's painted body. Whether they have the right to react. As he says in his last line, "Who owns this body, this body of work?"

The Quest

What did happen to Caballo Blanco, the famed long-distance barefoot runner who lived among the Tarahumara people in Mexico? He went off for a run in the hills and didn't come back. Barry Bearak set up his story about the famed Micah True's disappearance as a quest. We follow the searchers for the runner day after day, learning too about the man and his life and the fame he endured with the publication of the book "Born To Run," in which he was a main character. The story ends with the discovery of True's body by a stream and the delivery of his body to his companion.

J.R. Moehringer structured his story "Resurrecting the Champ" around his quest to find the famed boxer, and when he does, or thinks that he does, his quest is to learn if this homeless man claiming to be the champ really is.

Adventure writers such as Jon Krakauer follow this structure because it works so very well for their subjects. Chris McCandless a recent college graduate from a wealthy family, sells all his possessions, burns all his money, and takes off into the wilds of Alaska, only to die of starvation in the shell of a school bus. "Into the Wild" explores the why — why he pursued this fatal journey, why the journey ended in death, and the larger question of why some adventurers seek more risk than others.

The quest structure leads the reader on the search, raising his curiosity with each new stop, each new discovery, each new challenge. Will the protagonist succeed? How will the protagonist fail? What is at stake? What is the reward?

Structures inspired by topics and theme

Often, the topic or theme themselves will provide a structure. When constructing architecture to encompass a subject as broad as the 10th anniversary of 9/11,

New York magazine opted to create an encyclopedia of 92 entries that explore the horrific events, thoughts, and memories of that day. "A" included Airport Security and Artifacts. "J" focused only on Jumpers. "M" described Missing Persons Posters. "Q" was Quiet for the dumbstruck city. By approaching this enormous topic with a list, the story could cover more ground while allowing the reader to digest only pieces at a time if the memories were too painful.

The structures are as individual as the narratives. In "How I Met My Wife," novelist Robert Boswell provides 12 character-building techniques by telling the tale of how he met and married his wife, the writer Antonya Nelson. Each episode of his courtship represents a device, from meaningful sensory deprivation (Boswell played blind to Nelson's other boyfriends) to compare and contrasting different characters (Boswell, the hothead, wants to fight while his brother, the wise one, calms him down) to creating fictional versions, which is Method Number Nine:

> Later on, I would discover why Toni had developed an interest in me. (It was not my looks or sexual presence, so you know that I was disappointed.) A story I had submitted to workshop intrigued her. The story was one that I'd been working on for years. It was called "The Darkness of Love," and Toni fell for me while reading it. This may sound like an incident so specific to writers as to defy generalization, but I find the opposite to be true. She fell for a fiction that she attributed to the other, and that is precisely what is necessary for love. We fall in love with a fictional version of the other that we think they have authored, failing to see our own hand in the creation.
>
> Method number nine is to investigate the fictions to which a character clings.

In "The Pain Scale," essayist Eula Biss probes the meaning of pain by analyzing the numbers on the zero to ten scale doctors use to decipher a patient's discomfort. Biss opens the essay noting that there is no such thing as zero pain and shares thoughts and facts about zero that she collected through research and observation:

> Zero, on the Celsius scale, is the point at which water freezes. And one hundred is the point at which water boils.
>
> But Anders Celsius, who introduced the scale in 1741, originally fixed zero as the point at which water boiled, and one hundred as the point at which water froze. These fixed points were reversed only after his death.

The essay moves through the numbers in the same way, weaving in research, observation, and her personal experiences. It helps that her father is a doctor and provides her with some quote gems, such as "The problem with scales from zero to ten is the tyranny of the mean." Or in the section on number 10:

The digit ten depends on the digit zero, in our current number system. In 1994 Robert Forslund developed an Alternative Number System. "This system," he wrote with triumph, "eliminates the need for the digit zero, and hence all digits behave the same."

In the Alternate Number System, the tenth digit is represented by the character A. Counting begins at one; 1,2,3,4,5,6,7,8,9,A,11,12 ... 18,19,1A,21, 22 ... 28,29,2A ...

"One of the functions of the pain scale," my father explains, "is to protect doctors — to spare them some emotional pain. Hearing someone describe their pain as a ten is much easier than hearing them describe it as a hot poker driven through their eyeball into their brain."

Biss, like McPhee, is a master builder of narrative. Each sentence has a purpose. Each chunk builds on its predecessor. Despite the fact that Biss relies on images in much of her work and McPhee relies on scenes and facts, they share an ethic, that each subject deserves its own individual construction. As McPhee told the Paris Review: "Structure is not a template. It's not a cookie cutter. It's something that arises organically from the material once you have it."

TRY THIS

Think of a provocative question (e.g., In what situations does cellphone use irritate you and why?) and, using one of the structure styles listed above, write an answer to the question using scene, observation, reflection, and facts and stats collected from the Internet. Now write the essay using two other structures as framework. Which of the three creates the most engaging narrative?

6

What Are the Components?

> **Overview**
>
> A narrative comprises a matrix of components, all of which harbor an array of choices. What's the best opening? Who are the main characters? Who will tell the story? This chapter identifies the major components inherent in narrative — including beginnings, endings, point of view, character development, setting, and dialogue — and how various storytellers choose their approach to each.

STRUMMING THE KEYBOARD, I GLANCED AWAY from the blank computer screen and out the window of my third floor home office. Grey clouds gathered above the rooftops and an icy wind bent the bare trees sideways. I fantasized about a massive snowstorm, so white, so powerful that my attention would be directed to survival, not the taunting, blinking cursor. After a year of conducting hundreds of interviews, reading shelves of books and articles about the politics of abortion, the medical and emotional layers of abortion, of logging thousands of hours talking to abortion patients, observing procedures, and shadowing administrators and counselors and nurses, protesters and policeman, it was time to launch the narrative. And unlike the process Hemingway describes in "A Moveable Feast," the story was not writing itself.

I sighed. Perhaps, I thought, I should just make soup.

And then I remembered some advice the writing coach Don Murray had shared months before. Murray was entering The Library Restaurant in Portsmouth, New

Hampshire, as I was leaving one July evening and the poor guy didn't have a chance to utter hello before I plunged into hand-wringing self-pity about how could I possibly write *a whole book*? Eighty thousand words! Multiple chapters! Multiple themes! Accustomed to writers of all kinds — not just former students like myself — seeking his counsel, he stood at the top of the stone steps, his hand on the door handle, chuckling. He was a big man, over six-feet tall, with a round belly and a white beard. Think Santa Claus with heavy black glasses and a notebook tucked into his breast pocket.

"How do you eat an elephant?" he asked. "One bite at a time." And with that he turned his bulk toward the open door and entered the dark-paneled foyer.

One bite at a time.

Staring at my computer on that late winter day, I began chanting his advice like a mantra. And little by little, sentence by sentence, I began to write. By dividing the project into bites, or components, the challenge of spinning a cohesive tale of fact loomed far less daunting. The "bites" to consider for my book on a year in the life of an abortion clinic were the same as what I'd consider for a shorter piece. All narratives need a beginning and an end. In between that beginning and end, all narratives comprise a mix of components ranging from point of view to character to setting to dialogue.

It is often said that every word counts and so it goes with the components; each one serves a purpose, contributing in its own way to the narrative's meaning. Its purpose may be directly linked to the story's soul — a line of dialogue that reflects resolution — or it may simply be a detail that builds character, or contributes to plot. In all cases, it is up to the writer to select only the most worthy, the most substantial, the diamond in the coal that will turn the collection of facts and observations into a story that will engage the reader, leading him toward the story's finale.

But before we get to the finale, let's start at the beginning — with the beginning and the myriad of choices of how to start a narrative.

WHAT'S THE OPENING?

A few years back, Susan Orlean spoke at my university, and it seemed that in preparation for her visit, most students in the audience had read her profile "The American Man, Age Ten." A vocal crew up front demanded that she read the opening paragraph. Standing at the podium, her signature red hair cascading down her shoulders, she complied:

If Colin Duffy and I were to get married, we would have matching superhero notebooks. We would wear shorts, big sneakers, and long, baggy T-shirts depicting famous athletes every single day, even in the winter. We would sleep in our clothes. We would both be good at Nintendo Street Fighter II, but Colin would be better than me. We would have some homework, but it would not be too hard and we would always have just finished it. We would eat pizza and candy for all of our meals. We wouldn't have sex, but we would have crushes on each other and, magically, babies would appear in our home. We would win the lottery and then buy land in Wyoming, where we would have one of every kind of cute animal. All the while, Colin would be working in law enforcement - probably the FBI. Our favorite movie star, Morgan Freeman, would visit us occasionally. We would listen to the same Eurythmics song ("Here Comes the Rain Again") over and over again and watch two hours of television every Friday night. We would both be good at football, have best friends, and know how to drive; we would cure AIDS and the garbage problem and everything that hurts animals. We would hang out a lot with Colin's dad. For fun, we would load a slingshot with dog food and shoot it at my butt. We would have a very good life.

"Where did that come from?" one student asked.

Susan Orlean paused for a moment, as if mulling where indeed did that beginning — or any beginning for that matter — come from. And then she smiled, and shrugged, tossing up her hands. She had no answer.

One could infer from her silence that she didn't know, that her openings sprang from deep within her subconscious. Perhaps they do. There is always a bit of mysticism and magic about the creative process. Yet without deep thought and reflection the artistic magic wouldn't have direction. And without direction, how would words and images arrange themselves in a beginning? Susan Orlean had spent many hours with Colin Duffy, watching him, playing games with him, talking to him, talking to others about him. From that concentrated effort, the meaning behind the profile of this boy evolved, and when she sat down to write her beginning, she engaged both her imagination and concrete material that she had gathered from her research and reflection.

As with most aspects of creative writing, there's not one right approach to crafting beginnings, or leads as journalists call those first paragraphs. Some writers claim that the opening must be flawless before they can dive into the body of the piece. Others will start writing the middle of the piece first, hoping that an enticing beginning will emerge as the narrative gains traction. Some will write the end and then go back to launch the beginning. Yet *when* in the process those first paragraphs take shape isn't nearly as important as *how* they take shape. And how they take shape depends on the writer recognizing the one goal — the universal mission — of all beginnings: to lure the reader into the story.

This doesn't mean using tricks and clever devices that aren't connected to the tale. Rather, it means digging deep into the story's meaning and recreating a scene, an anecdote, a description, a line that entices and illuminates a core element. Or, to paraphrase John McPhee, the lead should shine a light into the story's soul.

While there are as many kinds of openings as there are stories, let's reduce the possibilities to a manageable number. Here are a few types to consider.

Begin with a scene

Often during the research and reflection stage, a scene will emerge that evokes the heart of the conflict. It could be a scene in which the main character confronts a crucial decision. Or a moment when a gentle disagreement turns to rage. Or a couple answering a Want Ad for a job that proves fatal. Through action, dialogue, and inner monologue, a scene grabs the reader and pulls her in, making her want to know what will happen next.

In "The Bravest Woman in Seattle," Eli Sanders opens with a scene from the trial of a man who broke into the home of a lesbian couple, raping both and murdering one. The prose is spare, neutral, but sprinkled with enough horror that the reader is sucked in:

> *The prosecutor wanted to know about window coverings. He asked: Which windows in the house on South Rose Street, the house where you woke up to him standing over you with a knife that night — which windows had curtains that blocked out the rest of the world and which did not?*
>
> *She answered the prosecutor's questions, pointing to a map of the small South Park home she used to share with her partner, Teresa Butz, a downtown Seattle property manager. When the two of them lived in this house, it was red, a bit run-down, much loved, filled with their lives together, typical of the neighborhood. Now it was a two-dimensional schematic, State's Exhibit 2, set on an easel next to the witness stand. She narrated with a red laser pointer for the prosecutor and the jury: These windows had curtains that couldn't be seen through. These windows had just a sheer fabric.*
>
> *Would your silhouettes have been visible through that sheer fabric at night?*
>
> *Probably. She didn't know for sure. When she and her partner lived in the house, she noted, "I didn't spend a lot of time staring in my own windows."*
>
> *Everyone in the courtroom laughed a small laugh — a laugh of nervous relief, because here was a woman testifying about her own rape, and the rape and murder of her partner, and yet she was smiling at the current line of questioning, at the weird perceptual cul-de-sac to which it led. She appeared to understand why people might need to hear these answers, though. What happened to her and Butz in that house in the early morning hours of July 19, 2009, is hard to comprehend. A juror, in order to ease into the reality of what occurred, might first need to imagine how the man picked these two women. At least, then, there'd be some sort of arc to the story.*

In these first five paragraphs, Sanders establishes character and plot; the reader yearns to learn how and why this evil happened, and, more important, how this young woman could summon the strength to survive the ordeal, let alone testify. The lead serves as a diving board into the body of the story, which takes the reader on a journey of the past (the woman's relationship with her partner, the night of the rape and murder), the present (the trial), and the future (the outcome and its consequences).

Similarly, Jo Ann Beard opens her much-anthologized essay "The Fourth State of Matter" with a scene that sets the stage for the tiers of drama that will follow:

> *The collie wakes me up about three times a night, summoning me from a great distance as I row my boat through a dim, complicated dream. She's on the shoreline, barking. Wake up. She's staring at me with her head slightly tipped to the side, long nose, gazing eyes, toenails clenched to get a purchase on the wood floor. We used to call her the face of love.*
>
> *She totters on her broomstick legs into the hallway and over the doorsill into the kitchen, makes a sharp left at the refrigerator — careful, almost went down — then a straightaway to the door. I sleep on my feet in the cold of the doorway, waiting. Here she comes. Lift her down the two steps. She pees and then stands, Lassie in a ratty coat, gazing out at the yard.*
>
> *In the porch light the trees shiver, the squirrels turn over in their sleep. The Milky Way is a long smear on the sky, like something erased on a blackboard. Over the neighbor's house, Mars flashes white, then red, then white again. Jupiter is hidden among the anonymous blinks and glitterings. It has a moon with sulfur-spewing volcanoes and a beautiful name: Io. I learned it at work, from the group of men who surround me there. Space physicists, guys who spend days on end with their heads poked through the fabric of the sky, listening to the sounds of the universe. Guys whose own lives are ticking like alarm clocks getting ready to go off, although none of us are aware of it yet.*

In this braided essay, Beard weaves together the death of her marriage, the impending death of her beloved dog, and the violent deaths of her coworkers in a university physics department when a depressed graduate student opens fire during a Friday afternoon meeting. It is a tale of loss and acceptance, of the ordinary and the extraordinary, all illuminated in this opening of a frail collie waking the narrator in the middle of a clear Midwestern night bright with stars. Through metaphor and imagery, the narrative tension is introduced.

Anecdotal starts

An anecdote is a mini story within a larger story, a brief account of an incident that illuminates a point about theme, character, issue, or place. It has a beginning, middle, and an end that often serves as a punch line, or the message that ties into the narrative. For instance, early in "Among Schoolchildren," Tracy Kidder establishes the character of the teacher, Chris Zajac, through anecdotes. One story, which depicts her playful side, describes Chris and her young son sneaking up to the radio and switching the channel from classical music to rock-and-roll when her husband wasn't looking. *"You're regressing, Chris," her husband would say.* Boom. Point made with the quote.

An anecdotal lead, then, is a short story that highlights an essay's core. The writer may glean the story from her own memory or from someone else's through interviews or research. For instance, while collecting content for a story on the challenges of raising gifted children, I talked to a mom who recalled an aha moment one morning when her daughter was two. Strapped to her highchair, the toddler watched her mother scurry from one side of the kitchen to the other to grab the toast from the toaster. "Mommy," she said, pointing to a spot on the counter, "wouldn't it be easier to put the toaster over there?" The mother was dumbstruck. First, her daughter was correct; the toaster would be more efficient in that place. And second, how could she possibly mentor a child whose brain worked twice as fast as her own? As she spoke, I knew this would be my lead — a mini-story that illustrated the central conflict.

When exploring the heroin deaths of teenagers in one affluent Texas town, Pamela Colloff heard an anecdote from a police officer that she used to open "Teenage Wasteland":

> *What struck him, he would later say, was that the boy didn't look anything like a junkie. Plano police Sergeant Aubrey Paul had driven north along Texas Highway 289, where Plano's gated communities and mirrored office parks abruptly give way to unruly stretches of buffalo grass, to check out a call he had received the day before from a detective in the neighboring town of Frisco. This was before he knew the full scope of the problem, before his heart would sink when calls like this came in, back when he knew more about heroin from watching "The French Connection," he recalled with a half-hearted grin, than he did from his twelve years as a cop. What awaited him in the brick police station in Frisco that day was a jarring revelation: crime scene photographs of a seventeen-year-old who had died of a heroin overdose only a few months after moving there from Plano. Paul studied the photos — an otherwise healthy-looking kid, nude and sprawled across a bathroom floor — and felt a kind of dread. Maybe this was the beginning of something much larger. Maybe there would be more pictures, these gruesome still-lifes, to come.*

By opening with this anecdote, Colloff provides the central mystery that propels the reader page after page: how has heroin infected the youth of a tony Texas suburb?

Steven Harvey, in contrast, had to go only as far as his own memory to resurrect an anecdote to begin "The Art of Self," which defends the merits of the personal essay in the world of letters:

> *On a flight recently I met a fiction writer. Both of us were on our way to a writer's conference in Portland, Oregon, and when I told her that I wrote personal essays she laughed. "Oh, I love the form," she said. "It's so easy." I heard the ice in our drinks rattle in the silence that ensued. I had plenty of time, before we landed, to think about what she had said. Confusion about the essay begins with a misconception: that art must be invented. To be creative — the argument goes — literature must be made up. Since the personal essay begins with a real life, it is less creative, less artistic, than fiction. Such a view, I think, is mistaken, based not only on confusions about writing, but on confusions about art as well. What makes writing — writing of any kind — an art is not invention, but shape. Shapeliness. The facts, the events, the invented flights of fancy do not make up a work of art. The shapeliness of the author's composition takes us to that level.*

Surely, Harvey had brooded plenty about the personal essay's place on the ladder of literary respect. But the comment by the woman on the plane, so blithe, so grating, spurred him not only to explore on the page his feelings about the essay's value, but also provided a vehicle to launch the narrative. Following this anecdote, he eloquently explains that the essay, like fiction, requires that writers make decisions about beginnings and endings, shape and pace and language. They both illuminate the human condition, one based on imagination and the other on experience. He writes: "Recognizing that art is in the shaping of language, not in inventing or being true to life, can be liberating ... any event, when fashioned in words, can have meaning."

Descriptive leads

Where scene and anecdotal openings have action that entices the reader with movement and dialogue, a descriptive lead establishes a mood through sensory detail that connects to the story's core. The mission is to provide enough sounds, smells, visuals, and tactile specifics for the reader to form an image. Those images should arouse enough curiosity for the reader to yearn to know more.

When opening with a description of place, writers may seek details that illustrate a visual backdrop, much the way the sweeping panoramic shot of the English countryside set the stage for the BBC's "Pride and Prejudice." Or they may seek specifics to illuminate something richer, deeper, an underlying tension. By focusing on key images, the writer can establish a sense of mystery that the rest of the tale will explore.

Lauren Markham opens "First the Fence, then the System," the harrowing tale of Mexican children crossing the Rio Grande, by describing the border between South Texas and Mexico:

Tiptoeing through the scrub brush of South Texas, everything sounds like a threat: wind rustling the palm fronds, a lizard skittering through the understory, a hawk's heavy flapping, one's own arm against a pantleg.

At the bottom edge of the Santa Ana National Wildlife Refuge slinks that fabled river, the Rio Grande, not two car lengths across. It is both astounding and totally unsurprising that Mexico, on the opposite bank, looks just the same as Texas, just a mirror image of nothing special. The park is a restored desert wetland, home to birds and armadillos and the endangered ocelot, with the occasional crossing of both Border Patrol trucks and those they are hunting. Thanks to uproar from the park staff and local environmentalist groups that had worked to restore and preserve this nearly lost habitat, the infamous border wall — a twelve-foot-high metal fence — stops at the Santa Ana's perimeter and starts up again on the other side. Next to the river, a sign reads: this corridor will allow animals to safely pass along and across the Rio Grande. Just east of the sign, you can see a narrow scramble path leading from the murky river up into Texas.

The gift shop at the Santa Ana Refuge sells T-shirts and postcards of Texas wildlife .... I asked the cashier, who was at the window spying for jays, whether immigrants ever crossed through here. She raised her eyebrows, registering that I was clearly from out of town.

"Every day!" she said. "You can find stashes of water and clothes and all sorts of stuff back there," she said, motioning to the park. "But you know, they aren't after us. They aren't trying to hurt us. They just want a better life. It's mostly families and kids," she said.

"Kids?"

From the opening sentence, we sense the danger. Employing sound (wind rustling through palm fronds) and visuals (the infamous border wall 12-feet high, the Rio Grande, not two car lengths across) we are at the border of two countries, two cultures. We envision panicked children and their parents scrambling through the brush. But no sooner has the picture formed than Markham tosses us into a brief scene that sends us to the heart of the narrative — the dangers children face as they seek a new life in the States.

Instead of describing setting, Jeff Sharlet opens his book "Sweet Heaven When I Die" with a description of the book's subject, Brad Will, an anarchist journalist:

Even before he was killed by a Mexican policeman's bullet, Brad Will seemed to those who revered him more like a symbol, a living folk song, than a man.

This is what the thirty-six-year-old anarchist's friends remember: tall, skinny Brad in a black hoodie with two fists to the sky, Rocky-style, atop an East Village squat as the wrecking ball swings; Brad, his bike hoisted on his shoulder, making a getaway from cops across the rooftops of Times Square taxicabs; Brad, locked down at City Hall disguised as a giant sunflower with wired-together glasses to protest the destruction of New York's guerrilla gardens. Brad (he rarely used his surname, kept it close in case you were a cop) wore his long brown hair tied up in a knot, but for the right woman — and a lot of women seemed right to Brad — he'd let it sweep down his back almost to his ass. Jessica Lee, a journalist for a radical paper called the Indypendent, met Brad at an Earth First! action in Virginia the summer before he was killed, and although he wasn't her type she followed him away from the crowd to a waterfall, where he stripped naked, revealing thighs thick with muscle and a torso long and broad. She kept her swimsuit on. He disappeared behind the sheets of cascading water. When she ducked behind the falls, too, and he moved to kiss her, she turned away. She thought there was something missing. "Like he was incomplete, too lonely." Or maybe just tired, after a decade and a half on the front lines of a revolution that never quite happened.

In one paragraph we meet our protagonist, see our protagonist, know how he died and a bit of how he lived. The character building begins immediately. We want to know more about him, why he made those choices that led to his death by bullet. The narrative is launched.

Background beginnings

Many kinds of narratives, including personal essays, benefit from an opening that offers the reader background. This kind of lead serves as a foundation from which the rest of the tale can build. Think of it as providing the Big Picture so that the reader can understand the narrative's specific trajectory. For instance Daniel Doen Silberberg begins his essay "Blue Rain" by explaining the complex dynamic of his young marriage:

I had recently married Shoshana. We lived in a first-floor apartment in a five-story building in the Bronx. It was an odd brick structure. Concrete stairs rose up out of a small, narrow courtyard and led to an entrance door framed with Byzantine curls of wrought iron. Shoshana was finishing up at Hunter College and doing some modeling. She had a hard-to-miss dignity unique for her years, and her black, waist-length hair made her exotic. Breck shampoo was popular and well known for their models. She had caught that company's attention and many other people's too. She had caught mine, but she hadn't held it. I was like a car skidding through a stop sign. I was past her already, but she didn't know it yet. A straight-forward and happy being, she was putting together a life.

His wife is lovely, happy, and secure in their union. He is not. We read on to learn why he is ready to leave when he seems to have so much.

Likewise, Ann Beattie chooses to begin her essay "My Life with Boxes" by providing her history as a dumpster diver. We read about her past to understand her future as a box collector:

> *I HAVE dumpster dived. I have walked my dog, pretending he is just looking for a place to pee, on trash night, to see what treasures people have left curbside. I have a great chair (circa Somerville, Mass., 1978), which cost me a fortune to reupholster, that the dog did not pee on and that I did get into the trunk of my car. Pride? Now I'd worry about bedbugs, but in my idealistic youth, I just wanted free furniture.*
>
> *Now my desires are humbler. All I want is free boxes.*

In "The Blind Faith of the One-Eyed Matador," a profile of a matador who continues to taunt bulls in the ring despite that one had gouged out his left eye, Karen Russell chooses to begin by explaining bullfight basics:

> *What does the bull see as it charges the matador? What does the bull feel? This is an ancient mystery, but it seems like a safe bet that to this bull, Marques — ashy black, 5 years old, 1,100 pounds — the bullfighter is just a moving target, a shadow to catch and penetrate and rip apart. Not a man with a history, not Juan Jose Padilla, the Cyclone of Jerez, 38 years old, father of two, one of Spain's top matadors, taking on his last bull of the afternoon here at the Feria del Pilar, a hugely anticipated date on the bullfighting calendar.*

We dive into this tale of loss and resilience (some might say hubris) by looking at the matador from the bull's point of view. Our sympathies are wrenched; do we root for the bull or the matador? Do we blame the bull for the matador's loss of vision in his eye, the potential end to a storied career, his livelihood? His passion?

Open with commentary

John Jeremiah Sullivan has said that he is tired of his own voice, the ever present "I" in his storytelling, but my guess is that he's hard pressed to find readers who agree. Who better to share insights than this clever writer who through humor, research, and polished prose entertains and educates us on subjects ranging from his ancient landlord Mister Lytle to horse racing to Cuba's confused identity? Because his voice is so strong and he is so clearly in charge of the narrative journey, he often opens by establishing his point of view on whatever subject he's exploring. The lead from his essay on Walt Disney World, "You Blow My Mind. Hey Mickey":

> *Something you learn rearing kids in this young millennium is that the word "Disney" works as a verb. As in, "Do you Disney?" Or, "Are we Disneying this year?" Technically a person could use the terms in speaking about the original Disneyland, in California, but this would be an anomalous usage. One goes to Disneyland and has a great time there, probably — I've never been — but one Disneys at the Walt Disney World Resort in Florida. There's an implication of surrender to something enormous.*

He doesn't have to state his feelings about Disney; the disdain is implicit. By opening with a reference to the iconic nature of the 25,000-acre theme park that is visited by over 52 million people each year, he entices the reader to join him on the family vacation to learn how his understanding of Epcot and the Magic Kingdom and the Animal Kingdom is — or is not — altered by the experience.

Similarly, Gary Smith captures the reader's attention in "Walking His Life Away" by sharing his fascination with the Olympic race walking competition. He lays out its absurdities (walking, not running) and the intensity. We aren't entirely clear where he's headed in this profile of racewalker Albert Heppner, who committed suicide after not qualifying for the Olympics, but because Smith's drive to understand the sport is so clear, the reader, too, is curious:

> *Who knows why? In two weeks they'll light the world's largest wick, let some white birds loose and then start lining up men and women from around the earth to see who can run the fastest from here to there. The fastest down straight-aways, around curves, over barricades, through puddles, even clenching metal sticks. Who knows why? For days you'll sit in front of your TV and watch all of these races. Except for one.*
>
> *It's the oddest and longest footrace, the one that forbids the competitors to go as fast as they can — in fact, that forces them to walk. It's the one Olympic race you'll scoff at, at first. Then ignore.*
>
> *That's the race I'll be watching closest. See, I know what happened one day five months ago in the race to get to this race. I know how much can be at stake when a man takes a four-hour walk: Everything.*

Smith doesn't feign objectivity, but rather leads the reader to his perspective using detail and fact — and strong point of view, which we get to next.

TRY THIS

1. Select five published works with openings you admire. Using material from your own research and reflection, imitate the structure, the cadence, the word choice of each model. Which works the best?

2. Close your eyes. Conjure up an image from your third grade classroom. Describe that image using sensory detail, zooming out and zooming in. How could that description launch a narrative?

3. Again, close your eyes but this time imagine a scene you have observed while researching a story. What about that scene reflects the conflict? Zero in on the action that illuminates that conflict and write the lead.

4. Write a lead of each form listed above: scene; anecdote; descriptive; background; commentary.

WHAT POINT OF VIEW WILL GUIDE THE STORY?

Choosing a point of view means choosing the narrator, or narrators. In short, who will tell the story? Is the narrator invisible, an Oz-like voice through the loudspeaker? Or is the narrator the author, telling the tale through her personal lens? Perhaps the narrator is a character, or multiple characters, who mold the material to promote their vision?

Point of view forms the lens through which the reader views the subject. If the author uses first person, which means she is the narrator, we see the world through her point of view, her opinions. An Oz-like omniscient narrator is more neutral, providing us with a more sweeping look at the action; this voice is God, with insights into the past, present, and future and possibly the ability to jump in and out of characters' heads. In contrast, third person narration, telling the tale from a character's lens, is, like the author's, limited to his own experiences. He has no psychic abilities to know what others are thinking and sees only the action before him. And, like the author, the character narrator has opinions.

Different subjects require different points of view, even at the hands of the same writer. For instance, in "Walking His Life Away" Gary Smith uses first person narration. He tells the story from his, the author's, vantage point. Smith is not a racewalker, but the competition fascinates him. His fascination serves as the vehicle to explore the sport, its demands, and the role it played in the suicide of one of its masters. In "The Man Who Couldn't Read," Smith's narrator is John Corcoran, who recounts for the reader his decades of deception, the tactics he employed to hide his illiteracy as he collected academic degrees, taught school, and built a lucrative real estate business. Because we are in his head and heart, we feel his anguish, his embarrassment, and ultimately his determination to overcome the disability. (*Which was worse, he wonders now sometimes, the stinging flesh ... or the never-ending silence? That was how his fourth grade teacher had tried to cure him, by asking him to read and letting one minute of quiet pile upon the next and the next until the little boy thought he must suffocate.*) And in "A Boy and His Bot," Smith is omniscient, the invisible voiceover showing with scene and telling with exposition how one boy with a ravaged immune system not only attends school but also becomes a sportscaster through a robot:

> **The bell rang.** *Striding straight toward the robot, as it motored toward math class, was Zaaaaak-eryyyyy Yorrrrrk, best athlete in the whole school, the soon-to-graduate shortstop who'd given the thumbs-up to those long, loud and controversial introductions that Lyndon howled over the P.A. system each time a Greyhound stepped to the plate.*
> *"Hey, Zak, how's it going?"*
> *"Good, Lyndon."*

Lyndon Baty, the boy operating the robot, has an immune system so compromised he must avoid crowds, which means he attends classes and hangs with his peers through technology. Smith's narrator is the camera, showing how Lyndon's life-through-a-bot works, following the robot through his day at school.

In certain kinds of tales, choosing the narrator is easy. A memoir requires first person. It is, after all, the author's journey, the author's opinion of the events she has lived. Likewise a personal essay employs the "I" since a personal essay is an exercise in self-exploration — of an idea, an experience, a perception. Who else but the author could narrate? Yet, as Gary Smith proves, a variety of options are at the ready for other kinds of tales.

Omniscient point of view

One form of omniscient narrator, that all-knowing, all-seeing storyteller looking down from above, is distant, a neutral guide who has no agenda other than to show the scenes and explain the facts. The goal is to let the reader arrive at his own conclusion without being guided by the narrator's opinion. This kind of omniscient voice relays the story as he observes it. The characters on the page are like characters on a screen; the reader sees them in action but doesn't have access to their internal thoughts. For example, here's the lead to Lenny Bernstein's Washington Post story about children surviving a tornado in Oklahoma:

> *It was the regular tornado drill, the one Alexander Ghassimi and other children in Moore, Okla., learn in school: Get to an interior hallway, get down, cover up. Then a teacher who had been watching the progress of Monday's*

storm outside Plaza Towers Elementary School came tearing down the hall, yelling to move as many children as possible into the girls' bathroom, and 11-year-old Alexander knew this was no ordinary tornado.

"We were in the hallway doing our procedure," Alexander said. " 'Get down. Put your hands over your head.' "

Perhaps 70 or 80 children jammed into the bathroom .... When the tornado hit, [some teachers] threw themselves on top of the children.

We see the children, hear the teacher shrieking. We know what 11-year-old Alexander is thinking only because he tells us. The distant omniscient narrator is like a camera — recording only what he sees and hears.

Yet other omniscient storytellers, such as Gary Smith in "A Boy and his Bot," exercise more power, shirking that objective tone in favor of a sharper, more defined voice. While the writer isn't physically present, his voice makes his point of view, his opinion of the subject, clear as a quartz crystal. Writing about Lyndon Baty's efforts to stay plugged into school, friends, and sportscasting through his robot, Smith's tone is warm, approving:

INCOMING CALL FROM....

The robot paused, as if it were considering the multitudes who might be dialing in to incarnate it. Lyndon, it finally declared.

A small camera flipped up at the robot's crown. White headlights flashed at its base, then blue and orange lights blinked on around its monitor. The robot disengaged from its charging station and began rolling toward a doorway.

A bell rang. The bot gathered speed lest it be late for its ninth-grade science class.

Coach Lawson approached the robot and grinned. He's a history teacher and baseball coach at a 68-student high school in Knox City, Texas, but you can't fool folks. He's still what he once was: a rodeo clown. He lifted a hand and high-fived the bot.

A voice came from its two speakers. "What time do I need to be at the game on Saturday, Coach?"

"One o'clock start," said Coach Lawson.

"Thanks!" said the bot.

Coach Lawson resisted the urge, this time, to cover the robot's camera lens with a sticky note. He smiled and watched the voice of yourrrrr Knox City Greyyyyy-hounnnnnds! whir down the hall.

Through his choice of images — the bot zipping down a school hall, the coach high-fiving the contraption, the voice asking about practice — Smith's narrator reveals humor and good will and not a little awe of the scene before him.

Another kind of omniscient narrator flexes even more muscle by zipping in and out of a character's head, or multiple characters' heads. This narrator has the power to read minds and understand motivation, providing the reader with the third person point of view.

Third person point of view

Tom Wolfe was surely not the first nonfiction writer to present scenes through the eyes of a character, but he was among the loudest advocates of employing the literary device in true stories. Third person point of view, he wrote in his introduction to the anthology "The New Journalism," "gives the reader the feeling of being inside the character's mind and experiencing the emotional reality of the scene he is experiencing."

In this way, third person narration allows the reader a deeper intimacy with the character, a stronger understanding of his dreams and fears. Through telling the aftermath of the Newtown shootings through the point of view of Mark Barden, the father of one of the 20 first graders killed on that December morning at Sandy Hook Elementary, Eli Saslow gives us access into the unfathomable in his story "After Newtown Shooting, Mourning Parents Enter into the Lonely Quiet":

> It sometimes felt to Mark in these moments like his grief was still deepening, like the worst was yet to come. After the gunfire, the funerals, the NRA protests and the congressional debates, they were finally coming into the lonely quiet. They were coming to the truth of what Newtown would become. Would it be the transformative moment in American gun policy that, in those first days, so many had promised? Or another Columbine, Virginia Tech, Gabby Giffords, Aurora — one more proper noun added to an ever-growing list? The FBI had closed its temporary Newtown office. Politicians in Washington were moving on to other issues. Scariest of all to Mark, he was starting to forget little things, too, losing pieces of Daniel to the recesses of his mind, so he had started a journal to log memories before they disappeared.

The effect is powerful. By feeling Mark Barden's grief, not just seeing it, the reader's empathy is deepened, the reading experience more profound.

Unlike fiction writers, who can make up what their characters think, nonfiction writers like Wolfe and Saslow, have to ask. And ask. Few people will respond in the detail required to recreate internal dialogue, which means the writer must press and probe to extract the coveted thoughts. It's a bit easier in immersion projects in which the writer is camped out over a long period, such as Katherine Boo's reporting in the Mumbai slum for her book "Behind the Beautiful Forevers." The writer observes a scene and can within hours, or even minutes, ask the subject what he or she was thinking. Yet even asking people to relive a recent moment requires writers to ask a litany of questions to elicit the necessary detail. Katherine Boo asked so many questions about the same moments that one of her teenage subjects wondered if she were dim-witted.

And sometimes, no matter how many questions you ask, you may still not get the detail you need. While researching a story about the problem with knees, I interviewed the man with the most famous leg joints in Boston: Bruins legend Bobby Orr. "What were you thinking when you stepped on the ice that first minute of that infamous Black Hawks game?" I asked.

"I don't know," he said. "It was a long time ago."

And so I pressed on, asking him the same question in multiple ways, from multiple angles about the collapse of his knee that night on Chicago ice, but he simply did not remember, or preferred not to remember. Fortunately, one of his surgeons *did* recall the specifics of Orr's knees. Instead of Bobby Orr narrating scenes, his surgeon, Dennis Griffin, did the honors. The story opens with Griffin preparing to operate on Orr's left knee for the fifth time:

Out Orr went under anesthesia, and just as he was sliced open, the doctor from Buffalo arrived and greeted the surgical team. Ugh, thought Dennis Griffin, then a young resident studying under Carter Rowe, as his eyes followed the visiting doctor's. The cartilage encasing Orr's bones was a dingy white, not a healthy creamy white, and instead of being smooth, it was as rough as a cobblestone street. Spurs littered the bone. And the two shock-absorbing cartilages between the leg bones were gone, removed during earlier operations. The left knee of 27-year-old Bobby Orr looked to Griffin like an elderly man's, ready for replacement.

Dennis Griffin's reactions and thoughts add dimension, insight that only the surgeon would have. Instead of just fact we get emotion.

The longer the piece, the more complicated the narrative, the more points of view the story can accommodate. In Tom Wolfe's "The Angels," an excerpt from his book "The Right Stuff," he tells the story of NASA training through the point of view of both an astronaut-in-training and the astronaut's wife. Tracy Kidder pops into the heads of the homeowners, the architect, and the builder in his book "House" — how else could he show through scene the personality conflicts and various snafus that are a part of every building project?

Katherine Boo shares the internal monologue and desires of multiple residents of the Annawadi slums, letting the children and their parents show what it takes to survive the corruption and poverty of modern day Mumbai. Interestingly, Boo has been criticized for not including herself in her narratives, that her point of view is so clear that she should be physically present. She, however, insists not. In an interview with her editor that is posted on her website, Boo said, "I long ago decided I didn't want to be one of those nonfiction writers who go on about themselves. When you get to the last pages of 'Behind the Beautiful Forevers,' I don't want you to think about me sitting beside Abdul in that little garbage truck. I want you to be thinking about Abdul."

First person point of view

Katherine Boo chooses to use "the eye" rather than "the I," but for other writers, the only option is to employ the latter. Who else but Ryan Van Meter can make sense of his childhood confusion, of feeling different? By definition memoir is the recreation of memory, of a writer examining an element of his or her life and leading the reader to an insight about the human condition. That element has conflict at its heart, a challenge to overcome — addiction, abandonment, scaling high peaks, living abroad, coping with disease. What is often forgotten, though, is that in memoir there are two narrators — the older wiser narrator reflecting on the younger narrator as she works her way through confusing or troubled times. "I now, I then," as Virginia Woolf said.

Ann Patchett was devastated when her friend, writer Lucy Grealy, died at 39 of a heroin overdose and, like many writers, turned to her craft to understand the death, but more important, their relationship. Lucy was a complicated friend, a complicated human. Diagnosed with cancer at age 9, she had had treatments that removed part of her face, and then undergone years of surgeries to rebuild her face. Bright and talented, loving and lively, she was an accomplished poet and memoirist in her own right, the author of "Autobiography of a Face." But she could also be jealous and selfish and occasionally hurtful. In "Truth & Beauty: A Friendship," Patchett tackles her own memories of their decades-long friendship, the competition between two writers, the love, the tension, the bond. Narrator Patchett is older, wiser as she plumbs the past of her younger self:

> I got a note from Lucy not long after receiving my acceptance letter from the Iowa Writers' Workshop. She said that initially when she heard I had gotten into the workshop she was sorry, because she had wanted to be the only student there from Sarah Lawrence. But then our mutual friend Jono Wilks had told her that I was going up early to find housing, and if this was the case, would I find a place for her as well?... I sat at the kitchen table and looked at her handwriting, which seemed oddly scrawny and uncertain, like a note on a birthday card from an elderly aunt. I had never seen her writing before, and certainly these were the only words she had ever addressed to me. While Lucy and I would later revise our personal history to say we had been friends since we met as freshmen, just for the pleasure of adding a few more years to the tally, the truth was we did not know each other at all in college. Or the truth was that I knew her and she did not know me. Even at Sarah Lawrence ... everyone knew Lucy and

everyone knew her story: she had had a Ewing's sarcoma at the age of nine, had lived through five years of the most brutal radiation and chemotherapy, and then undergone a series of reconstructive surgeries that were largely unsuccessful. The drama of her life, combined with her reputation for being the smartest student in all of her classes, made her the campus mascot, the favorite pet in her dirty jeans and oversized Irish sweaters.

Ann-Then is eager for Lucy's friendship. She does what is asked — finds an apartment — without a lot of reflection. In contrast, Ann-Now, the narrator, is ruminative, analyzing Lucy's handwriting, her lack of college identity compared to Lucy's celebrity, the reason for her celebrity. She adds details that she learned later, such as how they revised their history, claiming that they were friends in college, "just for the pleasure of adding a few more years to the tally." Without the reflection that comes with time and distance, the past would be merely action. With reflection, the narrator-now provides context and meaning.

In addition to mining the meaning of one's own life and thoughts, the "I" can also be a vehicle to analyze the events and lives of others. Call it an internal approach to the external. Kate Bolick reflected on her decades of dating as a launch pad to examine why more women, like her, choose to stay single. Cynthia Gorney based a story on the pros and cons of hormone replacement therapy on the deep depression she suffered during the depths of menopause. Tom Bissell explored the Vietnam War and its impact on the soldiers and their families through visiting the country with his father, a Vietnam veteran. Bissell sensed that if he had a better understanding of the war, he'd have a better understanding of his father, who could be loving one minute and brutally cruel the next. Bissell opens his essay "War Wounds" by weaving the external and internal together:

In the beginning was the war. Many children of Vietnam veterans, when they look back on their adolescence, feel this with appropriately biblical conviction. In the beginning was the war. It sits there, in our fathers' pasts, a dying star that annihilates anything that strays too close. For the growing-up children of many vets the war's remoteness was all but impossible to gauge because it had happened pre-you, before you had come to grasp the sheer accident of your own placement in time, before you recognized that your reality — your bedroom, your toys and comic books — had nothing to do with the reality of your father. Despite its remoteness, however, the war's aftereffects were inescapably intimate. At every meal Vietnam sat down, invisibly, with our families.

Using oneself as a literary device works when one's own experience enhances the understanding of the topic. Any writer could tackle the impact of PTSD on children of Vietnam vets through interviews and research, but the son of a

Vietnam vet can bring the emotional intelligence and firsthand observations of the lingering legacy of the Southeast Asian conflict.

Second person point of view

In second person, the author addresses the reader as "you." It is a conversation between writer and reader, a device that aims to create a bond, a sense of intimacy. Second person asks the reader to suspend disbelief and inhabit the story.

For instance, in "Bret, Unbroken," Steve Friedman profiles a middle-aged man who suffered brain and body injuries so severe from a childhood accident that few thought he would survive, let alone talk or walk, or finish high school, hold down a job, maintain an apartment — and compete in running races. Instead of an omniscient narrator reciting Bret Dunlap's history and

CHALLENGING CHOICES

Cynthia Gorney: Who? Me?

As a narrative journalist, Cynthia Gorney is often faced with the dilemma of whether or not she should be physically present in a story, whether she is the "eye" or the "I," and if the latter, how much should she invade the story's space. Does she hover at every junction or does she dip in only when absolutely necessary? Through decades of wrestling with the "I," she has arrived at a formula:

The first factor is how the publication tends to use first person as a narrative device. At The New Yorker, I, the person, doesn't exist. I'm merely a narrative device. "The first time I met him." "He told me." The "I" is strictly grammatical.

The second is how what I do might matter to the story. I'm a dedicated lap swimmer, but in my profile of Natalie Coughlin the reader doesn't know anything about me except that I follow Natalie around during an international swim championship. I'm not a character. But in one paragraph, a rumination in the center of the story, I talk about how fascinated people are with her swimming, that I am a dedicated lap swimmer and like researchers, I am fascinated with how complicated swimming is. That I'm fascinated by bodies and water is all you know about me. The writer uses a specific character trait that is useful to the reader's understanding.

I did a piece on a woman who runs a website for parents of Marines. She and I bonded over the phone, and I moved into her house for a week. We had similar personalities. We had sons the same ages. Mine was not deployed. I thought that was relevant to the story to show why she would open herself and her house up. She wanted people like me to understand what it was like to think all the time about a son at war.

The third factor is if your experience is the narrative of the story. In my New York Times Magazine piece on the conflict about hormone replacement therapy, sharing my experience was essential. But even then, you temper what you say. There's a very narrow slice of which part of yourself you write about.

observing him working and running, Friedman chose a second person narrator. This point of view — *If only you could have explained to people all you knew — about farming and animals and your cat and the designer chickens you planned to breed, about military history, and how you knew Latin and German, how you longed for a woman's touch...* allows the reader to lodge inside Bret Dunlap's head. Since Dunlap's injuries prevent him from articulating his thoughts fluidly enough to carry a narrative, second person narration allows the writer to tell the story for him.

> *You bought a new pair of shoes, the kind with the big N on them. You decided you had to strengthen the right side of your body. To do that, you needed to go to the gym. You took some of the money you had been saving and you applied for a membership at a local health club, and when you pulled out your credit card and asked if the club accepted it, the guy behind the desk — a big, muscle-bound guy — looked you up and down, at your short jeans and your old jacket and at the smile frozen on your face, and he said, "Well, sure, if it's your card," and you turned and left. But you didn't quit. Failure isn't getting knocked down. You joined Anytime Fitness, in downtown Rhinelander, and your first time there — after your 7 a.m. to 3 p.m. shift at the warehouse — the manager showed you around and explained the machines and you nodded, and you got on one of the treadmills.*

While second person point of view can be an effective tool to use from start to finish, as "Bret, Unbroken" proves, it is often hard to sustain. Consequently, writers often use it more sparingly, either in the lead (to lure in the reader) or in patches (to indicate a change in perspective.) For instance, Joe Wilkins' narration is first person for the bulk of his essay "Out West: Growing Up Hard," but weaves in chunks of second person narration, which ask the reader to assume the narrator's mantle. In the case of the Wilkins essay, it means the reader feels the metal of the gun, the crunch of dry prairie grass, elements of Wilkins' hardscrabble childhood:

> *NOW YOU'RE THIRTEEN, old enough to hunt by yourself, so you load an old, bolt-action .22 with shells. You walk north. There is little wind, the sun a white hole in the sky. Beneath your boots the bones of dry grass bend and crack. You feel good about this. Prairie dogs are bad for the fields. They spread disease. A sheep will snap a front leg in a doghole. Your father is dead, your grandfather is old, and you tell yourself you are just doing what a man does. You are taking care of the fields, keeping the stock safe. You tell yourself all kinds of things.*

The reader and Wilkins are one, feeling the same drama, the same confusion. Who wouldn't keep reading?

TRY THIS

1. Think back to a disagreement you had with a relative. Write the scene from your point of view. Now call your relative and find out what he or she was thinking during the argument. Why did he or she feel that way? Plumb for anecdotes. For instance, if you argued that all shoreline should be accessible to the public, find out why your aunt, uncle, or cousin believed otherwise. Ask if she has had any personal experiences that helped form the opinion. Now write the scene from your relative's perspective, weaving in the background as internal monologue.

2. Envision a tension-filled ride you once had in a car. We've all disagreed about directions, or where to stop for lunch, or when to change the music. Write the scene from a variety of perspectives. First, distant, objective omniscient. Then first person — your point of view. Then third person — from another rider's point of view. For the heck of it, try second person, as if you are writing a letter to an outside party, trying to make her understand what you are feeling and thinking.

WHO ARE THE CHARACTERS?

Character is story. It drives the action, the scene, the plot. We read to see how characters develop, change, learn from an experience. And by character we don't mean source, the one-dimensional talking head you find in news stories. He said. She said. A name (Andrea Egmont) followed by a title (director of Newburyport Youth Services). By character we mean a fully developed, multidimensional, flawed, engaging, complicated, contradictory human on the page.

As in fiction, true stories have major and minor characters; not every person on the page deserves a full court press. The major characters, the stars of the show, the protagonists for whom we root, and the antagonists, whose demise we cheer, earn the attention, the detail. The minor characters are more flat, deserving of a line or two of description, just enough to place them but not enough to overwhelm.

The question, then, is who deserves the spotlight?

A starting point is length. If you're writing an 800-word essay, you don't have room to develop more than one major character. That character could be the narrator exploring how an event or condition challenged and changed her (Bonnie Rough pondered in her New York Times "Modern Love" essay whether she, a carrier of a rare genetic disorder, should bear children) or how an event or condition challenged and changed someone else (GQ writer Chris Heath examines in a profile of the actor James Gandolfini how the actor evolved from a New Jersey kid to the star of "The Sopranos").

Longer, more intricate narratives can accommodate multiple rounded characters. As she developed her Modern Love essay into a book, Rough recognized the role other members of her family played in her reproductive deliberations, particularly her grandfather, who suffered from hypohidrotic ectodermal dysplasia (HED), and her mother, who like Rough, is a carrier of HED. Ridiculed as a child for his high forehead, thin hair, and tiny pointed teeth, the grandfather grew up isolated. Even his sisters didn't want to be seen with him. As an adult, he was a risk taker, a gambler, and a liar, who lost his life savings and his family. Rough's mother witnessed the demise and then, suspecting but not knowing for certain that she was a carrier, passed the disease on to her only son, Rough's younger brother. Through exhaustive research and interviews, Rough gathered enough details of her grandfather and her mother's experience to write chapters from their points of view, making them living, breathing characters with insights, motivations, and flaws.

Think of characters that have jumped off the page. Perry Smith of "In Cold Blood," the chain-smoking murderer with his short legs, tiny feet, and fantasies of buried treasure. Fred Brown, the Piney native in John McPhee's "Pine Barrens" who eats raw onion and pork chops in the morning wearing only his underwear and a pair of shoes. Just how Capote and McPhee made these guys come alive on the page doesn't boil down to one, or even two, secret ingredients. Instead, master storytellers dispatch a rich array of devices to create memorable personalities.

Description

Creating a life force requires physical description. The reader needs to know enough bodily attributes to conjure up an image. The success of that image, however, depends on avoiding the ordinary details that could describe a wide swath of human kind (tall with brown hair and a big nose) and instead zeroing in on defining characteristics. The long-tapered fingers of the violinist? The retired rugby player's smushed nose? Susan Orlean pens memorable physical descriptions, isolating just the right features and employing just the right metaphors. Meet "The Orchid Thief"'s main character:

> John Laroche is a tall guy, skinny as a stick, pale-eyed, slouch-shouldered, and sharply handsome, in spite of the fact that he is missing all his front teeth. He has the posture of al dente spaghetti and the nervous intensity of someone who plays a lot of video games. Laroche is thirty-six years old. Until recently he was employed by the Seminole Tribe of Florida, setting up a plant nursery and an orchid-propagation laboratory on the tribe's reservation in Hollywood, Florida.

But if the goal is to make the person stand out on the page, we need other elements besides slouch-shouldered and pale eyes. We need movement. By showing a person in action and providing some key background facts, the reader conjures up a more complete image. Does she walk with the bounce of a preschooler or the precision of a ballerina? Does he limp from an old football injury? Does he pour the brandy as carefully as a mother measures cough syrup? In Skip Hollandsworth's opening to "The Last Ride of Cowboy Bob," we watch Peggy Jo Tallas perform her morning routine:

PEGGY JO TALLAS WAS, BY ALL ACCOUNTS, the classic good-hearted Texas woman. For much of her adult life, she lived with her ailing mother in a small apartment in the Dallas suburbs. Every morning, after waking up and making her bed, always taking the time to smooth out all the wrinkles in the sheets with her hands, she'd walk into her mother's bedroom. She'd wrap a robe around her mother's shoulders, lead her to the kitchen, fix her cereal, and lay out her pills. For a few minutes, the two of them would sit at the table, making small talk. Peggy Jo, who didn't like to eat until later in the day, would often smoke a cigarette and drink Pepsi out of a coffee cup. Then, after her mother was finished eating, Peggy Jo would gently guide her back to her bedroom, prop a pillow behind her head, set a glass of tap water and her romance novel on the side table, and walk back into her own room to get dressed.

Usually, she liked wearing khaki pants, a simple blouse, and loafers. But on a lovely morning in May 1991, Peggy Jo, who was then 46 years old, decided to wear something different. She walked over to her dresser, the top of which held a few small glass sculptures of dolphins with iridescent eyes that she had been collecting off and on for more than a decade. She opened one of the lower drawers and pulled out a pair of men's pants and a dark men's shirt. From her closet, she grabbed a men's brown leather jacket that she kept on a hanger. She then reached for a Styrofoam mannequin's head that was on a shelf in the closet. A fake beard was pinned to it and on top was a white cowboy hat.

We see a middle aged woman solicitous of her mother, a woman who smokes cigarettes and drinks Pepsi for breakfast, who prefers khakis and simple blouses but on this day dresses as a cowboy. The ordinary turns extraordinary. Soon we read that when she leaves the house, she'll rob a bank. But before we get to that hook we have an image of a thoughtful daughter performing mundane morning tasks before she commits a felony. Add all the details together and we have a portrait of a complicated woman whose impact reaches far beyond her mother's bedside. As Aristotle said, "The whole is greater than the sum of its parts."

Anecdotes

Readers are demanding; they want proof of every statement. An anecdote goes a long way in providing the specifics that support a point the writer strives to make about a character. Instead of telling the reader that Dr. Paul Farmer, the central character in "Mountains Beyond Mountains," has a great sense of humor, Tracy Kidder shows Farmer's silly side by describing him once laughing so hard that he fell on his back, his legs slicing the air like scissors. Not exactly the image you'd expect from a Harvard doc who has devoted his life to providing medical care to the world's poor. The humor, it turns out, is a trait that has endeared Farmer to not only his patients, but also his medical colleagues, one of whom shared the anecdote.

Likewise, instead of just stating that orchid collector John Laroche is odd, Susan Orlean proves it with an anecdote from his childhood:

> *Laroche strikes many people as eccentric. The Seminoles, for instance, have two nicknames for him: Troublemaker and Crazy White Man. Once, When Laroche was telling me about his childhood, he remarked, "Boy, I sure was a weird little kid." For as long as he can remember he has been exceptionally passionate and driven. When he was about nine or ten, his parents said he could pick out a pet. He decided to get a little turtle. Then he asked for ten more little turtles. Then he decided he wanted to breed the turtles, and then he started selling turtles to other kids, and then he could think of nothing but turtles, and then decided that his life wasn't worth living unless he could collect one of every single turtle species known to mankind, including one of those sofa-sized tortoises from the Galapagos.*

Anecdotes are also useful in rounding out a personality. While it is easier to paint someone in one tone, on the page as in life few people are either pure goodness or pure evil. Stories of past actions go a long way in showing multiple layers. For instance, when Ben Montgomery was researching his series "For Their Own Good" about abuse at the Florida School for Boys, he was desperate to find some redeeming features for Troy Tidwell, the one-armed guard accused of beating boys senseless. Tidwell refused to talk. His granddaughter, however, shared some memories with Montgomery that, if not sanitizing, at least showed a human side:

> *Tidwell's granddaughter, Tiffany Pippin, says her family doubts the stories. They know a man who danced the fox-trot on Friday nights, who took his grandchildren fishing, who flirted with the ladies behind the perfume counter at the mall in Dothan, Ala. They know a man who always dressed sharp before*

*he left the house and sat quiet in the First Baptist Church on Sunday mornings.
"He's a good man," says Pippin, 29. "He loved his wife. He never beat his
children."*

*Tidwell's family lived in Bascom, a tiny town north of Marianna, Pippin
says. His father died when he was young. When Troy Tidwell was 6, he played
with his father's shotgun. He leaned on the barrel and accidentally fired the
gun, which severed his left arm.*

*He's self-conscious about it and sits with his arm facing the wall when the
family goes out to dinner. Pippin says her grandfather has worked hard his
whole life to overcome the handicap, and after more than 40 years at the school
he deserves a peaceful retirement. That's why the allegations burn.*

While the men who claim they retain scars from Tidwell's strap may not find
these stories of a loving grandfather comforting, the anecdotes provide the reader
with a slice of the guard's humanity, enough to recognize the complexity within
us all.

Speech

How a person speaks — her choice of words, phrases, clichés, inflection, restraint,
or lack of restraint — all contribute to building character. Too often we read
stories in which each character sounds the same. Quotes and dialogue are sani-
tized, rearranged to sound crisp and articulate. In truth, how many of us can
string together a verbal diatribe of coherent sentences?

Since we can't invent dialogue to reveal character, our mission as true storytellers is to capture people as they really sound. In most cases that may mean
quick snatches of dialogue or short quotes. In "Fourth State of Matter," Jo Ann
Beard shows the humor of and the friendship she shares with her friend and colleague through mere snippets of conversation.

*Christoph Goertz. He's hip in a professorial, cardigan/jeans kind of way. He's
tall and lanky and white-haired, forty-seven years old, with an elegant trace
of accent from his native Germany. He has a great dog, a giant black outlaw
named Mica, who runs through the streets of Iowa City at night, inspecting
garbage cans. She's big and friendly but a bad judge of character, and frequently runs right into the arms of the dogcatcher. Chris is always bailing
her out.*

"They don't understand dogs," he says.

*I spend more time with Chris than I ever did with my husband. The
morning I told him I was being dumped he was genuinely perplexed. "He's
leaving you?" he asked.*

And then there's accent. Tom Wolfe captured film director Otto Preminger's Austrian in "Radical Chic" through language. "I geeve a t'ousand dollars!" Preminger told the Black Panthers at the Park Avenue Fundraiser at the heart of Wolfe's satire on liberal causes of the 1960s. Chris Heath chose a different route in his profile of the late actor James Gandolfini, whose New Jersey accent in life and in his signature role as Tony Soprano begged attention. Instead of sounding out the accent through spelling (or misspelling), Heath just let Gandolfini speak for himself. With a little help from Heath's observations, we can hear the New Jersey in the New Jersey native:

> When I ask him something moronic about this newfound preference for grilled fish, he erupts with polite exasperation, the way he will whenever anything seems too personal or embarrassing or disrespectful or trivial. "Oh, who gives a fuck about any of this?" he asks cheerfully, but in a way — his eyes fixing on you, then darting about as the muscles around his mouth move through a repertoire of expressions — that unavoidably reminds you of Tony Soprano. "Seriously?"

A character's voice can also be captured from written prose. Letters, e-mail, blog posts, book scribbles, however thoughts are shared on the page or screen. While Mister Lytle, John Jeremiah Sullivan's 92-year-old erudite landlord, was eminently quotable, uttering phrases such as "Vanity has no claim on me," a passage from a letter he wrote Sullivan speaks to his very essence:

> "Now that I have come to live in the sense of eternity, I rarely know the correct date, and the weather informs me of the day's advance, but I believe it is late August," and went on to say, "I'm presuming you will live with me here."

Facebook, too, provides ample excerpts of a character's voice. Ian Shapira based an entire story on the Facebook postings of a new mom, from pre-delivery to the harrowing days following the birth in which she chronicled her failing health:

> I'm starting to go a bit stircrazy in our house. So many of you have been so generous in offering to cook, run errands, etc. But what I'd really love now is just some old-fashioned company. I can't stay up or talk long, but I would love to see you for 30 minutes this weekend or next week ....

The frustration in her voice is palpable, the phrasing informal, friendly. We can identify with that voice, making the ending, her death, that much more tragic.

Possessions

"Status life" is Tom Wolfe's phrase for possessions, a key ingredient he uses in both fiction and nonfiction to define his characters. The material things with which people surround themselves showcase their priorities, their lifestyle, their personalities. Wolfe is relentless with specifics. The "blue-gray nailhead worsted suit, custom-tailored in England for $1,800, two-button, single-breasted, with ordinary notched lapels. On Wall Street double-breasted suits and peaked lapels were considered a bit sharp, a bit too Garment District." The "round table with about eight hundred dollars' worth of flowered cotton fabric from Laura Ashley hanging to the floor and a piece of beveled glass costing $280 covering the top." When Wolfe wants to hammer in a point, he'll repeat specific features:

> *It was a big, wide room with Chinese yellow walls and white moldings, sconces, pier-glass mirrors, a portrait of Felicia reclining on a summer chaise, and at the far end, where Felicia was standing, a pair of grand pianos. A pair of them; the two pianos were standing back to back, with the tops down and their bellies swooping out. On top of both pianos was a regular flotilla of family photographs in silver frames, the kind of pictures that stand straight up thanks to little velvet- or moiré-covered buttresses in the back, the kind that decorators in New York recommend to give a living room a homelike, lived-in touch.*

Two grand pianos! Both with a flotilla of silver-framed family photographs! The plethora of status life details plants an image of Leonard and Felicia Bernstein's taste and luxury living in this excerpt from "Radical Chic," Wolfe's account of the New York elite wooing the Black Panthers.

Likewise, possessions can paint portraits of struggle. Go back to Dickens and his reports of the tattered clothes and cold fireplaces of the London poor to see the role possession played in storytelling. Over a century later, "Invisible Child" by Andrea Elliott shows the plight of homeless children through chronicling a year in the life of 12-year-old Dasani. We see her care for her baby sister in the squalor of their room in the shelter. We see her in the subway, dressed in a hand-me-down Patagonia jacket and purple Uggs.

> *She wakes to the sound of breathing. The smaller children lie tangled beside her, their chests rising and falling under winter coats and wool blankets. A few feet away, their mother and father sleep near the mop bucket they use as a toilet. Two other children share a mattress by the rotting wall where the mice live, opposite the baby, whose crib is warmed by a hair dryer perched on a milk crate.*

With details such as a bucket for a toilet and coats for blankets, the reader is saturated in proof of Dasani's dire circumstances.

WEB CHOICES

Filmmaker Stephen Maing on building character

When New York City council speaker Christine Quinn was the leading candidate for NYC mayor, Quinn agreed to allow a New York Times video team to shadow her campaign. For both Quinn and The Times, a documentary would chronicle an historic ascension; if elected, she would be the first woman, let alone the first openly gay woman, to rule New York from City Hall. But by early summer of 2013 when Stephen Maing, an independent filmmaker, joined the video crew, her campaign was unraveling. Dogged by external factors (decisions to extend mayoral term limits, to not eliminate Central Park carriage rides) as well as internal (an inability to separate herself from the incumbent, Mayor Michael Bloomberg, to reflect on voter animosity) she found herself in third place on primary night. Instead of recording history and analyzing the city's politics, as many of the journalists on his team envisioned, Maing saw their job instead as illuminating her character. Just how he and his team achieved this task in "Hers to Lose" was a combination of selecting key moments, structuring those key moments, and scrutinizing just what those key moments meant. Says Maing:

What caught my attention is that she is constantly talking. She's in control of her identity, her messaging. And so the first thing I scanned the material for were moments when she lost control. I scanned material for times when she wasn't talking, when an interview question gave her pause. The moments of intimacy and reflection were in the silences. That was a big discovery for me.

Her smile was painful in one sense. The camera is on and the smile comes out. It really turned me off. I got interested in the moments ramping up to the plastic smile and the moments ramping out of it. She's a polarizing figure — she's a female candidate, openly gay — and there was an awkwardness of reconciling some of the choices she made as a politician. We needed to find a way to represent that she was an individual who had not come to terms with how the public saw her. One analogy was her smile. That was a helpful way to cue the viewer to approach the things she was saying with a more layered reading.

We needed to linger, to live in her face. In the last interview I caught three different passes on her face. That is a useful way to punctuate an idea, and in this case the entire film.

For me, there was no single logical narrative for what actually was the cause for her campaign to fail. It was a fluid number of missteps and failures. The film needed to land the distinct moments in her campaign.

There's that scene in the car in which she's unwilling to talk about term limits (after a man at a campaign stop had blasted her for voting to extend them), which shows her inability to see how she comes across. This is an important moment. It is denial, which is at the crux of why she lost. To say I don't know is not a good enough answer. To be shocked reflects a critical lack of reflection.

If this was going to come out after she lost, we couldn't play out the win or lose suspense. Out front this was a story about someone who lost but could have been mayor. We would have to bookend the film with the loss and start with the juxtaposition of hopefulness in early interviews with the moment she loses. This is a portrait considering the peaks and valleys in this person's life. What are the factors that played into her choices?

I'm not interested in giving people concrete takeaways. I wanted to create a level of intimacy that hadn't been seen with her, to create moments that could be interpreted in multiple ways. Because she let the camera in, she lets us see her as a human being navigating a complex situation that she had created for herself.

This isn't a story about politics. It is a film about human nature. You're trying to understand one kernel of truth about a person.

TRY THIS

1. Paint a portrait of yourself by listing: 3 defining physical traits; 3 defining anecdotes; 3 phrases you often use; 3 material possessions that show your priorities. Now write this portrait in third person point of view — as if you were describing yourself in a narrative. Choose only the most telling details.

2. Watch "Hers to Lose." What are Christina Quinn's defining physical features? Her speech patterns? What do her clothes, her home say about her? What defining anecdotes can you glean from watching her interact with her staff, the public, and the interviewers? Paint her on the page as if you were writing a story about her.

WHAT IS THE SETTING?

During the years that my colleague Tom Haines was a travel writer for The Boston Globe, he realized that his main mission in telling stories about an Arctic island or a Moroccan market was not to wax eloquently about shimmering ice flows or bins of couscous, but instead to unearth the psychological tension of place. He loves that phrase. I love that phrase. It sums up brilliantly the role of setting. Whether place is merely a backdrop for action or is an integral part of plot and theme, the goals are the same: to provide the context and sensory detail that will spark an image in the reader's mind and move the narrative forward.

The first mission is to decide the setting's dominance. If its role is primarily background — the canvas on which the characters speak and move — its job is to provide a sense of time and geography, a few specifics to trigger an image. For instance, Ryan Van Meter's selection of setting particulars is sparse in his essay "Cherry Bars" but enough to place the reader at the moment:

We're lying on a blanket in the park, eating the cherry bars my grandma baked this afternoon and singing along to the whine of Simon and Garfunkel on my battery-operated tape player. It's summer 1992, we're seventeen. A heavy tree stretches over us, leaves so dense most of the sunlight is blotted out and can't reach our blanket.

We know just enough to envision two teenagers lying under a leafy tree on a summer afternoon, listening to pop ballads, and eating gooey sweets. That's all we need. The heart of the action is between the characters and the setting is nothing more than framework.

In contrast, setting may play a pivotal role. It could be *the* source of narrative tension. I think of "Killing Libby," Mark Levine's tale of a Montana town poisoned by exposure to asbestos. The setting — the mines, the industrial plant, the infected air hovering over the town — is the conflict. Or I think of Tom Haines' "Facing Famine," a tale of a land unable to sustain life. He shows us a wide view of the Ethiopian valley, the rocky road, the tattered town. And then he zooms in close when introducing character:

> *Travel often approaches boundaries of wealth and health. But what does it feel like to cross those boundaries and enter a place that is, everywhere, collapsing? What comes from knowing people who, with an empty grain basket or a thinning goat, edge closer to death?*
>
> *The route led first to Addis Ababa, a highland capital, then east and south, down into rolling stretches of the Great Rift Valley. In the tattered town of Ogolcho, Berhanu Muse, a local irrigation specialist, agreed to serve as translator and guide.*
>
> *A narrow road of rock headed south, through one village, then another, for one hour, then two.*
>
> *In late afternoon, before evening wind lifted dirt from north to south, east to west, we stopped and parked near a hilltop. A man and woman collected grain from a tall stick bin on the corner of their rectangular plot of land.*
>
> *Gebi Egato offered his hand from his perch inside the bin. Halima, his wife, smiled warmly, then carried a half-filled sack toward the family's low, round hut. Abdo, a 3-year-old with determined eyes, barreled out the door.*
>
> *I asked if we could stay.*
>
> *"Welcome," Gebi said.*

I think of Rebecca Solnit's Icelandic surroundings in her essay "Summer in the Far North." The arctic setting is the story, the heart of the essay's central question: what can one learn from living in the land of light and ice? She establishes place by telling us:

*The far north is an unearthly earth, where much of what those of us in temper-
ate zones were told is universal is not true. Everyone walks on water, which is a
solid. In winter, you can build palaces out of it, or houses out of snow. Ice is
blue. Snow insulates. Water crystallizes into floating mountains that destroy
whatever collides with them. Many other things turn hard as rock in the cold.
Nothing decays, and so time stops for the dead, if not the living. Cold is stability and warmth can be treacherous.*

*Trees dwindle; shrubs cling to the ground; and further north nothing remains
of the plant kingdom but low grasses, diminutive flowers, mosses, and lichens
hidden beneath the snow part of the year; and nearly every species but the rein-
deer and some of the summer birds is carnivorous. In winter, light can seem to
shine upward from the white ground more than from the dark sky where the
sun doesn't rise or rises for an hour or two a day. And at the poles themselves,
there are not 365 days per year but one long night and one long stretch of light,
and the sun rises once in the spring and sets once in the fall.*

Ice is blue. Trees dwindle. Light shines upward from the white ground. Language that evokes an image. Details that sing. The landscape seen through the
narrator's lens.

The setting can also be viewed from a character's point of view. When writing
"The Good Soldiers," David Finkel alternated between omniscient and third
person point of view telling the story of the final surge of the Iraq war. Finkel
embedded with a battalion and showed the horror of the conflict through these
soldiers. To set the stage of their new surroundings, he introduced the landscape
from the soldiers' initial sighting:

*Everything in Rustamiyah was the color of dirt, and stank. If the wind came
from the east, the smell was of raw sewage, and if the wind came from the west,
the smell was of burning trash. In Rustamiyah, the wind never came from the
north or the south.*

*They began learning this as soon as they landed. The air caught in their
throats. Dirt and dust coated them right away. Because they arrived in the
dead of night they couldn't see very much, but soon after sunrise, a few soldiers
climbed a guard tower, peeked through the camouflage tarp, and were startled
to see a vast landscape of trash, much of it on fire. One thing they had been told
before they arrived was that the biggest threat in their part of Baghdad would
be from homemade roadside bombs, which were referred to as improvised explosive devices, or more simply, IEDs. They had also been told that IEDs were often
hidden in piles of trash. At the time it didn't overly worry them, but now, as they
looked out from the guard tower at acres of trash blowing across dirt fields and
ashes from burned trash rising in smoke columns, it did.*

The soldiers smell raw sewage. They feel the air cloaked with dirt catch in their throats. They see the acres of burning trash and fear the danger that lies beneath. The setting provides a visceral experience for the reader; through describing the scene from the soldiers' eyes, we are the soldiers.

DIALOGUE OR DIRECT QUOTES?

In both fiction and nonfiction, readers yearn to hear characters' voices. Speech breaks up text, defines personalities, and contributes to plot points and theme. Speech adds color, opinion, life. It is a rare narrative that doesn't benefit from the sound of a human voice.

To exercise this literary device, writers choose between direct quotes, which appear in exposition, or dialogue, which is incorporated into scenes.

Direct quotes appear in isolation. Woven into the text, the quotes burst through the explanation, uttered to the narrator and the narrator alone. Glance at any daily media story and you'll find quotes sprinkled throughout. For instance, in a Boston Globe feature by Akilah Johnson about a former bad boy, Irlando Goncalves, turned college scholar, the narrator condenses the backstory and then highlights it with a quote:

> *There were constant phone calls home from the school about his behavior and, in turn, constant calls from his mother to his father, who was still in Cape Verde at the time, about their unruly child. Goncalves said his behavior was so bad that his mother temporarily sent him back to the African island nation for a dose of discipline.*
>
> *"My mom doesn't like me talking about it because it makes her feel bad," he says. "I was just a troublemaker."*

Following the anecdote, Goncalves' words show insight and humility. They support the narrator's point that he was out of control. Goncalves speaks to the

---

TRY THIS

1. Resurrect a photo from your archives that sparks memories of a particular place. List five details for each sense (sight, sound, taste, touch, smell) of the place. Think back to what happened at that place and write a scene, using the details collected to paint an image of the setting in the reader's mind.

2. Write a description of an urban setting without taking your pen off the page or your fingers off the keyboard. Then go back and erase all adjectives and adverbs (those "ly words," such as magnificently). Replace those words with sensory detail and action.

writer just as interviewees speak to the camera in a documentary. There is no interaction with other characters. Just quote.

In contrast, dialogue occurs between two or more people within a scene. This means that there is setting, and movement, and reaction. Think of your own conversations. You aren't frozen in a bubble as you bicker with your sister Maisy about who will set the table tonight. Chances are you stand in the kitchen, or perhaps the TV room. You may point your finger, wash your hands, click off the remote — something besides just argue. In turn, your sister Maisy gets flushed with anger and prepares to hurl dirty socks at you.

Note the interaction between the characters in this scene from Sarah Schweitzer's "Together Despite All, Glimpsing the Distant Finish." For 6 months Schweitzer chronicled the recovery of one of the Boston Marathon bombing victims, Marc Fucarile, embedding herself in his hospital room, his physical therapy sessions, his living room. Day after day she watched him interact with his fiancée Jen, his son, his family, his nurses, his social worker, his therapists as he learned to live as an amputee. By using the characters' verbal exchanges, in all their ragged honesty, Schweitzer shows the magnitude of the bombing's impact on its victims and their loved ones. Here a social worker has arrived to talk about Marc and Jen's son, but Marc begs off, pointing to his ears, which remain shattered from the explosion.

> *Jen takes the social worker's card, promises to follow up, and says goodbye. She makes her way to the foot of Marc's bed. She hunches over and chews her thumbnail. There is a half-moon of skin where her nail used to be.*
>
> *Marc's floor nurse flits into the room and above the hubbub calls out: Your ICU nurses want to pop in and say hi. Marc is straightening, pushing his torso as upright as it can go without disturbing his foot dangling off two pillows. "I'm dying to see them, and I need to see them. Eddie? Eddie, do you want to let them know?" he says, dispatching his older brother down the hall to retrieve the nurses.*
>
> *Jen stares in disbelief. Suddenly, for nurses, the old Marc is back? The charmer, the guy who has time for everyone and hates to disappoint anyone? She yanks her hair into a tight ponytail. Her eyes fix on him. He's a flirt. She knows that. He can flirt with any nurse he likes. But if he has energy for them, why couldn't he talk to the social worker about Gavin?*
>
> *"What?" Marc asks her.*
>
> *"You were extremely rude to the social worker. She doesn't think so, but I do."*
>
> *"I can't hear. I couldn't hear the conversation."*
>
> *"I understand that, but everybody else can wait when it has to do with our son."*

Told from Jen's point of view, we see her staring at Marc, feel her incredulity at his priorities. We see her chewing her already shredded thumbnail. In turn, we see Marc struggling to sit up straight, careful not to disturb his remaining foot, so injured that it, too, may be amputated. We hear his bafflement at Jen's words. Through action and dialogue, Schweitzer paints the pain both characters suffer, and, in turn, illuminates the narrative's central question: how do the victims of this very public tragedy and their families recover?

Capturing dialogue is the easiest, of course, when the writer is present at the moment of the verbal volley. But if you reflect on past scenes that either you or someone else experienced, the dialogue must be recreated. Many a memoirist will argue that the writer is qualified to restate what he or she remembers of the conversation. Memoir = memory, and the writer's memory will suffice. Others will argue that dialogue by nature involves another person and that person may, probably will, have a different memory. A quick fact check can clarify words on the page — as well as defuse a possible relationship rift. No one likes to be misquoted.

For scenes in which the writer wasn't present, there is no option but to ask the participants what they said. J. Anthony Lukas recreated the experiences of three families during the Boston bussing crisis in the 1970s for his book "Common Ground" and said that he tried to speak to all parties involved when reciting dialogue, but in some cases based the recollection on only one person's memory.

In all cases, recreating dialogue means asking the participants again and again what was said. Truman Capote would ask one of the doomed killers of "In Cold Blood" to recall a scene, then move to the other one's cell and ask him for the same. Remarkably, most of their accounts were mirror images. When they differed, Capote would continue to probe both parties for details to ferret out the most accurate portrayal as he could.

WHAT IS THE ENDING?

I've always liked the advice that the crucial job of a narrative ending is to leave the reader feeling satisfied. Sounds simple enough. But the truth is that to provide the reader with a fulfilling closure requires a Herculean amount of thinking and plotting.

In narrative storytelling the end is as important as the beginning. The end is the destination, the answer to the question, the mystery that lured the reader from page to page. Or in my sixth-grade teacher Mrs. Crawford's terms, if every

---

TRY THIS

Go on the website mediastorm.com and select one of the site's videos that is rich in dialogue. Select a scene and write it, weaving in dialogue, action, and setting. What verbal exchanges and details are key to creating a cinematic experience?

story is based on a problem, the end provides the problem's solution. Sometimes that solution is clear — my fiction colleague Tom Payne seeks epiphanies in his endings, insights gained by the characters from the challenges they have faced — and sometimes the solution is not so clear. The ending, then, acknowledges the shades of grey.

The difference between fact and fiction is that fiction writers can make up their endings. They can wrap up with a Hollywood kiss or they can go Dickensian bleak. They can unify or divorce. They can give life or squelch it. J.K. Rowling made headlines when she announced that she should have matched Hermione with Harry Potter and not Ron Weasley. Throughout the writing of the Harry Potter series she had envisioned Hermione and Ron ending up together, but in retrospect, she thinks that the driven Hermione would soon tire of laid back Ron and they'd spend their marriage in counseling.

Writers of true stories don't have the luxury of creating either scenario. They have only the events that have happened, or their conclusions about the events that have happened, to ponder as possible endings. Yet what they can do with that material is as infinite as the ways a sculptor can mold a blob of clay.

End by telling

Our instinct as storytellers is often to end a tale with a verbal wrap-up, a thoughtful summary of what we conclude from the experience we've just described, the question we've chased. But these endings are not the same as the ones your high school English teacher demanded — summaries of major points already stated. Rather, an explanatory narrative ending offers the reader something new. Unlike that high school essay formula, a narrative doesn't state its point at the beginning and then devote its body to proving that thesis. Rather, a narrative woos the reader with mystery, and an explanatory end tells the reader how that mystery is solved.

When Ann Patchett accepted the challenge to write about driving an RV across South Dakota and Wyoming for a week, her central quest was clear: would her suspicion of RVs and the people who love them change? A more personal question was how would she and her ex-boyfriend, who had agreed to travel with her as moral support, survive a week within the confines of a Winnebago? Scene by scene we follow her on this journey as she struggles to navigate her big tin box on narrow winding roads, star gazes from the motor home's roof, meets RV enthusiasts, visits the Badlands and Yellowstone, clashes and reconciles with Karl. And paragraph by paragraph, she leads us to the revelation with which she wraps up the essay:

I believe the Winnebago has set me free. It has made me swim and eat pancakes with strangers and turn down obscure roads with no worry about where I have to be and when. I believe it has set many people free, old people and people with children who go off and see what this country has to offer because of their motor homes. Maybe they don't all hike, maybe they don't shoot the rapids or explore the wilderness, but they are out there. Who am I to define how others should vacation?

I feel like I went out to report on the evils of crack and have come back with a butane torch and a pipe. I went undercover to expose a cult and have returned in saffron robes with my head shaved. I have fallen in love with my recreational vehicle.

And so it is with no small amount of sadness that we go back to Billings to return the Minnie. After we've wiped down the counters and turned over the keys, we find ourselves powerfully drawn to the sales lot. We could buy one. We could drive home, or drive in the direction of home and see where we end up. Karl, who possesses many good qualities, not the least of which is that his foot is exactly a foot long, begins to pace off different models to calculate their length. We have our eye on a 30-foot Airstream Classic. I know what would happen, what our friends would say. We would never be welcome to park in front of their homes. We would be drummed out of polite society. We would be refugees on the road. We wouldn't mind.

In the balance of show and tell, she shows us the trip through scene and then tells us her conclusion through exposition. No repetition. Just fresh insight. Making sense of all the puzzle pieces.

Instead of examining a single experience like driving an RV through the Tetons, Nancy Mairs explores in her essay "Sex and the Gimpy Girl" how society treats women who deviate from the preconceived norm. Opening with a scene at a woman's health clinic, Mairs describes her inability to access neither the reception counter nor the examination table from her wheelchair. From there she explores the question of how society's treatment of women as commodities impacts all women in general and women with disabilities in particular. Her ending summarizes the insights she's gained from her intellectual journey on the page:

I'll conclude the strain involved in balancing a disabled woman's significant differences with her equally significant similarities to the general female population — in the reproductive sphere as in all areas of human experience — but I also believe, true to my Yankee roots, in the virtue of hard work. Women with every kind of disability must learn to speak forthrightly about their needs and appetites even when society appears to ignore or repudiate their feelings. The nondisabled must accustom themselves to hearing their utterances without judging the "rightness" or "wrongness" of their realities. I am always dismayed when a parent snatches a curious child away from my wheelchair or shushes her when she asks, "Why do you use that?" I see in the making yet another adult who will, in the name of politeness, pretend there is nothing the matter with me while simultaneously but surreptitiously regarding me as an escapee from "The X-Files." Neither of these views is accurate, but she'll never find that out unless we talk.

End by showing

Scenes are also a powerful way to end a narrative. By capturing a moment that shows rather than tells the resolution, the writer aims to leave the reader with an ending that hits the reader viscerally as well as intellectually. Through scene we are able to imagine how the characters face their future, or how the place under siege will fare in the days to come. Through scene we feel and see the sensory detail that plants an image that will resonate and indicate the narrative's completion.

"A Civil Action" chronicles one specific lawsuit from the point of view of Jan Schlichtmann, the lead prosecutor. He's young and ambitious and arrogant when he tackles suing W.R. Grace for contaminating the waters around Woburn, Massachusetts, an act that is linked with the deaths of multiple local children from leukemia. Author Jonathan Harr shadows Schlichtmann over the years that the case winds through the criminal justice system, eventually bankrupting him. In the end, Schlichtmann is a shadow of the designer-suit clad, brash lawyer we met in the beginning. What has he learned from this experience? How will he face his future?

Kiley lent Schlichtmann the price of a round-trip plane ticket to Hawaii, and also gave him a little spending money. For a week or so Schlichtmann stayed in a grimy, dilapidated motel, twenty-seven dollars a night with the bathroom down the hall. Then he bought a backpack and a sleeping bag and set off hiking on the western island of Kauai. He walked over a mountain pass to a remote valley named Kalalau.

He spent several days camping on the white sand beach, completely alone. He cooked over campfires. He swam and lay in the sun. He told himself that he was purging his mind, but in truth he kept wondering how one would know if one had wasted one's life. He was afraid of finding the answer. He wasn't sure from one moment to the next just what he intended to do. On his third day at the beach, right around dusk he stripped off all his clothes and swam out into the open ocean. The sea was as smooth as glass, with only the gentlest of swells. He swam westward, toward the setting sun, for a long time, and when he finally turned to look back the island of Kauai was little more than a blur on the horizon. The water was warm and he was naked, and he felt completely at peace. He treaded water for a while, gazing back at the island. He thought of swimming on until he could no longer see land.

But then this thought turned on itself, and he began swimming slowly back.

In fiction terms, a narrative's end reveals character development, how the character has changed from the central problem, or problems on which the storyline is based. In this case, we see that Schlichtmann is devastated, but in the end proves resilient, that the vigor that propelled him into the drama in the first place will also help pull him through.

Dream scenes provide ample material for endings. By illuminating scenes from our subconscious they can provide a tidy way to sew up the meaning the writer hopes the reader will absorb. Tracy Daugherty returned to Bakersfield, California, a magnet for generations of his Oklahoma relatives, as well as the Joads from Steinbeck's "Grapes of Wrath." Although Daugherty has never lived in Bakersfield, or even been there before, he plants himself in the town to learn how this town at the base of the All-American Pipeline became Little Oklahoma in the 1930s and what this exploration will tell him about himself, and his family roots. Scene by scene we follow him through his days, meeting the locals, connecting what he sees and whom he meets with his own family, his own past. He analyzes the town's class and race divisions, its culture of oil drilling, its honky-tonk bars and cheeseburger cafes. He explores what it means to live in Bakersfield then and now. He concludes with a scene he dreamt:

> *In a dream I had, my last night in Kern County, I was sitting in a porch swing of an old wooden house, a house similar to my grandparents' Oklahoma home, rocking back and forth. A sloping lawn spread before me: each time I swung high, I could see, beyond the lawn a vast landscape, changing each new arc I made. Now a forested valley, then a sunny canyon, now a desert, then a spring-fed meadow. Fireflies and constellations swirled in the sky, now dawn, then dusk. Where am I? I thought, the age-old migration lament. Then: It doesn't matter. I can take it all inside me. I opened my mouth for a pleasurable scream.*
>
> *At that moment I awoke, feeling happy, comforted, expansive. Through my motel window a big Western sun hung in the east. By the road below an old mattress lay in a ditch and a glut of cardboard boxes, as if Tom Joad had just cluttered by in his truck, spilling junk.*

End with a quote

During my early feature writing days I ended every story with a quote. Quote endings worked. A key character uttered a provocative statement that summed up the point I wanted to make. And while my editor agreed that, yes, these endings succeeded, she suggested that I break out of my comfort zone and try different finales.

I did, but I maintained then and maintain now that ending with someone's voice, someone's opinion or insight, or even someone's question, can resonate like the final chord of a song.

In her essay "Mothers, Sisters, Daughters, Wives," Mimi Swartz analyzed the Texas legislature's continuing efforts to eliminate abortion and public funding for women's reproductive health care and how those efforts impact the state's publically funded health care clinics, and the women they serve. Swartz takes the reader on a journey of the state's history of family planning support, of the back role women play in Texas politics and the toughness they've developed, of the recent movement to slice public funding of abortion and birth control. She describes the state legislature's successful effort to pass a law requiring transvaginal sonograms for women seeking abortions. She ends the piece describing how Maria Naranjo, the director of a Houston Planned Parenthood, has dealt with the cuts to its budget, offering a pay-as-you-go plan for its services and also referring patients to private clinics that service the poor. But, she knows, it is not enough.

> The cycle Naranjo predicts is this: the state government prevents poor women from getting affordable health care and birth control, so there will be more abortions, more Medicaid births, more expensive complications, and more illnesses caught too late. This doesn't seem like a good outcome for anyone, much less fiscal conservatives or those who oppose abortion.
> "We are going backward instead of forward," Naranjo said with a pained shrug. And then, like generations of Texas women before her, she got back to work.

Swartz ends with Naranjo's frustration, which summarizes the response of health clinic personnel to the relentless budget cuts, and her own insights into the future of reproductive health care: Texas women are tough and strong and will keep fighting.

David Finkel wanted to understand the statistics of high unemployment among black males so he found an unemployed black male and hung out with him. He learned about his family, his previous jobs, his education. He followed him to job fairs and employment offices. Scene by scene we watch Chris Dansby meet rejection, until he doesn't. After months of trying, he snags a job moving furniture and boxes around government office buildings. Finkel ends the piece with a scene of Chris at work:

> He picked up the final box, carried it to a far wall and placed it under a window that happened to offer a breathtaking view to the south.
> Down there to the right was Ward 3, where the unemployment rate was 1.5 percent.
> And down there to the left was Ward 8, where the 16.3 unemployment rate no longer included Chris, who stood now at the window transfixed.
> He'd never seen things from such a perspective.

In a moment, he would get back to work. He would move some filing cabi-
nets. He would keep a job. He would learn how to love himself.
But right now, all he could do was stare.
"Damn," he said.

That final quote — "Damn" — leaves us feeling hopeful, that while we aren't guaranteed of his success, we see that Chris recognizes the opportunity he has been granted, and that his future doesn't have to be as bleak as his past.

End with ambiguity

Life is messy. Often challenges don't conclude with a clear victory or defeat. Sometimes the resolution is no resolution. And that's okay. It merely means the writer's job is to illustrate that sometimes there are no easy answers.

Say that you're a successful businessman in your 30s. You've had a number of relationships, none of which have worked for the long haul. But you want to be married, want to have a wife, perhaps a family. Since you've struck out in your native country, the USA, why not seek fresh faces in another country: Russia? You sign up with the Fortuna Marriage Agency, move to St. Petersburg, and meet 30 women in 30 days. Throughout the narrative describing this man, whom we only know as Spencer, and his quest, John Tayman zooms in on his indecisiveness, showing through recreated scenes how each woman becomes "The One" at some point, then drops back. Tayman ends "Project Wife" illustrating Spencer's fuzzy future:

> *His visa is expiring, he has obligations. He's running out of time. He wants*
> *to spend a few more days with Ela, settle in, see how it feels, see her as his*
> *wife. He says, I'm pretty sure about her, I am. He feels a little lost, at sea. He*
> *thought it would happen more quickly, happen with a click, like light*
> *blooming into a room. He thinks, Maybe things fall into place after you*
> *choose, maybe the confidence comes with the decision itself, maybe then I*
> *will know.*
>
> *He says, I like Elvira a lot. She's what I've been looking for. I should just do*
> *it. He says, Yeah, I feel fine about the process, yeah, heck yeah. He says, I think*
> *I'll marry her. I could marry her. He says, What do you think?*

Who knows from this ending which of the women — Elvira, Anna, Alla, Natasha, Maria, Ekaterina — he ends up with, if any of them.

In "The Incredible Buddha Boy," George Saunders flew to Nepal to observe a 15-year-old boy who had been, supposedly, meditating under a tree without food or water for 7 months. Curious to find out if this was a hoax, he visits the boy, spends the night outside near the boy, witnesses odd lights and flashes that he wonders might be miracles or perhaps tricks of his imagination. He studies the culture and talks to the villagers. He meets the boy's parents and his cousin who checks each morning to see if the boy is breathing. Saunders' suspicion morphs into awe, and he wonders if this boy has an awareness from which we could learn. Two months after Saunders returns home, he learns that the boy has disappeared, that he stood up, said he would return in 6 years, and walked into the jungle. Saunders concludes this piece:

> *So it's a mystery, even more than it was a mystery before, when it was already pretty damn mysterious.*
>
> *But I imagine him the night of his escape, making his way through the woods in the moonlight, weak on his feet from months of fasting and sitting, his eyes really open for the first time since May. The world, the beautiful world, is fleeing past, and he's seeing it in a way we can't imagine. He's come so far and is desperate to get somewhere beyond the reach of the world, so he can finish what he's started.*
>
> *He hasn't eaten in ten months, and isn't hungry.*

Was he for real? Does he have magical powers? Saunders doesn't know. So instead of a concrete ending he imagines one. Ambiguity at its finest.

End with surprise

Life is also surprising. What we anticipate will happen may not. Catching a reader off-guard with an end he doesn't expect is a powerful narrative tool.

In "The Love of My Life" Cheryl Strayed shares her journey of grief after her mother's sudden death, her years of adultery and promiscuity and heroin, doing whatever she can to dull the pain. After terminating a pregnancy, the result of an affair with a user, she hits bottom, and decides to find answers hiking the Pacific Crest Trail. She packs her mother's wedding ring, which she later loses as she rinses her hands in a stream. Recognizing the symbolism of this loss, but also the truth of the matter, she concludes the essay:

> ***IF THIS WERE*** *fiction, what would happen next is that the woman would stand up and get into her truck and drive away. It wouldn't matter that the woman had lost her mother's wedding ring, even though it was gone to her forever, because the loss would mean something else entirely: that what was gone now was actually her sorrow and the shackles of grief that had held her down. And in this loss she would see, and the reader would know, that the woman had been in error all along. That, indeed, the love she'd had for her mother was too much love, really; too much love and also too much sorrow. She would realize this and get on with her life.*

But this isn't fiction. Sometimes a story is not about anything except what it is about .... Losing my mother's wedding ring in the Tongue River was not OK. I did not feel better for it. It was not a passage or a release. What happened is that I lost my mother's wedding ring and I understood that I was not going to get it back, that it would be yet another piece of my mother that I would not have for all the days of my life, and I understood that I could not bear this truth, but that I would have to.

Healing is a small and ordinary and very burnt thing. And it's one thing and one thing only: it's doing what you have to do. It's what I did then and there. I stood up and got into my truck and drove away from a part of my mother. The part of her that had been my lover, my wife, my first love, my true love, the love of my life.

We expect an epiphany from this experience, meaning from the symbolism. But Strayed is too real, too wise. Grief doesn't just end, and a daughter doesn't miraculously recover from losing her mother. Instead, Strayed drives away, unchanged by the symbolic loss of the ring. It is up to the reader to ponder where she goes from there.

TRY THIS

1. For a piece in progress, write:

   a. a one-line end
   b. a scene end
   c. a quote end

   How would these endings reshape the story?

2. Think back to a moment when you felt triumphant. Write that moment as a short scene. What are the scenes that led to that ending? What is the lesson learned? Now try the same for a moment when you felt in total despair. What's the history? Insight gained?

7

Pulling It All Together

> ## Overview
>
> You have a compelling idea, rich material, a firm focus and structure, and have settled on all those key components discussed in Chapter Six. In these final pages we explore the decisions you will face as you pull the whole enchilada together, from the first draft to the last. Choices include how to launch that initial draft, to outline or not to outline, narrator's tone of voice, tense, what to expand, what to compress, and how to attack revision.

IN HIS LAST NOVEL "TIMEQUAKE," Kurt Vonnegut divided writers and their strategies for battling the blank page into two tidy categories. On one side there are the swoopers, the storytellers who toss everything down "higgledy-piggledy, crinkum-crankum, any which way." Once they have a draft they go back and revise, detail-by-detail, line-by-line, draft after draft until they get it right. On the other side are the bashers, who punch and pound their way through each sentence, adding and deleting, arranging and rearranging, not moving on until it shines. "When they are done," writes Vonnegut, "they are done"

Travel writer Rolf Potts is a basher. He'll revise and revise each passage until it says what he wants it to say and sounds like he wants it to sound. Much of his writing of shorter pieces occurs in his head so that when his fingertips touch the keyboard he's already thought through a first draft. For more complicated, longer narratives, he'll puzzle over organization until he's built what he feels is a firm frame. Only then will he jot down the first word. Writing is slow, painstaking.

But when the passage is polished he can move on to the next one, and when that is perfect, he can move on to the next. There may be some tinkering as the narrative unfolds, but his process is so purposeful that by the time he ends the draft he can press Send without a backwards glance.

I, on the other hand, am a swooper. For me, the act of putting pen to paper is a journey toward discovery and I need to get the whole damn thing down before I can even start to think about word choice and narrative flow. How can I mull metaphors and build tension before I see the pieces and know how they fit together? My first effort is, in industry slang, a vomit draft. Only after I have tossed on the page scenes and background, reflections and insights, stats and facts, dialogue and quotes can I begin to understand how best to tell the story. And it is only through rigorous revision that the piece evolves to reader-worthy.

It is like sculpting. From a blob of clay, a sculptor begins his work. At the end of the first stage he has molded the shape of a body. At the end of the second, limbs emerge. At the end of the third, there may be a nose and fingers, toes and calf muscles. Each time he toils, the shape is more defined until he has sculpted a dancer so finely detailed that we see the strands of her hair, the cleft in her chin, a crack in her lip. Likewise, a writer shapes that blob of a first draft by revising until every passage, every sentence, every word builds toward what she wants the reader to know. We may think we know the meaning when we sit down to write but only through pondering and pruning, embellishing and rearranging can we make that destination visible to the reader.

Clearly, swoopers and bashers share the same goal — to craft a rich tale that engages a reader from first line to last. While one minces and the other gallops, the bottom line is that they both write and rewrite to reach that goal. And that, alas, is the key to pulling together a vivid narrative.

Yes, dear reader, you, too, must pen multiple drafts.

In an ideal world, we would be one and done. We would be so smart, so visionary that the perfect words and images, structure and epiphanies would pour forth from our fingers on the first try. But the cold truth is that probably not one piece of polished prose has ever emerged unaltered from first to final draft. Writing, as Don Murray said, is revising. Be it sentence-by-sentence, passage-by-passage, or draft-by-draft. How do you know what works and doesn't work until there's something on the page?

Creating a narrative from ideas and notes, from scribbled scenes and sample structures, and then polishing to ensure clarity, brevity, meaning, and, of course, eloquence, is a journey full of twists and turns and digressions. At every juncture, a myriad of choices awaits. What is worth saving? What should go? Where should the pace increase? Should the tense switch?

At no point, however, are the deliberations as hair yanking as at the beginning when the choice is, quite simply, "How do I fill the page?"

WHAT WE TALK ABOUT WHEN
WE TALK ABOUT A FIRST DRAFT

A few summers back, a student I'll call Josh took my travel writing class in Cambridge, England. Thrilled to be studying abroad and earning credit to tell stories of his adventures, he could barely contain his enthusiasm. In class, his head bobbed in understanding, his hand forever raised. Yet when he sat down to write his essays of place, he froze. He didn't know what he wanted to say, other than that he really liked traveling to London to see musicals, or that punting on the River Cam was harder than it looked. So, like many writers desperate to complete an assignment, he plopped himself down and free-wrote, letting his fingers rip across the keyboard. The words poured out, the pages mounted. And then he pressed Send.

The good news about this method is that Josh had a draft. The bad news is that he assumed he was done. After listening to his classmates discuss his piece during workshop — some nice moments, but the focus was fuzzy, adjectives choked the storyline — he began to realize that what he thought was a clear, compelling travel essay about the White Cliffs of Dover was really a meandering collection of overly descriptive scenes attempting to connect the present to past summer vacations on the Maine coast. It made sense to him, but not to the reader. This draft was, as novelist Terry Pratchett says of all first drafts, "just you telling yourself the story."

That first attempt to tell yourself the story may not be pretty. In fact, it may be downright horrid. "The first draft of anything is shit," according to Hemingway. But the rough draft provides you with that blob of clay to mold. Without it, you're shaping air.

And while each writer has his or her own technique for firing up a draft, there lie some grounding considerations that we all mull, whether on the page or in our heads.

To outline or not to outline?

At almost every reading I've attended by a nonfiction author, someone in the audience will ask, "Do you outline?" At one, Mark Kramer, author of multiple books and magazine narratives, nodded and said, "Oh yes. But then once I begin writing I usually toss it and start again." At another, Jonathan Harr, author of "A Civil Action," said he outlines by ordering the scenes he wants to include. Adrian Nicole LeBlanc doesn't outline until after she writes the first draft, quite a feat considering that her book "Random Family" took her 11 years to research and was published at 432 pages.

Outlines for most storytellers, however, are not the Roman numeral I, II, III brand. Leave that to the academics and scribes of EPA regulations. Rather, writers penning narratives of fact define outlining as everything from listing themes to organizing passages in excruciating detail. Faith Adiele plots her essays by image. John McPhee isn't ready to write until he posts an intricate outline on the wall, ever visible for consultation. Each component is sketched separately with a dizzying amount of specifics. If McPhee is anything, he is thorough.

Ted Conover's outline is more of a mental checklist. Once he's completed typing up all his notes (for his book "Newjack," the tale of his months as a prison guard at Sing Sing, he compiled about 500 single-spaced typed pages), he'll devote several weeks to reading and annotating the material. Then he puts the highlighted notes aside and imagines how the chapters will fall. He says in the "New New Journalism," "The notes are unmediated experience, and now it is time to mediate it, give it a structure. I have to decide what I'm going to do with my experience." From his ruminations for "Newjack," he knew a beginning chapter would cover his training, and toward the end he'd focus a chapter on New Year's Eve and the fires inmates set in their cellblocks. In the middle, he'd place a chapter about the day he was slugged and spit on, the day he began to hate all the inmates, a pivotal moment in the narrative trajectory.

Once he envisions the chapters he begins filling in the list by plugging his notes into certain chapters. And then he revises these chapter notes. When he's ready to write a chapter, on his desk will be a hard copy of the most updated version of that chapter's notes, the original 500-pages of single-spaced notes, and the books he imagines he'll quote. Then he starts to write.

In addition to organizing by images, Faith Adiele creates a timeline for her essays. The daughter of a Finnish mother and a Nigerian father, she is a woman of multiple cultures. Her approach to writing is like her approach to life — from different angles. Once she has launched an essay, has attempted to find meaning from an image or an event that has haunted her, she'll list in chronological order her life events along with world events. This timeline helps her draw connections. When, for instance, she began writing about the day her mother told her the real story of her birth (her father wasn't dead, her parents weren't married, and her mother gave birth alone in a home for unwed mothers) she found the scene flat. They sat on a couch and talked. But on her timeline she saw that her chat with her mother coincided with Mt. St. Helens' eruption and the anniversary of the Dred Scott Decision. Two pivotal events she could use thematically. Shock and disbelief of the destruction caused by this beloved mountain. Entire ecosystems swept away. And the Dred Scott Case, an affront against African-Americans, launched the Civil War. Her grandfather had kicked her mother out of the house when he learned she was pregnant with the child of a black man. Her timeline, then, would blend the personal with the universal, a journey of self and other.

The purpose of any outline, be it a list of scribbled scenes, an intricate Ted Conover-type framework, or a map that emerges from a rough draft, is to create order out of chaos. That chaos may be years of research, or pages of reflection. It's simply a matter of figuring out what you want to say and where you want to say it.

TRY THIS

1. On little pieces of papers — 3x5 cards work nicely — isolate key scenes, placing one scene on each card. On another set, write on each card a piece of integral background. On another set, write key facts. On another set, key stats. You should have a thick stack of cards by the end. Place the cards on a large flat surface — dining room tables work well — and align stats and facts and background with certain scenes. How will those scenes build best toward meaning?

2. Find a quiet place and sit down, or lie down. Relax. Close your eyes. Now think through your material. What are your best scenes? What concrete material (stats, facts, background) supports and enriches these scenes? What order of these scenes creates the most tension? Offers rising and falling action? Arrive at resolution?

3. Make a timeline of your life's key events. Circle two of the most momentous, life altering. What else was going on in the world at that time? Add key regional, national, and world events. For fun, add objects (ones you remember, such as your grandmother's ear muffs, or ones from the period, such as U.S. flags flying everywhere after 9/11) and trends (music, food, fashion) to the timeline. What connections can you draw?

Hurdling the terror of the blank page

To move beyond paralysis, we have to, as my colleague the poet Mekeel McBride says, "turn off the inner editor." The voice that tells you you're an imposter, that you can't possibly write this story. There's nothing new. No one will read it.

Even the masters whose names appear in literary journals and magazines and on shelves of books suffer from it. In The New Yorker essay "The Writing Life: Draft 4," John McPhee recalled a letter he wrote to his daughter Jenny, who sought her father's advice on hurdling First Draft Block: *For me, the hardest part comes first, getting something — anything — out in front of me. Sometimes in a nervous frenzy I just fling words as if I were flinging mud at a wall. Blurt out, heave out, babble out something — anything — as a first draft. With that, you have achieved a sort of nucleus. Then, as you work it over and alter it, you begin to shape sentences that score higher with the ear and eye.* Recognize, too, he wrote, that the rough draft is the hardest, and takes the longest time. The first round of a long piece on California geology took him 2 years to write. The next three drafts took 6 months.

Some writers may say they enjoy the ride, but most of us admit to deep despair during that initial draft, of contemplating careers in flower arranging or FedEx delivery, anything that doesn't require placing words on a page.

Yet somehow, some way we plug on. Ann Patchett says that pretty much any dilemma is hurdled by sitting in that chair, and sitting some more. The indomitable Norah Ephron once wrote that her strategy was to write as fast as she possibly could and keep going until the momentum faded. That could be by Paragraph 3, but still that's three paragraphs more than she had at the opening bell.

The important thing is to get *something* on the page. And then keep going.

Draft for meaning

And that something may be better than one thinks *if* the writer has done the necessary ruminating. That first draft will be much less messy if the writer has mulled the material and determined the most important thing she's learned, or what she hopes to learn by writing the draft. The clearer the destination, the message she wants to share with the reader, the smoother the journey.

For external-based stories, the search for meaning begins during the research as the writer interviews and observes and collects data in pursuit of the answer to the central question. Along the way, patterns emerge and the writer begins to draw conclusions from those patterns. In the final lap, the writer starts to calculate where the story is headed, and makes a final push to collect every shred of evidence to support the point, the epiphany.

Sarah Schweitzer arrives at a narrative's meaning by talking. How she carved the story "On the Way to Catastrophe, trailing a Life of Wrong Turns" is a great example. On a sunny Saturday in early September, less than 12 hours after she was first stopped for speeding and driving without a license, 19-year-old Darriean Hess, high on fentanyl, sped her fiancé's car over a narrow bridge, crossing the double yellow line and plowing into a group of bicyclists on the first leg of an organized 100-mile ride. Bodies flew, bikes scattered, and Darriean sat sobbing in her boyfriend's Honda Civic, grasping her iPhone. Much had been written about the accident that killed two middle-aged women cyclists and gravely injured two others, but Schweitzer wanted her narrative to answer not what happened but *how* did it happen? How could one young woman make so many bad decisions that would lead to this kind of tragedy?

After spending months researching Darriean's past, Schweitzer found her brain churning with possible directions she could take this tale. And so she turned to her husband.

A lawyer, he's a thoughtful listener. Sometimes he offers suggestions. Sometimes he asks questions. And sometimes he doesn't have to mumble a syllable. Through articulating her thoughts — with or without his input — Schweitzer is able to sense the narrative's heart. In this case she told him a layered tale of abandonment and addiction, abuse and neglect, of a family that moved from one impoverished home to another, from a fishing village in Alaska to Seattle and then to Seabrook, New Hampshire, known more for its nuclear reactor and fireworks stores than its sandy coastline. She drew connections between the players of each generation and their role in Darriean's fate. And then it struck. "This is a story about shame," she said to her husband. "This is about a girl whose name is Darriean, whose father's name is Darrin, a man who raped her stepsister and spent years in prison. She sprang from a genetic mix of Darrin Hess. Is your life fated or do you chose your own path?"

As she spoke, the story's core began to fall into place. Darriean could have chosen a life different from her father, who was a violent drunk when home from his crab fishing trips, who plied her 10-year-old half-sister with beer before he assaulted her. Or she could have assumed she was doomed to follow Darrin's route. The question the story should try to answer, Schweitzer realized, was whether Darriean had the strength to rise above her past.

The answer: she did not. Raised as the youngest of four, Darriean was doted on by her siblings, but neglected by her mother. Twice as a child she was sent to live with relatives. Not long after 13-year-old Darriean returned to the family home in Seabrook, her mother died of an overdose, toppling face first into the garden dirt. Darriean barely knew her father; she was still a toddler when he was sent to prison after pleading guilty to three counts of rape of a child in the first degree. Her grandmother sought custody, neighbors found her jobs, but Darriean fled, finding solace with drugs and men. She was in a free-fall, Schweitzer realized, and something awful was bound to happen. The family shame had followed her. And the family shame formed the narrative arc that ended on a bridge over the Hampton River.

In contrast, because internal tales demand more rumination than research, ferreting out meaning is often easier once a draft is underway. Sometimes two or three drafts — or more. Personal essays and memoir require the author to have a distance from his younger self, to look impartially at the event, the image, and figure out the meaning. And sometimes that takes a while. Ryan Van Meter sent off his essay "Cherry Bars," thinking, or wanting to think, it was done. For him it captured a funny moment when he and a pal used his grandmother's dessert to vandalize a car. But rejection followed rejection (in one case an editor rejected it *twice*). Great writing. Wonderful characters. Nice scenes. But it doesn't go far enough. He'd return to it year after year, and finally, the meaning struck. Throughout the essay, the teenage Ryan and his pal exuded nostalgia — John Lennon glasses, Pink Floyd, Simon & Garfunkel — and he realized that the essay was about holding back, looking to the past because the future and its inevitable hard choices were on the horizon. Quarterly West published the essay in Fall/Winter 2006/7.

Once the meaning is determined, the writer's job is to stick to it, to ensure that every passage builds to that message. Best for all if that message can be summed up in a succinct sentence. My habit is to write that sentence on a

3x5 card. Where I go (or go to write), the card goes, an ever-present anchor to stay tethered. Other writers type the sentence at the top of their story. In the book industry, it is called a high concept sentence, the universal theme with a fresh pitch. For instance family shame is an age-old story. To summarize the fresh angle to the Darriean Hess tale, the high concept sentence could read: A legacy of family shame leads a 19-year-old over a bridge and into a self-fulfilling tragedy.

Draft for story flow

One of my favorite assignments for undergrads is to send them out to record a scene, to talk to three people, and chronicle a mini event. When they return to the writing lab, I tell them to put away their notes. Jaws drop. "Whaaa???" But then they write. Free of their notebook's shackles, of clinging to facts and quotes, they write from the heart, or at least the subconscious. The words flow, the cadence is strong. When they have a draft they then pull out their notes and revise for accuracy.

Writing without notes is liberating. It allows the inner storyteller to emerge. Scenes and reflections tumble forth without the fact-check pause that breaks the momentum. Veracity comes later — after the draft is done.

Assigned to write a story about the 100th anniversary of the venerable New Hampshire Historical Society's headquarters in downtown Concord, New Hampshire, I aimed to bring the reader back in time, to suspend disbelief and feel like he was part of the process that created a building that had been heralded as one of the most magnificent examples of stonework in the nation. To do that, I focused on the man who instigated the effort, writing the first paragraphs of the first draft from memory of what I had learned during the weeks of research. The pile of notes and books beside me lay unopened. Within the text I wrote myself notes to attend to later.

> *Then, as now, New Hampshire's glory to many was found in its mountains, its seacoast, its verdant valleys and forests and clear blue lakes. But to William C. Todd, New Hampshire's richness lay in its history. He wasn't immune to his native state's natural beauty, but for Todd, a bachelor schoolteacher from Atkinson, there was much to be celebrated in New Hampshire's role in the Revolutionary War, in its production of famous men such as Daniel Webster and Franklin Pierce, in its contributions to architecture, literature, and woodworking.*
>
> *Clear-eyed and dapper in his starched shirts and black ties, Todd was an active member of the New Hampshire Historical Society, attending its annual meetings and corresponding regularly with other members, many of who, like Todd, were Dartmouth College graduates. He had a long, narrow face with a*

high forehead and a thick white mustache. <u>And he was passionate about the</u>
<u>*Society, passionate about its role in preserving the state's history, passionate about*</u>
<u>*ensuring the Society's role in preserving the history for the future [rewrite].*</u> *By*
the time he was elected president of the Society in 1898, he recognized that the
institution was at a critical crossroads, that if something weren't done quickly,
the treasures collected by the Society could be lost. Forever.

In a voice described by his friend and fellow Society member Benjamin
Kimball as squeaky and husky, Todd announced at the annual June meeting in
1900 that <u>its current facility, a former bank building on Main Street in Con-</u>
<u>*cord [check]*</u>, *was no longer adequate. Crammed with over 3,000 books and*
pamphlets, the space was too small and not fireproof.

Writing, I knew I needed more details, more facts to make this passage accurate and livelier. But what I was after was a rhythm and a point of view. Facts came later as you can see from the final version:

For William Cleaves Todd, New Hampshire's glory did not lie in Franconia
foliage or Squam Lake at sunset or even the craggy seashore. While he admired
his native state's natural bounty, what Todd cherished above all was its history.
For Todd, a Dartmouth man and a bachelor school principal, there was much
to be celebrated in New Hampshire's role in the Revolutionary War (two-thirds
of the soldiers at Bunker Hill hailed from the Granite State), in its production
of famous men (Daniel Webster and Franklin Pierce), in its contributions to
art (Thomas Cole's "Notch of the White Mountains"), and invention (the Con-
cord Coach).

With such a passion for the past, it was fitting that Todd was a devoted
member of the New Hampshire Historical Society, and that he would become
the Society's president in 1898, the year that he and the Society both celebrated
their 75th birthdays. Dapper in his starched shirts and black ties, his thick
white mustache perfectly trimmed, Todd presided over the annual June meetings
and it was at the first meeting of the new century that he made the announce-
ment that would change the Society — and New Hampshire's architectural
reputation — forever.

A crisis was brewing, he told his 170 members. Crammed with over 3,000
books and pamphlets, the Society's headquarters, a former bank building on
Concord's North Main Street, was too small. Worse, it was not fireproof; all of
the Society's treasures, which included volumes of Daniel Webster's unpublished
letters, could be lost with the strike of a match.

The first draft established the flow. The subsequent drafts established the facts. Without notes I could begin to tell the story of this man and this remarkable building. With notes, I could complete it.

TRY THIS

Visit the nearest grocery store. Think of one thing you want to know about this place — What's it like stocking shelves for six hours? What happens to expired items? Who is the sushi chef and how did he arrive behind the deli counter? Ask the management if it is okay to hang out and ask employees questions, and then hang out and ask employees questions. Take lots of notes on what you hear and observe. Back at your desk, put away the notes. Write 500 words about what you learned from the experience. Finished? How's the flow? Where's the meaning? Fiddle for style and then return to your notes for specific numbers and quotes and facts. Accuracy.

Draft for voice

What storyteller's voice will narrate the tale? Will the voice be sarcastic? Empathetic? Formal? Intimate? Distant? How the narrator tells the story — the tone — impacts the message as much as the story itself. The first draft is the place to experiment and find that voice.

News stories are traditionally told in a neutral voice. Just the facts. No interpretation. No opinion. But narratives are stories, and the narrator has a personality. Depending on what message she wants to get across, that personality may be cajoling and coy, or smart and forceful.

Take for instance, Caitlin Flanagan's voice in her piece "The Dark Powers of Fraternities":

> One warm spring night in 2011, a young man named Travis Hughes stood on the back deck of the Alpha Tau Omega fraternity house at Marshall University in West Virginia, and was struck by what seemed to him — under the influence of powerful inebriants, not least among them the clear ether of youth itself — to be an excellent idea: he would shove a bottle rocket up his ass and blast it into the sweet night air. And perhaps it was an excellent idea. What was not an excellent idea, however, was to misjudge the relative tightness of a 20-year-old sphincter and the propulsive reliability of a 20-cent bottle rocket. What followed ignition was not the bright report of a successful blastoff, but the muffled thud of fire in the hole.
>
> Also on the deck, and also in the thrall of the night's pleasures, was one Louis Helmburg III, an education major and ace benchwarmer for the Thundering Herd baseball team. His response to the proposed launch was the obvious one: he reportedly whipped out his cellphone to record it on video, which would turn out to be yet another of the night's seemingly excellent but ultimately misguided ideas. When the bottle rocket exploded in Hughes's rectum, Helmburg was seized

by the kind of battlefield panic that has claimed brave men from outfits far more illustrious than even the Thundering Herd. Terrified, he staggered away from the human bomb and fell off the deck.

The narrator is an adult mocking the twisted thinking of a drunken college student at a fraternity party. Her tone is factual, but her word choice belies her attitude. "An excellent idea." "Misjudge the tightness of a 20-year-old sphincter and the propulsive reliability of a 20-cent bottle rocket." "His response to the proposed launch was the obvious one: he reportedly whipped out his cellphone to record it on video." Of course! Why wouldn't you want to chronicle a bottle rocket up the butt for posterity?

When using third person point of view, the author's choice on narrative voice will determine if the character is a protagonist, someone we root for, or an antagonist, someone we wish will fall on a spear. In "The Bravest Woman in Seattle," Eli Sanders chose the former when he narrated from inside the head of the young woman on the witness stand testifying against the man that raped and stabbed her and killed her female partner:

The prosecuting attorney asked something like: How'd it go at Weight Watchers? Without missing a beat, without shame, she framed her body with her hands, moved them up and down, and said: "Well..."

As if to say: Look at me. Go ahead, look at all of me. It's okay. Laugh at the awkwardness of this, as everyone in the courtroom is doing right now, if that's what you all need to do. It's okay. Really. Look at me. And thank you for looking, because later on in this trial, the prosecutor will step up to the witness stand and pull my straight black hair back from my neck so that I can more easily point out, for all of you who are looking, the four slashing scars that run from below my left ear toward my throat, the scars from when the man cut and stabbed me with his knife. I am not scared. I have nothing to hide here. Not anymore. Not for something as important as this, the opportunity to put him away.

She is not fearful. She is not enraged. She wants justice. And because we so admire her strength and honesty, her calm thoughts as she faces her attacker and the public, we want her to win, to find relief in a guilty verdict, to move on with her life.

In memoir and personal essay, the narrator is the author, but the author has the flexibility to alter the way she chooses to tell a particular tale. Mary Karr recreates her past in "The Liar's Club" through the lens of the child Mary, sharing with the reader her pet peeves, sibling jealousy, and confusion. Ryan Van Meter, too, chooses to tell the story of a car ride from his 5-year-old perspective in

"First," articulating his affection for his playmate, the wish to hold his hand, his parents' disapproval.

> *In the car Ben and I hold hands. There is something sticky on his fingers, prob-ably the strawberry syrup from the ice cream sundaes we ate for dessert. We have never held hands before. I have simply reached for his in the dark and held him while he holds me. I want to see our hands on the rough floor, but they are only visible every block or so when the car passes beneath a streetlight, and then, for only a flash. Ben is my closest friend because he lives next door, we are the same age, and we both have little brothers who are babies. I wish he were in the same kindergarten class as me, but he goes to a different school — one where he has to wear a uniform all day and for which there is no school bus.*
>
> *"I love you," I say.*

We see what a 5-year-old sees, understand his relationship with Ben as 5-year-old Ryan understands it. An adult would articulate the kind of private school Ben attends, but all a child knows is that his friend wears a uniform and doesn't take a bus.

One of the reasons that Cheryl Strayed's memoir "Wild" became a bestseller and book club favorite is, I believe, her voice. In her essays as well as her memoir, she has the intimate voice of a friend, admitting to bad behavior — a little her-oin, a lot of infidelity — but by explaining why she needs the physical release of bodies and drugs, and the humor she employs describing her often misguided adventures, we cheer her on to better choices and a happy, stable life. She isn't evil; she's just confused.

From "Heroin/e":

> *The first time I smoked heroin it was a hot, sunny day in July. I got down on my knees in front of Joe where he sat on the couch. "More," I said, and laughed like a child. "More, more, more," I chanted. I had never cared much for drugs. I'd experimented with each kind once or twice, and drank alcohol with mod-eration and reserve. Heroin was different. I loved it. It was the first thing that worked. It took away every scrap of hurt that I had inside of me. When I think of heroin now, it is like remembering a person I met and loved intensely. A person I know I must live without.*

From "Wild":

> *How could I carry a backpack more than a thousand miles over rugged moun-tains and waterless deserts if I couldn't even budget it an inch in an air-con-ditioned motel room? The notion was preposterous and yet I had to lift that pack. It hadn't occurred to me that I wouldn't be able to. I'd simply thought*

that if I added up all the things I needed in order to go backpacking, it would equal a weight that I could carry. The people a REI, it was true, had mentioned weight rather often in their soliloquies, but I hadn't paid much attention. It seemed there had been more important questions to consider. Like whether a face muff allowed a hood to be cinched snug without obstructing my breathing.

She is honest in the first, admitting why in the wake of her mother's death, her father's abandonment, separation from her husband, she found solace in heroin. In the second, we watch her try to lift the backpack she'll carry during her 1,000-mile journey across the Pacific Crest Trail. She doesn't expect sympathy since she readily admits that she played the fool, caring more for accessories than the critical factor of a backpack's heft. But because she is so honest, so self-deprecating, we root for her in the long run — to finish the journey — and the short-run — to lift the pack she calls "Monster" onto her back and start the journey.

Draft for tense

What tense does the narrative need for maximum impact? Does it require the immediacy of present tense, of allowing the reader to follow the action in real time? Or would it be more effective to tell the story in hindsight, offering interpretations and explanations?

Some narratives are obvious. John Sedgwick had no choice but to write in past tense his book "In My Blood," which delves back centuries as he traces the mental illness that threads through generations of his family. Likewise, Sarah Schweitzer chose past tense for the Darieann Hess tale. Schweitzer sensed the narrative strength lay in leading the reader from the beginning, using the cycling accident as the inevitable crisis. Her opening:

SEABROOK, N.H. — *Two decades ago, the Hess family was on the run, fleeing the Pacific Northwest where the unthinkable had engulfed them, branded them, and left them grasping for a new life.*

They settled into a ragged corner of this tough, working-class town in the lowlands of New Hampshire's Seacoast. Their house's porch sagged and its dirt driveway turned to rutted mud in rain.

But here, in the heart of old Seabrook, where people's struggles were their own and questions weren't asked, the family believed their secrets were safe and their past had been left behind.

You can almost hear the drumbeat of the background music, thumping the harbinger of catastrophe.

In contrast, Schweitzer opted for present tense for her narrative chronicling the relationship of a couple devastated by the Boston Marathon bombings. Immersed in their world for months, Schweitzer lets the story unfold in real time:

> *A social worker comes to Marc's bed. She holds a thick folder and starts to talk with him and Jen Regan, his fiancée, about their 5-year-old son, Gavin. I can't hear, Marc interrupts, pointing to his ears. His blown-out eardrums make everything sound like a watery underground tunnel.*
>
> *Jen and the social worker step aside to talk. Marc can do only what he can do. But in moments like this — especially in a moment like this — Jen can't help wanting more. She wants the old Marc who shared the load with her. Now she can't imagine burdening him: She hasn't told him that after Gavin smiled through his first visit to the hospital room a few days earlier, he had collapsed at the elevators, into her arms, sobbing.*
>
> *Jen takes the social worker's card, promises to follow up, and says goodbye. She makes her way to the foot of Marc's bed. She hunches over and chews her thumbnail. There is a half-moon of skin where her nail used to be.*

The disadvantage of present tense is that it doesn't allow for the reflection that comes with time and distance. The advantage, however, is the inherent sense of urgency, of the reader joining the characters on a journey, knowing what they know, hearing what they hear. Ryan Van Meter writes "First" in present tense, placing the reader on the back seat of the station wagon with him and Ben. Nick Flynn employs present tense for most of the sections in his memoir "Another Bullshit Night in Suck City," even if the scenes he describes date back decades, back to before he was born:

> *My father drives back to Scituate one day and everything's been replaced. Houses have changed color and there are more of them — the bookstore's now a knick-knack shop, the bookie's a barber, the package store's a bank. He digs his heel in below the gas pedal as he steers, his heel wears a hole in the carpet, beneath the carpet is steel. Sweat drips from his ankle in summer, collects in the hole, eats away at the steel. Without thinking he will end up outside the house he grew up in, he will look at the front door but he will not enter. His legs will not carry him, his hand will not work the latch, as in the dream when you come to the threshold you know you must pass but cannot. Open your mouth to scream but nothing comes out.*

Readers may be jarred by this use of present tense in a scene that occurred when the narrator was a toddler, clearly decades before the author sat down to craft this memoir. But it is also refreshing by allowing Flynn to get inside the car and drive with his father.

TRY THIS

1. Whip out some more 3x5 cards. On the first card, write a paragraph describing a pivotal moment you observed once in school (any grade will do). Do not let your pen off the page or fingers off the keyboard. Turn off the inner editor and write. On the second card, rewrite the moment for meaning, adjusting it to mean what you want it to mean, adding and deleting content. On the third card, rewrite it for voice. How does the narrator sound? How do you want the narrator to sound? On the fourth card, focus on word choice.

2. Try writing the first three paragraphs of a narrative in four different voices: distant, sarcastic, angry, informal. Which works best?

3. Read a narrative aloud in present tense. Then read it in past tense? Which flows more naturally?

WHAT WE TALK ABOUT WHEN WE TALK ABOUT REVISING

Emerging writers don't like to revise. Or at least most don't. Like Josh from my travel writing class, they deem writing a one and done deal. Even after their piece is workshopped, after their peers have identified content holes, confusing passages, blurry meaning, the idea of facing that story again is torture. My colleague Janet Schofield asks the students in her fiction and nonfiction workshops to list what they loathe about revising. They like what they wrote. It makes sense to them. There's so much to change they're overwhelmed. They don't know where to start. It's hard.

Of course it is hard. But it is not in the stratosphere of Rough Draft Hard. In fact, once you get going, revising can be fun. Truly. And while Janet knows from decades of teaching that few students will concede the fun factor in rewriting, she also knows that they can overcome their resistance to it.

Once their grievances are aired, she narrows the list to ten common complaints and writes them on the board. She says, pointing to #1/ How to Start, "This is something everyone struggles with when they revise. Has anyone found a strategy that has helped him or her get through it?" Hands rise. Suggestions fly. "Start with the comments from workshop that rang your bell the loudest." "Highlight the best stuff." "Start with a blank screen. The good things sneak back in and the bad things are forgotten." "I never believed that revision was my friend until I finally stopped thinking of it as punishment."

Don Murray spent a lifetime in the classroom and on the page spreading that message: Revision isn't a penalty. Instead, he preached, "Writing evolves from a sequence of drafts, each one teaching the writer how to write the next." Revision is problem solving.

For most of us, the first draft is, as Terry Pritchett says, for ourselves. We write to get the material down, to see what we have. The second, third, fourth, fifth and, yes, maybe sixth and seventh drafts are for the reader, each version becoming clearer, sturdier, more complete, less cluttered, more on message, more colorful.

There's not one path to that final, polished version. But there are some common approaches and core questions the writer must ask of the draft.

Is the meaning clear?

Readers enjoy a good yarn, elegant prose, evocative images, but ultimately will feel robbed if they end a narrative that doesn't harbor a message that resonates with someone besides the author. This means that revision's first order of business is to ensure that the central point forms the spine of the narrative and that every scene, reflection, sentence, and word builds toward that epiphany. Everything else goes.

In "The Goldfish History," Ryan Van Meter explores the symbolism of the pet goldfish he nurtured and the evolution of two relationships — his roommate Kim and his boyfriend Geoffrey — during the goldfish's life. He writes of his deep bond with Kim, a female friend since college, the first person to whom he had said, "I'm gay." He writes of Geoffrey's suspicion that Kim is in love with the narrator. He writes of Kim moving out when Geoffrey moves in. He writes of his extraordinary efforts to keep the goldfish alive (e.g., peeling a pea for fish food) and its death on his sixth anniversary with Geoffrey, who soon leaves him.

Van Meter writes his first drafts in longhand, aiming to make sense of an image, or an event, such as Rufus' death on his anniversary with the boyfriend who left him. In the case of "The Goldfish History" his early drafts sought to understand the effort he exerted to keep Rufus alive. "I was interested in dissecting that metaphor and seeing what it would reveal," he says. His subsequent drafts, typed on the computer, showed people struggling to make sense of loss. He framed the essay around Rufus' life, pursuing the transformation of thought during those years. How did his thinking towards Kim, and Geoffrey, and Rufus change? In draft after draft, he planted the key thoughts in what he hoped were the right spots on the timeline, drawing the narrative tension from his reflections. But still he hadn't nailed the insight he sought.

Until he took a walk with his Boston terrier around his neighborhood in Iowa City. While rounding the corner of Muscatine and Seventh, he realized the essay's message: that you could be sure of something and still be wrong.

An aha moment like that, however, demands recalibrating the essay. As Van Meter says, "It becomes so startlingly obvious what belongs and what doesn't."

You have to be vigilant and, as Faulkner warned, you may have to kill your darlings. "You may have really good stuff," Van Meter says. "Save it and maybe it will seed a new essay."

The first draft, too, may lead to a surprise revelation, a focus so dramatically different than the original vision that every passage requires reevaluating. When Rolf Potts plotted out in his head a travel essay about Lebanon, he envisioned a narrative centered on how the country has evolved from decades of war, and that this funny man he met, Mr. Ibrahim, would serve as a slice of humor. But as he wrote he realized that the eccentric Mr. Ibrahim, who paraded only the positive about his beloved city Beirut and rebelled loudly against any challenge, was a tragic figure, much like the city itself. The man proved the metaphor for the place. "It was a longer and more serious story than I expected," says Potts.

Out went any anecdote or detail that didn't support his new direction.

Revising for meaning is much like home renovation. Once you've rethought your needs — an open design for easy entertaining, a music room for your band, lots more windows for lots more light — all the walls and doors and ceilings that don't support this new vision end up in the dumpster.

Is the structure solid?

A narrative's framework has one major goal: to lure the reader to the finale. Passages build on each other, the first leading to the second, the second leading to the third, and so on until you reach the end. The question posed to a first draft, then, is whether those passages are organized in a way that creates the suspense to hold the reader.

If the narrative hinges on a central question, the building blocks, or passages, mount to answer that question. Does each passage provide the material that contributes to the message? Does the reader have enough information to understand the next section? If not, what needs to be inserted?

The first draft may provide merely one layer, and subsequent drafts will strive to provide more depth. Sometimes the first draft is merely action; future drafts will add the layers of reflection and context. Faith Adiele knows this well. As a woman born of multiple cultures, Adiele doesn't look at any of her personal narratives with

---

TRY THIS

Write a one-sentence thesis statement at the top of a first draft. The ONE thing you want the reader to know. Highlight all the passages that support that statement. Cross out everything else. What is left? Make a list of other anecdotes, facts, stats, background, and reflection needed to complete that message in the next draft/s.

what she calls "the black and whiteness and linearity of Western tales." Instead, her drafts strive to weave in the range of ways she views her past and present, the different perspectives adding the necessary structural layers. "I'll tell the story once, stop, break, and then retell the story through another cultural lens," she says. "It's sort of cubist, always circling around."

In some cases, all the material is there and the writer's charge is to rearrange. Katy Butler struggled with the structure of "What Broke My Father's Heart," a blend of memoir (her parents' end-of-life experiences) and reporting (the medical community's approach to caring for the terminally ill). Should she lead with the Big Picture? With technological advancements that keep people alive against their will, or the will of their loved ones? Or should she lead with her mother's dilemma: should she turn off the pacemaker that keeps her husband, disabled from a stroke and mute from dementia, alive? If she started with the former, the reader may be bored. If she started with the latter, the reader may find her mother repugnant. And that ran counter to her goal, which was to make the reader care about her parents enough to read to the end to see what happens to them. Ultimately, she chose to open with a scene in her parents' home:

> One October afternoon three years ago while I was visiting my parents, my mother made a request I dreaded and longed to fulfill. She had just poured me a cup of Earl Grey from her Japanese iron teapot, shaped like a little pumpkin; outside, two cardinals splashed in the birdbath in the weak Connecticut sunlight. Her white hair was gathered at the nape of her neck, and her voice was low. "Please help me get Jeff's pacemaker turned off," she said, using my father's first name. I nodded, and my heart knocked.
>
> Upstairs, my 85-year-old father, Jeffrey, a retired Wesleyan University professor who suffered from dementia, lay napping in what was once their shared bedroom. Sewn into a hump of skin and muscle below his right clavicle was the pacemaker that helped his heart outlive his brain. The size of a pocket watch, it had kept his heart beating rhythmically for nearly five years. Its battery was expected to last five more.
>
> After tea, I knew, my mother would help him from his narrow bed with its mattress encased in waterproof plastic. She would take him to the toilet, change his diaper and lead him tottering to the couch, where he would sit mutely for hours, pretending to read Joyce Carol Oates, the book falling in his lap as he stared out the window.

Her mother is portrayed as gentle, refined, and thoughtful. When she asks for help to unplug her husband's pacemaker, we understand. She has won our empathy.

Yet even if the reader is engaged, yearning to find out if her parents are allowed to control their end of life care, Butler worried that the reader might become so mired in the medical ethics and background she wove in for context that he'd abandon the tale. By restructuring to allow the family-based passages to dominate, to insert only the facts and stats that pertained to her family, Butler hoped that the reader would gladly follow the drama as her father lingered, thanks to the pacemaker, in a haze of dementia and immobility, until pneumonia finally got him. Meanwhile her mother, worn out from caring for her spouse, chose not to undergo surgery for her own leaking heart valves. Within months, she too died — but on her own terms. This provided Butler with an ending that trumpeted her message:

A week later, at the same crematory near Long Island Sound, my brothers and I watched through a plate-glass window as a cardboard box containing her body, dressed in a scarlet silk ao dai she had sewn herself, slid into the flames. The next day, the undertaker delivered a plastic box to the house where, for 45 of their 61 years together, my parents had loved and looked after each other, humanly and imperfectly. There were no bits of metal mixed with the fine white powder and the small pieces of her bones.

For years, both in life and on the page, Butler wrestled with how we die. Through rethinking her structure, she was able to end her piece — which later evolved into her book "Knocking on Heaven's Door" — with a symbol of the conclusion she drew: No metal, no shards of technology, influenced her mother's death. As her mother wished. As Butler argued it should be.

WEB CHOICES

Multimedia artist Galen Clarke on Finding the Arc Among the Footage

Galen Clarke had never thought too much about the parallels between his work as a multimedia artist and his grandfather's authorship of medical books. He creates visual stories with still and moving images, and his granddad wrote text. But that changed one Thanksgiving while visiting his family in Atlanta. As Clarke spread out on the floor pieces of paper, each containing elements of the video narrative he was in the midst of producing, his grandfather noted, "That's exactly what I did." He had typed up each narrative section separately and then laid them out on the floor, arranging and rearranging to find the proper order. How very similar, Clarke had to agree.

(Continued)

(Continued)

Based in Denver, Clarke has traveled the world shooting visual projects that have appeared in media outlets from MSNBC.com to The National newspaper in Abu Dhabi. Recently he has produced a documentary about hiking the entirety of the Appalachian Trail and also "Remember These Days," a video detailing the world of one of the last seltzer deliverymen in New York. It is on this last project that he focused his thoughts on the challenges of pulling together a visual narrative from reams and reams of footage, which, he admits, mirror many of the challenges his grandfather — and all writers — face, too.

I struggle the most with paring down my ideas, settling on one direction to move in. The seltzer man could have gone in any direction. The focus was found in the pre-interview; this guy Walter wanted to talk about his kids and their relationship with seltzer bottles. As I pried him about his kids, I learned that they weren't interested in being seltzer men so I started investigating that angle. During the real interview with the camera rolling he surprised us. He brought out a lot more detail about his grandfather, his father, his kids.

Everything has a role in mind as we film. We knew that we'd bring the family in. Walter telling stories of his father. Scenes of taking the bottles out with his kids. Scenes of him delivering the seltzer.

(After the filming) the first thing I do is transcribe the A-roll (the interviews). I print out the transcript and cut it into little pieces of paper and then I move those around until I have a sensible script. That script is usually way too long and then I have to pare it down to a reasonable length. I let the story determine the length but there are some rules of thumb, such as an Internet video can't be too long, 3 to 4 minutes max, to keep a viewer's attention. There are exceptions; "Remember These Days" is closer to 10 minutes and The Hike is close to 15.

Once I get the A-roll rolled out I'll check out the B-roll (background footage) and see what works together. The goal is to draw connections to illustrate or complement what's being said.

We piece together the visuals and what he's saying in the interview. It takes a lot of fiddling. You categorize things in your mind. There will be a father section. A kid section. Scenes of him working, delivering. You need to build a sequence that's six or seven clips long with each clip holding the screen for 5 to 10 seconds. Each section of the story is a couple of minutes. In the introduction (Walter talking amid his 7,000 seltzer bottles) we pieced together six or seven chunks of video (from a 2-hour interview) that would transition into each other and tell the story of his father with his hopes for his children. Then the music comes in. The introduction tells you what the story is about.

I'm always seeking a conflict in my subjects. If I don't have a conflict that unfolds, I can't do much. Once I find the conflict, the resolution takes care of itself. Does the cancer patient live or die? Does the Seltzer Man's business carry on? Since none of his kids want to do it, it dies. That's the resolution.

What to expand and what to compress?

We all know people who know no proportion — every sniffle is pneumonia, every fender bender Carmageddon. In humans, that trait is annoying. In story-telling, a lack of proportion is lethal; not everything deserves the same amount of attention. A successful narrative requires a balance of compression and expansion — compressing the supporting background and minor players while expanding the key moments and starring characters.

What screams for more?

On a writer's shoulder perches the reader, forever chirping, "Prove it! Prove it!!" For every statement, scene, and character portrayed, the reader demands concrete evidence supporting the point the writer strives to make. This may mean adding more facts, anecdotes, and examples to exposition or sensory details, dialogue, and action to scenes. Or all the above.

For instance, to build her parents into rich, multidimensional characters, Katy Butler spent months revising "What Broke My Father's Heart," adding details, anecdotes, and explanation. We see her mother meditating and reading a self-help book on patience. We read her journal entries: "The Jeff I married ... is no longer the same person." We hear her fiercely refuse to move him to a nursing home, and instead struggle to move his bulk from bed to toilet. We watch her weep at his bedside, holding his hand. The details paint not a cold, calculating wife anxious to be rid of her burdensome husband, but a complex woman hon-oring her wedding vows and cracking under the pressure of his care.

She describes the man her father was before the stroke, the brain hemorrhage, the dementia, through facts and stories, how as a university professor he loved to debate, how he built floor-to-ceiling bookcases, coached rugby, and sailed Long Island Sound. She told how when she was a child he would wake her with verses from the Persian poet Omar Khayyam and quote Hamlet as he tucked her in at night. The man she describes is an intellectual, an athlete, and a doting dad, a sharp contrast to the man who wished to die after the first stroke that left him unable to utter a complete sentence or button a shirt. After the brain hemor-rhage, the loss of hearing, the loss of vision, the blood clots that short-circuited his brain, the incontinence, he was merely a vessel of his former self.

As Butler builds her case through specifics, the reader understands viscerally as well as intellectually the Butler family conflict. We understand why a devoted wife wishes to end her husband's compromised existence. And after his death by pneu-monia and she is diagnosed with her own heart ailment, we understand why she declines medical intervention. Through detailed scene and summary, through action and journal entries and dialogue, Butler shows her mother's will and lucidity:

The doctor sent her up a floor for an echocardiogram. A half-hour later, my mother came back to the waiting room and put on her black coat. "No," she said brightly, with the clarity of purpose she had shown when she asked me to have the pacemaker deactivated. "I will not do it."

She spent the spring and summer arranging house repairs, thinning out my father's bookcases and throwing out the files he collected so lovingly for the book he never finished writing. She told someone that she didn't want to leave a mess for her kids. Her chest pain worsened, and her breathlessness grew severe. "I'm aching to garden," she wrote in her journal. "But so it goes. ACCEPT ACCEPT ACCEPT."

While her mother's choice may make readers uncomfortable, we have enough ammunition to respect the reasons she makes it.

Recognizing what additional material a narrative craves begins early in the writing process. Hunched over my laptop, I keep a piece of paper by my side as I compose a first draft. On that piece of paper I write questions that I need to answer, holes I'll need to fill, in subsequent drafts. Fearful of losing momentum, I'll postpone plugging the content holes until the revision. Often, many of those questions are answered later in the draft, or turn out not to be necessary. Yet just as often, the narrative insists that I insert those details — and more. What does it feel like to wait on the steel examining table for the doctor to arrive? How many women will wait in the same room for the same doctor in the course of a day? What sound does the paper beneath your back make when you move? What music played in the background? What did the room smell like? Lysol?

The magic is in the details.

What to condense?

Some of the best advice I ever received was to tell the reader only as much as he needs to know. And no more. Sounds simple enough. But then, think about it: how much, exactly, *does* the reader need to know??? What in that first draft is necessary and what can the reader live without?

Too much explanation?

Because we know our topic inside and out, and because we often want the reader to know everything that we know, all the cool details and background, we are quick to toss everything on the page. That's what a vomit draft is for. Get it all down. But, in truth, does the reader really need to know the number of dwarf conifers in Golden Gate Park's botanical gardens for an essay about San Francisco homelessness? Great fact, and perhaps a runaway teen may have once found shelter under the little tree, but include that detail? Not necessary.

CHALLENGING CHOICES

Faith Adiele Confronts Revision in 6 Easy Steps

WRITING & REVISING PAGE 1 OF YOUR
MEMOIR IN 6 EASY STEPS

STEP 1: FREEWRITE (161 Words)

First Line Exercise: Come up with a bold claim/mystery
that hooks your reader, establishes the theme, and sets
something in motion. Then write whatever details you can recall.

I GREW UP THINKING *BIAFRA* WAS A CURSE WORD.   Late at night
in the living room, over dinner, my mother and other grownups whispered
the word. What distinguished it from other things my mother didn't want to
know was the way she looked. Normally my mother seemed fearless.

During the years of *Biafra* my mother played a lot of Joan Baez, and
eventually I confused the frightening issues she sang about with *Biafra*.

In time I came to understand that *Biafra* was not a curse but a place. With
no television and my mother busy keeping magazines from me, I had no
visual image. It was years before I realized that *Biafra* was also a war,
one of the bloodiest and most controversial of the 20th century, before
I learned that *Biafra's* infamous starving children could have been my
playmates, and that while I tossed in bed at night, first in California and
then in Washington, my father was there.

STEP 2: INTERROGATE THE TEXT

Research Exercise: Circle examples of vagueness in the
draft and note any gaps in the story, then research for
authenticating details and potential metaphor.
3-Lines Exercise: Add 3 lines after each sentence
to further develop the idea or emotion.
1-Image Exercise: Add an image to each sentence,
particularly sensory detail to <u>show</u> what you've already <u>said</u>.

I GREW UP THINKING *BIAFRA* WAS A CURSE WORD. Late at night in
the living room, over **dinner**, my mother and other grownups whispered
the word. What distinguished it from other things my mother didn't want
me to know was the way she **looked**. Normally my mother seemed
fearless.

During the years of *Biafra*, my mother played a lot of Joan Baez, and
eventually **I confused the frightening issues she sang about with**
Biafra.

In time I came to understand that *Biafra* was not a curse but a place. With
no television and my mother busy keeping magazines from me, I had no
visual image. It was years before I realized that *Biafra* was also a war, one

Comment: One image: How does *dinner* smell?

Comment: One image: How does *the word* sound?

Comment: One image: Let readers *see* how mother **looked**

Comment: 3 Lines that *show/* prove her *fearlessness*

Comment: Research opp: What **years?**

Comment: One image: How does *Joan Baez* sound?

Comment: Research opp: What **songs** did she sing about which **issues?** 3 Lines that *show* this **frightening confusion**

Comment: Research opp: Which *magazines*? One image: What does *keeping magazines* look like?

(Continued)

(Continued)

of the bloodiest and most controversial of the 20th century, before I learned that *Biafra's* infamous **starving** children could have been my playmates, and that while I tossed in bed at night, first in California and than in Washington, my father was **there**.

> **Comment:** One image: How does *starving* look?

> **Comment:** One image: settings for *California* and *Washington*

STEP 3: WRITE FIRST REVISION (332 words, exactly twice the length)

> **Comment:** Research opp: What does *being there* mean? What did my mom know?

I GREW UP THINKING *BIAFRA* WAS A CURSE WORD. Late at night in the living room, over **the rich aroma of groundnut stew**, my mother and other grownups whispered the **breathy, frightening series of vowels**. What distinguished it from other things my mother didn't want me to know was **the way her sleepy eyes woke and darted at the sound**. My mother was not a woman who scared easily. **The apple-cheeked daughter of Nordic immigrants who'd thrown her out for bearing a black child, she stood arms akimbo, all 5-foot-2 of her, at the edge of playgrounds, blue eyes glittering behind thick spectacles,** just daring the white kids and their parents to say something: *Say anything, Just breathe the letter N...*

At times, when I was **between the ages of 4 and 7—**the years of *Biafra*—during a pause in Joan Baez **wailing about Bangladesh** on the hi-fi, my mother's voice would seep into the hallway: *Biafra*. I had no idea what the curse meant, but it frightened me too, at one point fusing in my mind with what was happening in Bangladesh, and seemed to go on happening for years, long after **the tsunami, the famine, the civil war,** had ended, as long as Joan kept singing.

In time I came to understand that *Biafra* was not a curse but a place. With no television and my mother **busy tearing the covers off** *Life* **and** *Time* **magazines,** I had no visual image. It was years before I realized that *Biafra* was also a war, one of the bloodiest and most controversial of the 20th century, before I learned that *Biafra's* infamous starving children, with their **distended bellies and spindly legs, eyes shining at the news camera,** could have been my playmates, and that while I tossed in bed at night, first in **rural** California and then in **rural** Washington, **my father was missing.**

STEP 4: DO EDITING & REVISION EXERCISES

Scenes Exercise: Choose a key moment in the plot or a character's development and develop it into a real-time scene, so that readers can see/hear/feel for themselves. Include: (1) Direct Dialogue; (2) Description (of Character of setting); and (3) Choreography (movement, facial expression, gestures, body language)
Re-Envisioning Exercises: Try switching point of view (POV), first to third or second person, child to adult narrator, past to present tense, etc. Read aloud for rhythm, assonance, alliteration. Does it sound like it feels?
Endings Exercise: Come up with an image or other literary device that ties everything together, returns us to the opening but in a slightly different position, brings home your message without stating it heavy-handedly.

> **Comment:** Murder your darlings: Even though the first line sparked the whole memory/story, how can I SHOW rather than TELL, begin in *media res* and allow the reader to experience it as a present-tense SCENE?

I GREW UP THINKING *BIAFRA* WAS A CURSE WORD. Late at night in the living room, over the rich aroma of groundnut stew, my mother and other grownups whispered the breathy, frightening series of vowels. What distinguished it from other things my mother didn't want me to know was the way her sleepy eyes woke and darted at the sound. My mother was not a woman who scared easily. **The apple-cheeked daughter of Nordic**

immigrants who'd thrown her out for bearing a black child, she stood arms akimbo, all 5-foot-2 of her, at the edge of playgrounds, blue eyes glittering behind thick spectacles, just daring the white kids and their parents to say something: *Say anything , Just breathe the letter N...*

At times, when I was between the ages of 4 and 7—the years of *Biafra*—during a pause in Joan Baez wailing about Bangladesh of the hi-fi, my mother's voice would seep into the hallway: *Biafra*. I had no idea what the curse meant, but it frightened me too, at one point fusing in my mind with what was happening in Bangladesh, and seemed to go on happening for years, long after the tsunami, the famine, the civil war, had ended, as long as Joan kept singing.

In time I came to understand that *Biafra* was not a curse but a place. With no television and my mother busy tearing the covers off *Life* and *Time* *magazines*, I had no visual image. It was years before I realized that *Biafra* was also a war, one of the bloodiest and most controversial of the 20th century, before I learned that *Biafra's* infamous starving children, with their distended bellies and spindly legs, eyes shining at the news camera, could have been my playmates, and that while I tossed in bed at night, first in rural California and then in rural Washington, **my father was missing**.

> **STEP 5: WRITE SECOND RE-ENVISION (330 words, essentially the same length)**

I AWAKE AT NIGHT TO SOMEONE CURSING **IN THE LIVING ROOM.** Mom, who is trying to keep him quiet, sounds scared. I know she must look it. Every time she hears this particular **curse**, her **sleepy blue eyes wake up and dart** about.

"*Bi-a-fra!*" he says, the **breathy vowels** slipping down the hallway, and she rebukes him sharply: "*Sssh*, Faith!" Her feet pad quickly across the carpet, and then the arm of the stereo cranks, vinyl slaps vinyl, and the needle hits a fuzzy scratch. Sounding both powerful and helpless, **Joan Baez** (Mom's favorite) begins to **wail about** Guernica or **Bangladesh.**

I am four/five/six/seven and pop from my mattress/climb down from my bed, soaked in sweat. I'm not sure if I want to cry because of the **famines and floods and killings** Joan is singing about or because of the cursing in the living room that's slid into my sleep. I creep down hallway, following the nutty, oily **aroma of groundnut stew**. It's an African night.

Mom and an African man are **whispering**, heads together over bowls of peanut chicken. He is not my father. No one is my father. Now they are both cursing, their voices low, urgent, throbbing: *Biafra!* I turn and flee back to my room.

With no TV and Mom tearing the covers off *Life* **and** *Time* **magazines** and stepping in between me and bus-stop newsstands, I have **no image** to accompany this feeling crawling through my stomach. I am 11 before I realize that *Biafra* **is not a curse word, but a place and a war**, one of the ugliest **of the 20th century, before** I learn that *Biafra's* **children** staggering on spindly legs, bellies distended, are my cousins and age-mates, and that while I thrash at night, **first in a rural California** housing project and then in a trailer home in **rural Washington, my father is missing**, presumed dead on the killing fields I don't even know I'm dreaming about: *Biafra!*

> **STEP 6: SHOW TO READERS WHO DON'T KNOW *YOU* KNOW**
>
> I added the 2 sentences above after a student asked me who The African Man was. Immediately I realized/remembered that, for a child never having seen her father, investigating all unfamiliar African men would have carried more emotional weight than some war!

SOURCE: © Faith Adiele.

My colleague Tom Payne's advice is wise: never digress so far into background or description or facts and stats that the reader loses sight of the narrative arc — the action. Keep in mind that the scenes are the stepping stones and the exposition — the reflection and background, the explaining — is the mortar. And what you want is to avoid a pathway overflowing with cement.

Veteran writers of research-based tales know that if they've done the job right, they will toss at least 60 percent — and probably more — of the content so painstakingly acquired. Only the richest material makes its way into the narrative, the material that feeds the action and breeds understanding of character and place and issue. For instance, Amy Ellis Nutt accrued files and files of facts and background on the geology of Gloucester, Massachusetts, while researching her book "Shadows Bright as Glass." To Nutt, geology was a metaphor for this tale of Jon Sarkin, a successful chiropractor who awoke from a stroke a different man. Like the formation of Earth, he had shifted dramatically, from a calm, disciplined doctor and happy father to a volatile, manic, obsessive artist. She, however, devoted only two or three lines to what she learned about the rocks and land of Gloucester, Sarkin's home turf. More and she would have veered too far from the story line. The rule, she knows, is only include the details that are pertinent; in this case, details that enhance the reader's understanding of Sarkin.

"Narrative arc, narrative arc, narrative arc," she says is the mantra that keeps her from deep digression.

In personal narratives, the challenge is determining the right amount of reflection, of guiding the reader to meaning. Ryan Van Meter fears that he tends to over-tell, to work too hard connecting images for the reader. Through practice and working with other writers, he is learning to trust the reader to pick up on the subtleties, to recognize that in his essay "Youth Group" he doesn't need to explain to the reader that he experienced a symbolic baptism when he was held under water by a boy he admired. It's clear in the details.

What material might work in a sidebar?

In traditional print publications, writers have the option of creating sidebars to elaborate on certain points, perhaps a slice of history, or a timeline, or a character's troubled past. Sidebars zoom in on elements that warrant attention, but might pull too far away from the main storyline if woven into the main narrative. For instance, a story on famed Boston mobster Whitey Bulger's arrest after decades on the run would feature sidebars on his past crimes and profiles of his victims — great content that would threaten the narrative flow if included in the main story. The range and depth of sidebars in print publications are often determined by space, which is finite.

Digital publications, however, provide a dizzying opportunity for narrative enhancements. Through animated graphics, videos, podcasts, slideshows, and photo galleries, technology has created avenues to add content that once would have languished on the cutting room floor. Readers have the options of clicking on the sidebar links as they read, or if they fear digital distraction, can ignore the slideshows and interactive timelines until they finish the text.

For instance, in the narrative of "Snowfall: The Avalanche at Tunnel Creek," we read the chronology of the expedition that killed three expert skiers in Washington's Cascade Mountains in February of 2012. The Pulitzer-winning story is riveting, weaving in character and action and the history of avalanches in the area. But what grabbed the public's attention were the multimedia enhancements: the interactive graphics illustrating how avalanches form and where the skiers were on their descent when the avalanche struck; videos shot by the skiers as they began their backcountry ski; videos of the survivors detailing their experience; photo galleries of the skiers and the mountains. The narrative would have sunk with details about the build-up of hoar frost or the weather system that brought 32 inches of new snow to the Cascades, but by weaving them into multimedia enhancements, the reader gets the best of both worlds — a spellbinding text propelled by action and sidebars crammed with facts and stats and a wealth of perspectives.

Personal narratives, too, benefit from extra detail lodged in multimedia sidebars. In Atavist's "My Mother's Lover," for example, the text follows David Dobbs' effort to unravel the mystery of Angus, the man his mother mentioned on her death bed. All Dobbs knew of Angus was that he was a surgeon his mother loved during World War II and that he was killed when his plane was shot down over the Pacific. But when his mother asked to be cremated and that her ashes be tossed into the Pacific to join Angus, Dobbs' curiosity ignited. A dogged researcher, he talked to Angus' relatives, friends, and former squadron mates. As his investigation unfurled, he gathered not only material that he could use for his textual tale but also photos, videos, and audio. Woven into the narrative, the rich media creates a layered experience for the reader. To better envision the characters Dobbs describes on the page, the reader can tap on icons that link to photo galleries of Dobbs' mother and Angus. Tap on the name of a place and a map pops up. Tap on the name of a secondary character and a mini profile with a photo appears. Between chapters is video footage of the Fourth Emergency Rescue Squadron, Angus' team, flying over the Pacific. The reader can hear the planes, see the young WWII pilots in their gear, resting in their cabins. By the story's end, the reader feels an intimate connection with all the characters and the tragedy of war and unfulfilled love.

What words should go?

William Zinsser wrote that "clutter is the disease of American writing." Clutter is any word that doesn't enhance the narrative, one that repeats something already said or implied, that tells rather than shows. This includes adjectives and adverbs, those "ly" words such as "meaningfully" or "beautifully." As Stephen King says in "On Writing: A Memoir of the Craft," "The road to hell is paved with adverbs."

Kill adverbs. Kill adjectives. Kill clutter.

Why do you need to say, "We currently live here?" Present tense implies that you live here. No need for currently. What are gorgeous eyes? Wouldn't a brief description of carefully chosen specifics — almond shaped, blue as lapis — paint an image stronger than the adjective gorgeous?

Rough drafts ooze with clutter. In our zeal to get the narrative down, we don't pay much attention to economy. During the next phase of revision comes the attack on the unnecessary.

Here, for instance, is a short passage from the first draft of an essay about the Tower of London. The author, a former student, is clearly bright, has a keen eye for contradiction, and a vocabulary that is the envy of his classmates. But his penchant for adverbs and adjectives, for telling rather than showing, clogs the flow.

> *"Any ill words against the Monarchy and it was off with the bloke's bloody head it was!" the Yeoman Warder yells to a group of <u>enthralled</u>, <u>wryly-eyed</u> sightseers. His <u>guttural</u> inflection and <u>flamboyant</u> gestures are <u>relatively</u> theatrical for such a <u>gruesome</u> divulger referencing an <u>actual</u> phase in British history. Nevertheless, throughout the tour he was <u>flexibly</u> insightful and <u>affably relatable.</u>*

How much stronger would this colorful scene be if the underlined adjectives (enthralled, flamboyant, gruesome) and adverbs (flexibly, affably) were tossed and replaced with specifics? What does an enthralled sightseer look like? And what is wryly-eyed? How is this Yeoman Warder affable? A return to the drawing board produced a much tighter scene:

> *"Any ill words against the Monarchy and it was off with the bloke's bloody head it was!" the Yeoman Warder yells to a group of tourists, their focus riveted to this Tower of London guard. He speaks from the gut, a deep baritone, as his hands slice the air. Odd that such a gruesome phase of British history is illustrated with such theatrics. Still, the visitors stare spellbound, and follow this Beefeater in his black robe with deep red trim through the Tower, nodding at his insights and chuckling at his jokes.*

By focusing on action and specifics rather than adjectives, the writer avoids choking the reader with excess and instead wins him over with detail.

What needs polishing?

Once the clutter is vanquished the writer is left with the task of inserting just the right words in just the right way, a way that is lyrical, eloquent, captivating. If language is music, revision fine-tunes each note. Every word counts.

Age-old rules apply to all crafters of true stories. Active tense (I sing vs. I am singing). Active verbs (sprint vs. run fast). Specific nouns (Rolex vs. watch). But if a narrative's mission is to build pictures in readers' minds, the nonfiction writer needs to employ the imagery of a poet.

Enhancing description.

By carefully choosing the right combination of verbs and nouns the writer creates a sensory impression. Rose Whitmore, a graduate of the UNH MFA in Writing program, delivered a wallop with this sentence from her essay "The Odds of Injury":

> *But mostly I love the way the horses run, that long-evolved economy of movement, the low thrum of hooves, the rush of the last hundred yards.*

"The economy of movement" paints an image of those long legs gracefully galloping. "The low thrum of hooves" instills sound. "The rush of the last hundred yards" provides the sensation of wind.

Little in life is as excruciating as watching one's child suffer, and Kelley Benham endured more than her share during the months she and her husband, the writer Tom French, watched their micro-preemie daughter (born at 23 weeks) struggle to survive. In the first part of her series "Never Let Go" she describes seeing her daughter for the first time:

> *Tom wheeled me to her portholed plastic box. The nurse introduced herself as Gwen, but I barely heard her. There, through the clear plastic, was my daughter. She was red and angular, angry like a fresh wound. She had a black eye and bruises on her body. Tubes snaked out of her mouth, her belly button, her hand. Wires moored her to monitors. Tape obscured her face. Her chin was long and narrow, her mouth agape because of the tubes. Dried blood crusted the corner of her mouth and the top of her diaper. The diaper was smaller than a playing card, and it swallowed her. She had no body fat, so she resembled a shrunken old man, missing his teeth. Her skin was nearly translucent, and through her chest I could see her flickering heart.*

We see the bruises, the tubes, the dried blood, the skin so translucent Benham could see her daughter's flickering heart. Devastating. Yet that last detail, the flickering heart, brings the narrator — and the reader — a slice of hope.

The power of metaphor.

Benham also employs comparisons to create images that resonate. Metaphors are key tools of the creative writer, but as my novelist friend Carolyn Coman warns, they have to be the right metaphor to be effective. Otherwise, they should be jettisoned. Rule: if you write a metaphor that sounds familiar, it probably is. Think "cold as ice." "Hard as steel." Of course they are great — why else would they be used so much as to become clichés?

In that one paragraph, Benham creates comparisons that conjure up images so vivid that few readers could leave the page unmoved: a diaper smaller than a playing card; a baby so emaciated that she looks like a shrunken old man with missing teeth.

Metaphors depend on concrete images. Think of this example from Ryan Van Meter's essay "Youth Group": "*His body feels like the slick stones we lifted from the river when we rafted.*" Or this from David Foster Wallace's "How Tracy Austin Broke My Heart":

> *Plus they're beautiful: Jordan hanging in midair like a Chagall bride, Sampras laying down a touch volley at an angle that defies Euclid. And they're inspiring. There is something about world-class athletes carving out exemption from physical laws a transcendent beauty that makes manifest God in Man.*

A body as smooth and slippery as wet stones. A basketball player as ethereal as one of Marc Chagall's airy brides. The mind grabs the comparison. The image forms.

Sentence length.

Not all sentences are created equal. The length of the sentence determines the pace of the narrative. Long, ponderous sentences slow the speed; they allow the reader to pause, take a breath, think. Short clipped sentences accelerate the flow, leaving the reader breathless. Exposition is often home to the former and action scenes benefit from the latter.

That said, passages of all long sentences are laborious and those comprising all abrupt statements are jumpy. Brittle. A blend of both, even in fast-paced scenes, gives the reader the best of both worlds. Using a blend of quick, active sentences interrupted with slower, longer thoughts, Rose Whitmore keeps the reader riveted as she captures a moment at the horse track with her dad:

> *I am white-knuckled with excitement when the horses round the last corner of the track, the pack all mud and brawny bodies pushing toward the finish line.*

Fevered cries rise from the crowd. In the home stretch the jockeys whack the horses' haunches with their crops. And then a horse goes down. And a second horse and a third. The jockeys who've been flung to the ground leap to the side, trying to save their lives. My father cups his hand around my head and presses me to his chest, but I've already seen enough.

At 27 words, the first sentence establishes action and setting. At six words, "Fevered cries rise from the crowd," picks up the speed. Intensity builds with three more clipped statements. And then a reprieve as the jockeys scramble for salvation and her father pulls her close in protection.

There is perhaps no writer alive who has mastered narrative cadence as powerfully as Joan Didion. Read a passage aloud and marvel at the rhythm of each sentence, at the force of the symphony of the whole.

How better to end this book on narrative storytelling than to excerpt the opening of Didion's "Slouching Towards Bethlehem." Read it once silently and again aloud.

The center was not holding. It was a country of bankruptcy notices and public-auction announcements and commonplace reports of casual killings and misplaced children and abandoned homes and vandals who misspelled even the four-letter words they scrawled. It was a country in which families routinely disappeared, trailing bad checks and repossession papers. Adolescents drifted from city to torn city, sloughing off both the past and the future as snakes shed their skins, children who were never taught and would never now learn the games that had held society together. People were missing. Children were missing. Parents were missing. Those left behind filed desultory missing-person reports, then moved on themselves.

The first sentence, borrowed from William Butler Yeats' poem "The Second Coming," sets the stage. The rest of the paragraph explains why in a blend of long — 33 words in one — sentences and short — People were missing. Children were missing. The pull of her prose is as melodic as a Debussy symphony.

And while most of us can only dream of crafting prose so elegant, we should remember that lyric sentences such as Didion's don't just write themselves. Instead, they emerge after additions, deletions, adjustments. They emerge after revision. And, like those toned sentences, a well-told narrative of fact demands the same scrutiny, from the opening line to the last period. Without revision, we have prose blobs. With revision, we have art.

May our pencils, as Vladimir Nabokov once wrote, outlive our erasers.

TRY THIS

1. On a draft, highlight all the adverbs and adjectives. What is the intent of each? What impression do you want it to form in the reader's imagination? Delete them all and replace with detail, image, fact, and anecdote.

2. On that same draft, underline every "is," "are," "was," and "were." Note the passive construction. Revise in active tense with active verbs.

3. Circle every sentence-ending period. What's the pattern? Too many short sentences in a row? Too many long? Adjust the length to alter the cadence.

REVISION CHECKLIST

- Is the meaning/focus clear? Could you write a title, subtitle, and one-sentence statement depicting the story's message?
- Does the structure lead the reader from beginning to end, luring him or her with a strong tension line?
- Does the opening capture your interest? Does it leave the reader with a question he or she will pursue?
- Does the piece have a strong point of view?
- Are the scenes vivid? Place the reader in real time and place? Suspend disbelief?
- Are the primary characters developed fully into living, breathing beings, rich with complexity?
- Where else would sensory detail benefit the narrative?
- What other facts and stats and background does the narrative demand?
- Are quotes used well? Is the dialogue appropriately placed?
- How is the story's pace? Where could it speed up? Slow down?
- Are the tenses consistent?
- Are the verbs active?
- What metaphors would enhance the images?
- What clutter can you kill?
- Is the setting detailed enough to immerse the reader in place?
- Does every statement prove its point to the reader?
- What do you notice when you read the passages aloud?

References

CHAPTER 1: WHAT'S THE BIG IDEA?

Abel, Isaac. "A Frat Boy's "Gay Experience."" *Saloncom RSS*. 20 Apr. 2014. Web.

Baker, Will. "My Children Explain the Big Issues." *In Short: A Collection of Brief Creative Nonfiction*. New York: W.W. Norton, 1996. 133–35. Print.

Balf, Todd. *The Last River: The Tragic Race for Shangi-la*. New York: Crown, 2000. Print.

Biss, Eula. *Notes from No Man's Land: American Essays*. Saint Paul, MN: Graywolf, 2009. Print.

Bookman, Marc. "This Man Is about to Die Because an Alcoholic Lawyer Botched His Case." *Mother Jones*. 22 Apr. 2014. Web.

Boynton, Robert S. *The New New Journalism: Conversations with America's Best Nonfiction Writers on Their Craft*. New York: Vintage, 2005. 366–8, 159–60. Print.

Branch, John. "Snowfall: The Avalanche at Tunnel Creek." *The New York Times*. The New York Times 20 Dec. 2012. Web.

Campbell, Joseph. "Joseph Campbell Foundation." *Joseph Campbell Foundation*. Joseph Campbell Foundation, n.d. Web. 02 Oct. 2014. http://www.jcf.org/new/index.php?categoryid=31

Didion, Joan. "Why I Write." *The Writer on Her Work*. New York: Norton, 1981. 17–26. Print.

French, Thomas. *Zoo Story: Life in the Garden of Captives*. New York: Hyperion, 2010. Print.

French, Tom. "Angels and Demons." St. Petersburg Times. Web. Oct. 1997.

Hertz, Sue. "Do, Re, and Me." *Boston Globe Magazine*. N.p. 22 June 1986. Print.

Hertz, Sue. "Who Cares for the Child?" *Boston Magazine*, March 1989. Print.

Hertz, Sue. *Caught in the Crossfire: A Year on Abortion's Front Line*. New York: Prentice Hall, 1991. Print.

Jones, Chris. "The Things That Carried Him." *Esquire*. 30 Aug. 2010. Web.

Kidder, Tracy. *Among Schoolchildren*. Boston: Houghton Mifflin, 1989. Print.

Kidder, Tracy. *The Soul of a New Machine*. Boston: Little, Brown, 1981. Print.

Mairs, Nancy. "Sex and the Gimpy Girl." *The River Teeth Reader*. 10. 1–2, Fall 2009/ Spring 2009. University of Nebraska Press, 2009. 3–10. Print.

Montaigne, Michel De, and William Carew Hazlitt. *Michel De Montaigne: Selected Essays*. Mineola, NY: Dover Publications, 2012. Print.

O'Connor, Flannery. "Mystery and Manners Quotes." *By Flannery O'Connor*. Goodreads, n.d. Web. 03 Oct. 2014. http://www.goodreads.com/work/quotes/3267475-mystery-and-manners-occasional-prose

Rough, Bonnie J. "His Genes Hold Gifts. Mine Carry Risk." *The New York Times*. The New York Times, 29 Jan. 2005. Web.

Salmon, Jacqueline L. "Holiday Rush a Tradition Some Can't Do Without." *The Washington Post*, 22 Dec. 1997. Web.

Sampsell, Kevin. "I'm Jumping off the Bridge." *Salon.com*. 3 Aug. 2012. Web.

Silvio, Ann. "NBA Woos a World Audience." *NBA Woos a World Audience*. Boston.com, 10 June 2010. Web.

Waldron, Jan L. *Giving Away Simone: A Memoir*. New York: Times, 1995. Print.

Wickersham, Joan. *The Suicide Index: Putting My Father's Death in Order*. Orlando: Harcourt, 2008. Print.

Williams, Terry Tempest. *Refuge: An Unnatural History of Family and Place*. New York: Vintage, 1992. Print.

CHAPTER 2: WHAT IS THE FORM?

Baker, Will. *In Short: A Collection of Brief Creative Nonfiction*. By Judith Kitchen and Mary Paumier. Jones. New York: W.W. Norton, 1996. N. pag. Print.

Balf, Todd. "Daddy Knows Least." *The New York Times*. The New York Times, 13 Sept. 2008. 27 May 2014. Web.

Bearman, Joshuah. "Baghdad Country Club." *Atavist*. No. 10. December 2011. Web.

Bearman, Joshuah. "Duty Calls." *This American Life*. NPR, 1 June 2007. Web.

Bissinger, Buzz. "After Friday Night Lights." *Byliner*. Byliner, n.d. Web.

Bolick, Kate. "All the Single Ladies." *The Atlantic*. Atlantic Media Company, 30 Sept. 2011. Web.

Boynton, Robert S. "Ted Conover." *The New New Journalism: Conversations with America's Best Nonfiction Writers on Their Craft*. New York: Vintage, 2005. 3-30. Print.

Campbell, Katie. "The Egg and I." *The Best Creative Nonfiction*. By Lee Gutkind. New York: W. W. Norton, 2008. 131-45. Print.

Caramanica, Jon. "Pitched to Perfection: Pop Star's Silent Partner." *The New York Times*. The New York Times, 29 June 2012. Web. http://nyti.ms/RllfMt

Corrigan, Kelly. *The Middle Place*. New York: Voice/Hyperion, 2008. Print.

Didion, Joan. "Slouching Towards Bethlehem." *Slouching towards Bethlehem*. New York: Farrar, Straus & Giroux, 1968. 84+. Print.

Dubus, Andre. "Writing & Publishing a Memoir: What in the Hell Have I Done?" *River Teeth: A Journal of Nonfiction Narrative* 14.1 (2012): 41-61. Print.

Gannaway, Preston, and Chelsea Conaboy. "Remember Me: A Multimedia Documentary about One Family's Struggle to Deal with the Loss of a Parent." *Concord Monitor*. Dec. 2007. Web.

Gutkind, Lee. "Difficult Decisions." *The Truth of the Matter: Art and Craft in Creative Nonfiction*. By Dinty W. Moore. New York: Pearson/Longman, 2007. 167-73. Print.

http://azstarnet.com/app/images/flash/garbage/. Arizona Daily Star, 2009. Web.

Karr, Mary. *The Liars' Club: A Memoir*. New York: Viking, 1995. 7. Print.

Kidder, Tracy. *Among Schoolchildren*. Boston: Houghton Mifflin, 1989. Print.

LeBlanc, Adrian Nicole. *Random Family: Love, Drugs, Trouble, and Coming of Age in the Bronx*. New York: Scribner, 2003. 34-35. Print.

Lobsinger, Megan. "The Art of Being Concise: A Conversation with Brevity's Dinty Moore." *The Blog: Issues on Publishing Innovations, Issues, and the Writing Life*. Pubmission.com, 29 Sept. 2011. Web.

Lopate, Phillip. "Against Joie De Vivre." *Against Joie De Vivre: Personal Essays*. New York: Poseidon, 1989. 42-63. Print.

Lopate, Phillip. "The State of Nonfiction Today." Introduction. *To Show and to Tell: The Craft of Literary Nonfiction*. New York: Free, 2013. 3-16. Print.

McClanahan, Rebecca. "Book Marks." *The Best American Essays 2001*. Boston: Houghton Mifflin, 2001. 165-180. Print.

McCourt, Frank. *Angela's Ashes: A Memoir*. New York: Scribner, 1996. Print.

McDougall, Christopher. *Born to Run: A Hidden Tribe, Superathletes, and the Greatest Race the World Has Never Seen*. New York: Alfred A. Knopf, 2009. Print.

McGuigan, Brian. "I Wasn't the White Boy Everyone Thought I Was." *The Rumpusnet*. The Rumpus, 3 May 2014. Web.

McPhee, John. "Encounters with the Archdruid." *The John McPhee Reader*. By William L. Howarth. New York: Farrar, Straus and Giroux, 1976. 189-231. Print.

Miller, Brenda. "The Date." *Touchstone Anthology of Contemporary Creative Nonfiction: Work from 1970 to the Present*. By Lex Williford and Michael Martone. New York: Simon & Schuster, 2007. 381-88. Print.

Moore, Dinty W. "History." *TriQuarterly*. 16 Jan. 2012. Web.

Nutt, Amy Ellis. "The Wreck of the Lady Mary." *The Star-Ledger*. 21 Nov. 2010. Web.

Nutt, Amy Ellis. *Shadows Bright as Glass: The Remarkable Story of One Man's Journey from Brain Trauma to Artistic Triumph*. New York: Free, 2011. Print.

Remnick, David. "Long-Form Storytelling in a Short-Attention Span World." *ProPublica. org*. ProPublica and the New School, 17 Mar. 2011. Web.

Rumore, Kori. "Welcome to StarNet."

Sheff, David. *Beautiful Boy: A Father's Journey through His Son's Addiction*. Boston: Houghton Mifflin, 2008. Print.

Smith, Gary. "Shadows of a Nation." "The Man Who Couldn't Read." *Intimate Journalism: The Art and Craft of Reporting Everyday Life*. Ed. Walt Harrington. Thousand Oaks, CA: Sage Publications, 1997. 3-17. 19-42. Print.

Solnit, Rebecca. "The Archipelago of Arrogance." *TomDispatch.com*. TomDispatch, 13 Apr. 2008. Web.

Steinberg, Michael. "Michael Steinberg Has a Blog." *BREVITYs Nonfiction Blog*. Brevity, 30 Apr. 2012. Web.

Strauss, Darin. *Half a Life*. San Francisco, CA: McSweeney's, 2010. Print.

Sullivan, Andrew. "Why I Blog." *The Atlantic*. Atlantic Media Company, 01 Nov. 2008. Web.

Sullivan, John Jeremiah. "The Ballad of Geeshie and Elvie." *The New York Times*. The New York Times, 12 Apr. 2014. Web.

Sullivan, John Jeremiah. "Upon This Rock." *Pulphead*. New York: Farrar, Straus and Giroux, 2011. 3-41. Print.

Swidey, Neil. *Trapped Under the Sea: One Engineering Marvel, Five Men, and a Disaster 10 Miles into the Darkness*. Crown Group (NY), 2014. Print.

Walls, Jeannette. *The Glass Castle: A Memoir*. New York: Scribner, 2005. Print.

Wolfe, Tom. "Appendix." *The New Journalism*. New York: Harper & Row, 1973. 37-52. Print.

Woolf, Virginia. "The Death of the Moth." *The Lost Origins of the Essay*. By John D'Agata. Minneapolis, MN: Graywolf, 2009. 447-49. Print.

CHAPTER 3: WHAT IS THE CONTENT?

Balf, Todd. "The Story Behind the SAT Overhaul." *The New York Times*. The New York Times, 08 Mar. 2014. Web.

Bearak, Barry. "Caballo Blanco's Last Run: The Micah True Story." *The New York Times*. The New York Times, 20 May 2012. Web.

Bissell, Tom. "War Wounds." *Harper's Magazine*, December 2004. Web.

Bissell, Tom. *The Father of All Things: A Marine, His Son, and the Legacy of Vietnam*. New York: Pantheon, 2007. Print.

Blair, Elizabeth. "The Strange Story Of The Man Behind 'Strange Fruit'"*NPR*. NPR, 5 Sept. 2012. 07 May 2014. Web.

Bolick, Kate. "All the Single Ladies." *The Atlantic*. Atlantic Media Company, 30 Sept. 2011. Web.

Boo, Katherine. "Behind the Beautiful Forevers: Q&A with Katherine. "*Behind the Beautiful Forevers: Q&A with Katherine*. Behindthebeautifulforevers.com. Web.

Butler, Katy. "What Broke My Father's Heart." *The New York Times*. The New York Times, 19 June 2010. Web.

Eggers, Dave. *Zeitoun*. San Francisco: McSweeney's, 2009. Print.

French, Tom. "Your World Is Your Story." *Poynter*. Poynter, 2 Mar. 2011. Web.

Gorney, Cynthia. "Too Young to Wed: The Secret World of Child Brides."*National Geographic*. National Geographic, June 2011. Web.

Gross, Terry. "Bill O'Reilly." *NPR*. NPR, 8 Oct. 2003. Web.

Hertz, Sue. "Dominick Dunne: Success and Tragedy Rework Him." *Hartford Courant,* 21 Oct. 1984. Print.

Hertz, Sue. "Lessons From Loss." *Lessons From Loss*. UNH Magazine, Fall 2009. Web.

Hertz, Sue. "The Mission." *Boston Magazine* (Dec., 1988): 75+. Print.

Kidder, Tracy. *Mountains beyond Mountains*. New York: Random House, 2003. Print.

Lopate, Phillip. "Research and Personal Writing." *Creative Nonfiction* 43. 65-66. Fall/Winter 2011. Print.

Rough, Bonnie J. *Carrier: Untangling the Danger in My DNA*. Berkeley, CA: Counterpoint, 2010. 23. Print.

Sanders, Eli. "The Bravest Woman in Seattle by Eli Sanders." *Seattle Features*. The Stranger, 15 July 2011. Web.

Schwartz, Mimi. "Michael Steinberg." *Blog*. Michael Steinberg, 23 July 2012. Web.

Shapira, Ian. "A Facebook Story: A Mother's Joy and a Family's Sorrow." *Washington Post*. 9 Dec. 2010. Web.

Skloot, Rebecca. "The Truth about Cops and Dogs." *The Best of Creative Nonfiction*. By Lee Gutkind. New York: W.W. Norton, 2007. 88-101. Print.

Steinberg, Michael. *Still Pitching: A Memoir*. East Lansing: Michigan State UP, 2003. Print.

Strayed, Cheryl. *Wild: From Lost to Found on the Pacific Crest Trail*. New York: Alfred A. Knopf, 2012. Print.

Sullivan, John J. "A Prison, a Paradise." *NYTimes.com*. The New York Times, 23 Sept. 2012. Web.

Wallace, Mike, and Gary Paul. Gates. *Between You and Me: A Memoir*. New York: Hyperion, 2005. 259-60. Print.

Zamora, Amanda. "Free the Files." *Top Stories RSS*. ProPublica, 12 Dec. 2012. Web.

CHAPTER 4: WHAT'S THE FOCUS?

Boo, Katherine. *Behind the Beautiful Forevers*. New York: Random House, 2012. 223. Print.

Brennan, Emily. "Reporting Poverty." *Guernica / A Magazine of Art & Politics*. Guernica, 4 Sept. 2012. Web.

Campbell, Katie, and Ashley Ahearn. "How We Got Into Such A Mess With Stormwater · EarthFix · KCTS 9." *How We Got Into Such A Mess With Stormwater · EarthFix · KCTS 9*. KCTS, Oct. 2012. Web.

Campbell, Katie, and Michael Werner. "Undamming the Elwha." *Home*. Earthfix KCTS 9. KCTS, Apr. 2012. Web.

Campbell, Katie. "The Egg and I." *The Best Creative Nonfiction*. By Lee Gutkind. New York: W. W. Norton, 2008. 131-45. Print.

Cramer, Richard Ben. *What It Takes: The Way to the White House*. New York: Random House, 1992. Print.

Didion, Joan. "Some Dreamers of the Golden Dream." *Slouching towards Bethlehem*. New York, NY: Farrar, Straus and Giroux, 1968. 3-28. Print.

Faludi, Susan. "Where Did Randy Go Wrong?" *Mother Jones* 14.9 (1989): 22-32. Web.

Gornick, Vivian. "Chapter One." *The Situation and the Story: The Art of Personal Narrative*. New York: Farrar, Straus and Giroux, 2001. 12-14. Print.

Heath, Chris. "18 Tigers, 17 Lions, 8 Bears, 3 Cougars, 2 Wolves, 1 Baboon, 1 Macaque, and 1 Man Dead in Ohio." *Terry Thompson and the Zanesville Ohio Zoo Massacre*. GQ.com, Mar. 2012. Web.

Hemley, Robin. "Chapter One: Immersion Memoir." *A Field Guide for Immersion Writing: Memoir, Journalism, and Travel*. Athens: U of Georgia, 2012. 16-17. Print.

Jones, Chris. "Animals." *Print*. Esquire.com, Mar. 2012. Web.

Lowery, Wesley. "The Race Is On: Republican Gabriel Gomez Hopes Frequent Road Races Help Him Top Ed Markey in Senate Campaign." *BostonGlobe.com*. Boston Globe, 18 June 2013. Web.

Meter, Ryan Van. "First." *If You Knew Then What I Know Now*. Louisville, KY: Sarabande, 2011. 7-10. Print.

Montaigne, Michel De, and William Carew Hazlitt. *Michel De Montaigne: Selected Essays.* Mineola, NY: Dover Publications, 2012. Print.

Pitzer, Andrea. "Mark Bowden on Discovering Narrative and the Value of Beginner's Mind: "Only If You Are Truly Ignorant Can You Ask the Truly Ignorant Question." *Nieman Storyboard A Project of the Nieman Foundation for Journalism at Harvard.* Nieman Storyboard, 30 July 2010. Web.

Pitzer, Andrea. "Tom French on Zoo Stories, Narrative Nonfiction and the Pleasures of Playing Anthropologist." *Nieman Storyboard A Project of the Nieman Foundation for Journalism at Harvard Tom French on Zoo Stories Narrative Nonfiction and the Pleasures of Playing Anthropologist Comments.* 10 Sept. 2010. Web.

Potts, Rolf, and Justin Glow. "Videos." *No Baggage Challenge.* Rolf Potts, 2010. Web.

Potts, Rolf. "My Beirut Hostage Crisis." *Marco Polo Didn't Go There: Stories and Revelations from One Decade as a Postmodern Travel Writer: With Special Commentary Track.* Palo Alto, CA: Travelers' Tales, 2008. 251–255. Print.

Pritchard, Melissa. "A Soldier's Story - US Women Soldiers in Afghanistan."*Oprah.com.* O. The Oprah Magazine, May 2010. Web.

Talbot, Jill. "Brevity Craft Essays 38." *Brevity Craft Essays 38.* Brevitymag.com, Winter 2012. Web.

Taylor, Evan. "Isabel Wilkerson Lecture Illuminates Writing Process." *The Pioneer News.* Whitman College, 4 Oct. 2012. Web.

Walls, Jeannette. *The Glass Castle: A Memoir.* New York: Scribner, 2005. Print.

CHAPTER 5: WHAT'S THE STRUCTURE?

Altmann, Jennifer G. "McPhee Reveals How the Pieces Go Together - 4/30/2007 - PWB - Princeton." *Princeton University.* Princeton Weekly Bulletin, 30 Apr. 2007. Web.

Bearak, Barry. "Caballo Blanco's Last Run: The Micah True Story." *The New York Times.* The New York Times, 20 May 2012. Web.

Biss, Eula. "The Pain Scale." *Notes from No Man's Land: American Essays.* Saint Paul, MN: Graywolf, 2009. 145–70. Print.

Bolick, Kate. "All the Single Ladies." *The Atlantic.* Atlantic Media Company, 30 Sept. 2011. Web.

Boo, Katherine. "The Marriage Cure." *The Marriage Cure | NewAmerica.org.* The New Yorker, 18 Aug. 2003. Web.

Boswell, Robert. "How I Met My Wife." *Tin House.* Summer Reading 56, 2013. Web.

Boynton, Robert S. "Ted Conover." *The New New Journalism: Conversations with America's Best Nonfiction Writers on Their Craft.* New York: Vintage, 2005. 3–30. Print.

Capote, Truman. *In Cold Blood: A True Account of a Multiple Murder and Its Consequences.* New York: Random House, 1966. 13–24. Print.

Church, Steven. "Speaking of Ears and Savagery." *Creative Nonfiction.* Summer 45, 2012. Web.

Ehrenfreund, Max. "Edward Snowden, NSA Leaker, Could Remain in Russia Indefinitely." *Washington Post.* The Washington Post, 24 July 2013. Web.

Faludi, Susan. "Where Did Randy Go Wrong?" *Mother Jones* 14.9 (1989): 22–32. Web.

Hart, Jack. *Storycraft: The Complete Guide to Writing Narrative Nonfiction*. Chicago: U of Chicago, 2011. Print.

Hertz, Sue. "The Lure of Tuckerman!" *The Lure of Tuckerman!* UNH Magazine, Winter 2006. Web.

Hertzel, Laurie. "Setting the Scene." *Above the Fold: A Newsletter on Writing and Editing*. 1–8. Jan/Feb 2006. Web.

Hollandsworth, Skip. "The Last Ride of Cowboy Bob." *Texas Monthly*. Texas Monthly, Nov. 2005. Web.

Jones, Chris. "Roger Ebert: The Essential Man." *Esquirecom Article*. Esquire, 16 Feb. 2010. Web.

Jones, Chris. "The Things That Carried Him." *Esquire*. 30 Aug. 2010. Web.

Karr, Mary. *The Liars' Club: A Memoir*. New York: Viking, 1995. 7. Print.

Kerrane, Kevin, and Ben Yagoda. *The Art of Fact: A Historical Anthology of Literary Journalism*. New York, NY: Scribner, 1997. Print.

Kidder, Tracy. *Among Schoolchildren*. Boston: Houghton Mifflin, 1989. Print.

Kidder, Tracy. *House*. Boston: Houghton Mifflin, 1985. Print.

Kidder, Tracy. *Old Friends*. Boston: Houghton Mifflin, 1993. Print.

Kingsolver, Barbara. "Infernal Paradise." *High Tide in Tucson: Essays from Now or Never*. New York: HarperCollins, 1995. 194–206. Print.

Knight, Lania. "An Interview With Creative Nonfiction Writer Phillip Lopate." *Poets & Writers*. Www.pw.org, 16 May 2008. Web.

Krakauer, Jon. *Into the Wild*. New York: Anchor, 1997. Print.

Lopate, Phillip. "Against Joie De Vivre." *The Art of the Personal Essay: An Anthology from the Classical Era to the Present*. New York: Anchor, 1994. 716–31. Print.

Lopate, Phillip. "The State of Nonfiction Today." *To Show and to Tell: The Craft of Literary Nonfiction*. New York: Free Press, 2013. 3–16. Print.

Mackall, Joe. *Plain Secrets: An Outsider among the Amish*. Boston: Beacon, 2007. 48. Print.

McCourt, Frank. *Angela's Ashes: A Memoir*. New York: Scribner, 1996. Print.

McPhee, John, and William L. Howarth. *The John McPhee Reader*. New York: Farrar, Straus and Giroux, 1976. Print.

McPhee, John. "Encounters with the Archdruid." *The John McPhee Reader*. Ed. William L. Howarth. New York: Farrar, Straus and Giroux, 1976. 189–231. Print.

McPhee, John. "Structure: Beyond the Picnic Table." *The New Yorker*. The New Yorker, 14 Jan. 2013. Web.

McPhee, John. "Travels in Georgia." *The John McPhee Reader*. Ed. William L. Howarth. New York: Farrar, Straus and Giroux, 1976. 268–308. Print.

McPhee, John. *Silk Parachute*. New York: Farrar, Straus and Giroux, 2010. Print.

Meter, Ryan Van. "First." *If You Knew Then What I Know Now*. Louisville, KY: Sarabande, 2011. 7–10. Print.

Moehringer, J.R. "Resurrecting The Champ." *Los Angeles Times*. Los Angeles Times, 04 May 1997. Web.

Morales, Angela. "The Girls in My Town." *The Best American Essays 2013*. Ed. Cheryl Strayed and Robert Atwan. New York, NY: Houghton Mifflin Harcourt, 2013. 171–87. Print.

"The 9/11 Encyclopedia." *New York Magazine*. New York Magazine, 27 Aug. 2011. Web.

Reitman, Janet. "Jahar's World." *Rolling Stone*. Rolling Stone, 17 July 2013. Web.

Shanahan, Mark. "Anthony's Pier 4, Vestige of City's Old Waterfront, to Close in August - The Boston Globe." BostonGlobe.com. Boston Globe, n.d. Web. 06 July 2013. Web.

Shields, David. "36 Tattoos." *New York News and Events*. Village Voice, 15 Oct. 2002. Web.

Skloot, Rebecca. *The Immortal Life of Henrietta Lacks*. New York: Crown, 2010. Print.

Smith, Zadie. "Joy." *New York Review of Books*. New York Review of Books, 10 Jan. 2013. Web.

Strayed, Cheryl. "The Love of My Life." *Touchstone Anthology of Contemporary Creative Nonfiction: Work from 1970 to the Present*. By Lex Williford and Michael Martone. New York: Simon & Schuster, 2007. 500–13. Print.

Toledano, Phillip. "A Shadow Remains." *MediaStorm*. 12 June 2012. Web.

Toledano, Phillip. "Days with My Father." *Phillip Toledano - Days with My Father*. www.dayswithmyfather.com, 2010. Web.

CHAPTER 6: WHAT ARE THE COMPONENTS?

Beard, Jo Ann. "Personal History: THE FOURTH STATE OF MATTER." *The New Yorker*. The New Yorker, 24 June 1996. Web.

Beattie, Ann. "My Life With Boxes." *The New York Times*. The New York Times, 16 Feb. 2013. Web.

Bernstein, Lenny. "Children Survive Oklahoma Tornado in Elementary School Bathroom." *The Washington Post*. The Washington Post N.p., 22 May 2013. Web.

Bissell, Tom. "War Wounds." *Byliner*. Harper's, Dec. 2004. Web.

Boo, Katherine. "Behind the Beautiful Forevers: Q&A with Katherine."*Behind the Beautiful Forevers: Q&A with Katherine*. Behindthebeautifulforevers.com, Web.

Boo, Katherine. *Behind the Beautiful Forevers*. New York: Random House, 2012. 223. Print.

Colloff, Pamela. "Teenage Wasteland." *Texas Monthly*. Texas Monthly, Jan. 1999. Web.

Daugherty, Tracy. "Bakersfield." *River Teeth Reader*. University of Nebraska Press, 2009. 11–22. Print

Elliott, Andrea. "Invisible Child." *The New York Times*. The New York Times. 9 Dec, 2013. Web.

Finkel, David. "The Meaning of Work." *Washington Post*. The Washington Post, 19 Nov. 2006. Web.

Finkel, David. *The Good Soldiers*. New York: Sarah Crichton /Farrar, Straus, and Giroux, 2009. 17. Print.

Friedman, Steve. "Bret, Unbroken." *Runner's World & Running Times*. Runner's World, 3 May2013.Web.http://www.runnersworld.com/runners-stories/bret-dunlap-discovered-running-and-it-changed-his-life?page=single

Haines, Tom. "Facing Famine." *Boston.com*. The New York Times, 20 Apr. 2003. Web.

Harr, Jonathan. *A Civil Action*. New York: Random House, 1995. 492. Print.

Harvey, Steven. "The Art of Self." *Fourth Genre: Explorations in Nonfiction,* Spring 1.1. 1999. 140–42. Print.

Heath, Chris. "11 Moments with James Gandolfini." *GQ.* GQ, Dec. 2004. Web.

Hertz, Sue. "What's a Joint Like You Doing in a Race Like This?" *The Boston Globe Magazine.* Boston Globe, 17 Apr. 1988. Web.

Hollandsworth, Skip. "The Last Ride of Cowboy Bob." *Texas Monthly.* Texas Monthly, Nov. 2005. Web.

Johnson, Akilah. "One Teen's Journey from the Margins to a College Scholarship - The Boston Globe." *BostonGlobe.com.* Boston Globe, 3 Feb. 2014. Web.

Kidder, Tracy. *Among Schoolchildren.* Boston: Houghton Mifflin, 1989. 5. Print.

Kidder, Tracy. *House.* Boston: Houghton Mifflin, 1985. Print.

Kidder, Tracy. *Mountains beyond Mountains.* New York: Random House, 2003. Print.

Levine, Mark. "Killing Libby." *Mensjournal.com.* Men's Journal, Aug. 2001. Web.

Maing, Stephen. "Hers to Lose." *The New York Times.* The New York Times. 26 Sept, 2013. Web. Video. http://www.nytimes.com/video/nyregion/100000002461740/hers-to-lose.html

Mairs, Nancy. "Sex and the Gimpy Girl." *River Teeth Reader.* University of Nebraska Press, 2009. 3–10. Print

Markham, Lauren. "First the Fence, Then the System." *VQR Online.* Virginia Quarterly Review, Summer 2013. Web.

McPhee, John. *The Pine Barrens.* New York: Farrar, Straus & Giroux, 1968. Print.

Meter, Ryan Van. "Cherry Bars." *If You Knew Then What I Know Now.* Louisville, KY: Sarabande, 2011. 91–108. Print.

Montgomery, Ben. "For Their Own Good: A St. Petersburg Times Special Report on Child Abuse at the Florida School for Boys." *Tampa Bay Times.* Tampa Bay Times, 17 Apr. 2009. Web.

Orlean, Susan. "The American Man, Age Ten." *The Bullfighter Checks Her Makeup: My Encounters with Extraordinary People.* New York: Random House, 2001. 3–14. Print.

Orlean, Susan. *The Orchid Thief.* New York: Random House, 1998. 3–4. Print.

Patchett, Ann. "My Road to Hell Was Paved." *Outside Online.* Outside, June 1998. Web.

Patchett, Ann. *Truth & Beauty: A Friendship.* New York, NY: HarperCollins, 2004. Print.

Rough, Bonnie J. "His Genes Hold Gifts. Mine Carry Risk." *The New York Times.* The New York Times, 29 Jan. 2005. Web.

Rough, Bonnie J. *Carrier: Untangling the Danger in My DNA.* Berkeley, CA: Counterpoint, 2010. Print.

Russell, Karen. "The Blind Faith of the One-Eyed Matador." *GQ.* GQ, Oct. 2012. Web.

Sanders, Eli. "The Bravest Woman in Seattle." *Seattle Features.* The Stranger, 15 July 2011. Web.

Saslow, Eli. "After Newtown Shooting, Mourning Parents Enter into the Lonely Quiet." *The Washington Post.* The Washington Post, 11 Dec. 2013. Web.

Saunders, George. "Longform Reprints: The Incredible Buddha Boy by George Saunders." *Longform.* GQ, June 2006. Web.

Schweitzer, Sarah. "Together despite All, Glimpsing the Distant Finish." *BostonGlobe.com.* Boston Globe, 13 Oct. 2013. Web.

Shapira, Ian. "A Facebook Story: A Mother's Joy and a Family's Sorrow." *The Washington Post*. The Washington Post 9 Dec. 2010. Web.

Sharlet, Jeff. "Quebrado." *Sweet Heaven When I Die: Faith, Faithlessness, and the Country in between*. New York: W.W. Norton, 2011. 84–85. Print.

Silberberg, Daniel Doen. "Blue Rain." *Gettysburg Review*. Gettysburg Review, Winter 2011. Web.

Smith, Gary. "A Boy And His Bot." *Sports Illustrated*, 1 Aug. 2011. 23 Web. May 2014.

Smith, Gary. "The Man Who Couldn't Read." *Intimate Journalism: The Art and Craft of Reporting Everyday Life*. Ed. Walt Harrington. Thousand Oaks, CA: Sage, 1997. 3–17. Print.

Smith, Gary. "Walking His Life Away." *SI.com - Magazine - Olympic Sports: Is Olympian Albert Heppner Walking His Life Away? - Tuesday April 19, 2005 5:54PM*. Sports Illustrated, 26 July 2004. Web. http://www.si.com/vault/2004/07/26/377589/walking-his-life-away-for-race-walker-albert-heppner-making-the-2004-us-olympic-team-was-all-important--perhaps-in-the-end-too-important

Solnit, Rebecca. "Summer in the Far North." *MotherJones.com*. MotherJones, 13 June 2013. Web.

Solnit, Rebecca. "*Tomgram: Rebecca Solnit, The Art of Not Knowing Where You Are*." *TomDispatch.com*. TomDispatch, 13 June 2013. Web.

Strayed, Cheryl. "The Love of My Life." *Touchstone Anthology of Contemporary Creative Nonfiction: Work from 1970 to the Present*. By Lex Williford and Michael Martone. New York: Simon & Schuster, 2007. 500–13. Print.

Sullivan, John Jeremiah. "Mister Lytle." *Pulphead*. New York: Farrar, Straus and Giroux, 2011. 62. Print.

Sullivan, John Jeremiah. "You Blow My Mind. Hey Mickey." *The New York Times Magazine*, The New York Times, 8 June. 2011. Web.

Swartz, Mimi. "Mothers, Sisters, Daughters, Wives." *Texas Monthly*. Texas Monthly, Aug. 2012. Web.

Tayman, John. "Project Wife." *Byliner*. Byliner, n.d. Web.

Wilkins, Joe. "Out West." *Growing Up in the West*. Orion, Sept.–Oct. 2009. Web.

Wolfe, Tom. "Appendix." *The New Journalism*. New York: Harper & Row, 1973. 37–52. Print.

Wolfe, Tom. "New York Magazine." *Tom Wolfe on Radical Chic and Leonard Bernstein's Party for the Black Panthers—*. New York Magazine, 8 June 1970. Web.

Wolfe, Tom. "The Angels." *The Literary Journalists*. Ed. Norman Sims. New York: Ballantine, 1984. 89–102. Print.

Wolfe, Tom. *The Bonfire of the Vanities*. New York: Farrar, Straus Giroux, 1987. Print.

CHAPTER 7: PULLING IT ALL TOGETHER

Adiele, Faith. "Fire - An Origin Tale." *PBS*. PBS, n.d. Web.

Adiele, Faith. *Meeting Faith: The Forest Journals of a Black Buddhist Nun*. New York: W.W. Norton, 2004. Print.

Benham, Kelley. "Micro Preemie Parents Decide:Fight or Let Go of Their Premature Baby?" *Micro Preemie Parents Decide Whether or Not to save Premature Baby*. Tampa Bay Times, 6 Dec. 2012. Web.

Boynton, Robert S. "Adrian Nicole LeBlanc." *The New New Journalism: Conversations with America's Best Nonfiction Writers on Their Craft.* New York: Vintage, 2005. 227–47. Print.

Boynton, Robert S. "Ted Conover." *The New New Journalism: Conversations with America's Best Nonfiction Writers on Their Craft.* New York: Vintage, 2005. 3–30. Print.

Branch, John. "Snowfall: The Avalanche at Tunnel Creek." *The New York Times.* The New York Times 20 Dec. 2012. Web.

Butler, Katy. "What Broke My Father's Heart." *The New York Times.* The New York Times, 19 June 2010. Web.

Clarke, Galen. "Remember These Days." *Blog.* Mediastorm.com, 12 Apr. 2012. Web. http://mediastorm.com/training/remember-these-days

Didion, Joan. "Slouching Towards Bethlehem." *Slouching Towards Bethlehem.* New York: Farrar, Straus & Giroux, 1968. 84. Print.

Dobbs, David. "My Mother's Lover." *Atavist.* June 2011.

Flanagan, Caitlin. "The Fraternity Problem." *The Atlantic* 313.2 (2014): 72+. Print.

Flynn, Nick. *Another Bullshit Night in Suck City: A Memoir.* New York: W.W. Norton, 2004. 33–34. Print.

Hertz, Sue. "Temple of History. "New Hampshire Home Magazine, Nov./Dec. 2011. 75–81. Print.

Karr, Mary. *The Liars' Club: A Memoir.* New York: Viking, 1995. 7. Print.

King, Stephen. *On Writing: A Memoir Of The Craft.* New York: Scribner, 2000. Print.

McPhee, John. "The Writing Life: Draft 4." *The New Yorker.* The New Yorker 29 April, 2013. 32. Print.

Meter, Ryan Van. "Cherry Bars." *If You Knew Then What I Know Now.* Louisville, KY: Sarabande, 2011. 66–77. Print.

Meter, Ryan Van. "First." *If You Knew Then What I Know Now.* Louisville, KY: Sarabande, 2011. 7–10. Print.

Meter, Ryan Van. "The Goldfish History." *If You Knew Then What I Know Now.* Louisville, KY: Sarabande, 2011. 111–126. Print.

Meter, Ryan Van. "Youth Group." *If You Knew Then What I Know Now.* Louisville, KY: Sarabande, 2011. 53–65. Print.

Nutt, Amy Ellis. *Shadows Bright as Glass: The Remarkable Story of One Man's Journey from Brain Trauma to Artistic Triumph.* New York: Free Press, 2011. Print.

Patchett, Ann. *The Getaway Car.* N.p.: Byliner Originals, 2011. Print.

Potts, Rolf. "My Beirut Hostage Crisis." *Marco Polo Didn't Go There: Stories and Revelations from One Decade as a Postmodern Travel Writer: With Special Commentary Track.* Palo Alto, CA: Travelers' Tales, 2008. Print.

"A Quote by Terry Pratchett." *Goodreads.* N.p., n.d. Web. http://www.goodreads.com/quotes/644139-the-first-draft-is-just-you-telling-yourself-the-story

Sanders, Eli. "The Bravest Woman in Seattle by Eli Sanders." *Seattle Features.* The Stranger, 15 July 2011. Web.

Schweitzer, Sarah. "On the Way to Catastrophe, trailing a Life of Wrong Turns." *BostonGlobe.com.* Boston Globe, 23 Feb. 2014. Web.

Schweitzer, Sarah. "Together despite All, Glimpsing the Distant finish - The Boston Globe." *BostonGlobe.com.* Boston Globe, 13 Oct. 2013. Web.

Sedgwick, John. *In My Blood: Six Generations of Madness and Desire in an American Family*. New York: HarperCollins, 2007. Print.

Strayed, Cheryl. "Heroin/e." *The Best American Essays 2000*. By Alan P. Lightman and Robert Atwan. Boston, MA: Houghton Mifflin, 2000. 169–81. Print.

Strayed, Cheryl. *Wild: From Lost to Found on the Pacific Crest Trail*. New York: Alfred A. Knopf, 2012. 42. Print.

"20 Great Writers on the Art of Revision." *Flavorwire*. N.p., n.d. Web.

Vonnegut, Kurt. *Timequake*. New York: G.P. Putnam's, 1997.137. Print.

Wallace, David Foster. "How Tracy Austin Broke My Heart." *Consider the Lobster and Other Essays*. New York: Little, Brown, 2005. 142–43. Print.

Whitmore, Rose. "The Odds of Injury." *The Sun* February 458 (2014): 28–31. Print.

Zinsser, William Knowlton. *On Writing Well: An Informal Guide to Writing Nonfiction*. New York: HarperPerennial, 1994. Print.

Index

⑤SAGE researchmethods

The essential online tool for researchers from the world's leading methods publisher

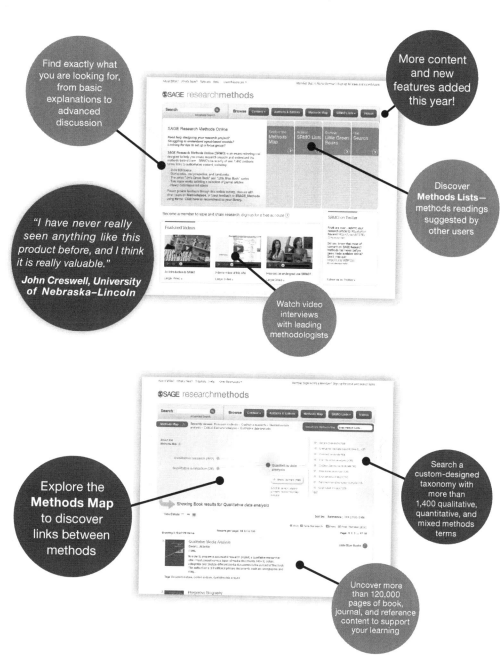

Find exactly what you are looking for, from basic explanations to advanced discussion

More content and new features added this year!

Discover Methods Lists—methods readings suggested by other users

"I have never really seen anything like this product before, and I think it is really valuable."

John Creswell, University of Nebraska–Lincoln

Watch video interviews with leading methodologists

Explore the **Methods Map** to discover links between methods

Search a custom-designed taxonomy with more than 1,400 qualitative, quantitative, and mixed methods terms

Uncover more than 120,000 pages of book, journal, and reference content to support your learning

Find out more at
www.sageresearchmethods.com

CQ Press, an imprint of SAGE, is the leading publisher of books, periodicals, and electronic products on American government and international affairs. CQ Press consistently ranks among the top commercial publishers in terms of quality, as evidenced by the numerous awards its products have won over the years. CQ Press owes its existence to Nelson Poynter, former publisher of the *St. Petersburg Times,* and his wife Henrietta, with whom he founded *Congressional Quarterly* in 1945. Poynter established CQ with the mission of promoting democracy through education and in 1975 founded the Modern Media Institute, renamed The Poynter Institute for Media Studies after his death. The Poynter Institute (*www.poynter.org*) is a nonprofit organization dedicated to training journalists and media leaders.

In 2008, CQ Press was acquired by SAGE, a leading international publisher of journals, books, and electronic media for academic, educational, and professional markets. Since 1965, SAGE has helped inform and educate a global community of scholars, practitioners, researchers, and students spanning a wide range of subject areas, including business, humanities, social sciences, and science, technology, and medicine. A privately owned corporation, SAGE has offices in Los Angeles, Boston, London, New Delhi, and Singapore, in addition to the Washington DC office of CQ Press.

Made in the USA
Middletown, DE
30 August 2024